THE ENLIGHTENED EYE

Qualitative Inquiry and the Enhancement of Educational Practice

ELLIOT W. EISNER

Macmillan Publishing Company
New York

Collier Macmillan Canada, Inc.
Toronto

Maxwell Macmillan International Publishing Group
New York   Oxford   Singapore   Sydney

Editor: Robert B. Miller
Production Editor: Ben Ko
Art Coordinator: Vincent A. Smith
Purchasing Buyer: Pamela D. Bennett
Text Designer: Anne Daly
Cover Designer: Russ Maselli

This book was set in Palatino.

Macmillan Publishing Company
866 Third Avenue, New York, New York 10022

Collier Macmillan Canada, Inc.

Library of Congress Catalog Card Number: 90-45207
International Standard Book Number: 0-023-32125-3

Printing: 3 4 5 6 7 8 9   Year: 2 3 4

For Steve and Linda—
Beethoven said it best:
"From the heart
may it return again to the heart"

A Word of Thanks

In writing this book, I received the support of many people and institutions whose contributions I wish to acknowledge. From September 1987 through August 1988 I was a Fellow at the Center for Advanced Study in the Behavioral Sciences in Stanford, California. If there ever was a paradise for scholars on this earth, it surely must be this happy place. Its then director, Gardner Lindzey, and its associate director, Bob Scott, through their own good qualitative judgment, managed to create just the right mix of social and intellectual structure and the kind of unobtrusive support that makes intellectual life a joy. My deep appreciation goes to them and to the Spencer Foundation, especially to its president, Larry Cremin, for support of my work as a Spencer Fellow during my year of residency at the center.

Fellows sometimes need fellows with whom they have a special relationship. I was fortunate to be able to establish warm and personally satisfying relationships with several fellows. My neighbor at the center, David Berliner, was a constant source of stimulation—our enthusiasms over intellectual matters run deep. Gary Marx and Barry Schwartz are two of the most perceptive sociologists I know. Both are tough-minded in their own way; they challenged and supported the ideas I shared with them about my work, and I learned much from theirs. Nancy Scheper-Hughes is an anthropologist of keen insight and deep social commitment, and a writer whose style shimmers. Her comments about her own work in Brazil gave me assurance that others outside of my own field shared some of my views. Nate Gage, a colleague at Stanford and a fellow at the center, has always been a person whose ideas challenged and stimulated others. Our discussions and debates have a long and productive history. Marcia Johnson, a model experimental psychologist, also contributed to my thinking. Also at the center was Fred Dretske, a philosopher of science, whose views about virtually any philosophic matter are 180 degrees from my own but with whom I have had some of the most satisfying and

v

stimulating discussions of the year. Each of these scholars—and friends—gave much to me, and for that they have my gratitude.

Those who contributed to my work go well beyond the boundaries of the center. Professor Michael Connelly and his team at the Ontario Institute for Studies in Education were good enough to read the first three chapters and to discuss them with me over a three-hour seminar in Toronto. This was followed by many notes and letters. I wish to say thanks publicly. Don Arnstein, Barbara Arnstein, and David Flinders gave careful attention to several chapters in this book from the vantage point of their specializations in philosophy of education and curriculum, respectively. They took seriously my request for a critique, and I wish to thank them as well.

I also want to express my deep appreciation to my friend Alan Peshkin, who read this manuscript with care and commented upon it with insight. He contributed in an important way to its final form.

In addition I wish to thank Roger Shuy and Jim Kuntz, S. J., for their permission to include their work in my book. I am most grateful for their generosity. Also, I am grateful to Peggy Hagberg, who as a graduate student prepared at my suggestion the paper quoted at length in chapter 5.

During the course of my fellowship at the Center I met regularly with my doctoral students. Choya Wilson and Rebecca Hawthorne read and commented on the early drafts of the first three chapters. Marcy Singer and Bruce Uhrmacher commented on and discussed with me in detail virtually the entire manuscript and provided assistance in getting books and articles I needed to do my work. They have my very deep gratitude.

Four other people, each in her own way, made among the most significant contributions to my work. Kathleen Much, a talented editor, read the manuscript from cover to cover and helped make it better. Evy Schiffman provided meticulous attention to details that matter and made valuable suggestions about matters of style. Nancy Baumann, more than any other single person, helped make this book possible. Nancy drove up to the center to get manuscript material, prepared the text, revised material I had edited, provided encouragement, and kept my mind free from the distractions that would otherwise have made it difficult for me to concentrate on reading and writing. To Kathleen, Evy, and Nancy I say a heartfelt thank you.

Books are not written simply by reading, writing, and editing text, as important as those tasks are. Books are written by human beings who need to be nurtured, cared for, at times coddled, and always encouraged. My wife, Ellie, provided that kind of support in her usual generous, loving way. She understood when I was preoccupied, shared enthusiasms, and reassured me when my intellectual well ran dry. Her contributions to my work infuse every page.

Elliot W. Eisner
Stanford, California
January 1990

Contents

Contents

Introduction

Aims, Issues, and Overview

The title of this book, *The Enlightened Eye*, is intimately related to my life as a painter, and my life as a painter is intimately related to the ways in which I think about inquiry. Although I haven't painted for more than a quarter of a century, my engagement in the visual arts from age six onwards and my studies at the School of the Art Institute of Chicago and later at the Illinois Institute of Technology's Institute of Design did much to shape the ways in which I think about seeing and solving problems. If the visual arts teach one lesson, it's that seeing is central to making. Seeing, rather than mere looking, requires an enlightened eye: this is as true and as important in understanding and improving education as in creating a painting.

Vision, at least initially, depends upon the existence of qualities that can be seen. These qualities may be aspects of the world we inhabit or products of our imagination. To imagine is to generate images; to see is to experience qualities. Both the content of the world and the content of our imagination are dependent upon qualities. It is through the perception of qualities—not only those we can see, but those we experience through any of our senses—that our consciousness comes into being. *The Enlightened Eye* is about the perception of qualities, those that pervade intimate social relations and those that constitute complex social institutions, such as schools. It is also about the meaning of those qualities and the value we assign to them.

But seeing qualities, interpreting their significance, and appraising their value are only one side of the coin. The other pertains to that magical and mysterious feat through which the content of our consciousness is given public form. I am convinced that we take this accomplishment much too much for granted. Just how do we share with others the feel of a

1

summer afternoon in Florence, Italy—or Dubuque, Iowa, for that matter? What must we do to tell the world about the excitement of a classroom we have seen, a discussion we have heard, a school we have visited? How do we recreate the event so that it can be known by those who weren't there? And how do we acquire the skills to do so? Are they the offspring of experience? Can they be taught? My book is about these matters as well.

The roots of this subject are about as old as history itself, for history, if it is anything, is a way of telling people stories about the past that will help them understand what it was like and how it came to be that way. These roots are even older than written history, for the drawings of animals on the walls of the caves of Lascaux were efforts humans made some twenty thousand years ago to tell of their experience and, perhaps, of their aspirations and fears.

The arts and the humanities have provided a long tradition of ways of describing, interpreting, and appraising the world: History, art, literature, dance, drama, poetry, and music are among the most important forms through which humans have represented and shaped their experience. These forms have not been significant in educational inquiry for reasons that have to do with a limited and limiting conception of knowledge. My aim in this book is to explore some of the ways in which the methods, content, and assumptions in the arts, humanities, and social sciences might be used to help us better understand our schools and classrooms. My aim is to expand the ways in which we think about inquiry in education, and to broaden our views about what it means to 'know'. But my ultimate aim goes beyond these: it is to contribute to the improvement of education. For me, the ultimate test of a set of educational ideas is the degree to which it illuminates and positively influences the educational experience of those who live and work in our schools.

I do not believe improvement of our schools is likely if we distance ourselves from their problems or their achievements. Detachment and distance are no virtues when one wants to improve complex social organizations or so delicate a performance as teaching. It is important to know the scene. And because the scene in organizations like schools is a mix of interacting factors, improving schools means knowing how the major features or dimensions of schools interact. It is impossible to understand the human pancreas, if it is studied without reference to the rest of the body. It can only be understood as a part of a system. Classrooms are fundamentally no different. What teachers and students do is influenced by their location in a system. Thus methodological pluralism and organizational holism are two conceptual pillars upon which my work is built.

These concepts have been pondered by social scientists like Erving Goffman, who as much as anyone has made social life vivid in some of our most important social institutions; Bruno Bettelheim, whose work with autistic children displayed one of the most enlightened eyes in the field; William Foote Whyte, whose observations of Italians in North Boston became the classic, *Streetcorner Society*. These are some of those whose work participates in a humanistic tradition. In education, Philip Jackson, Sarah Lawrence Lightfoot, Theodore Sizer, and Alan Peshkin have all directed their intellectual attention to schools and communities in ways that Lincoln and Guba (1985) call "naturalistic inquiry."

These scholars not only study intact settings in their "natural state," but they try to make sense of those settings through language that is not tied to formalism or to theories that abstract the vivid particulars into oblivion. Each tries to tell a story that has the ring of truth without compromising figurative or interpretive language.

There is another practical tradition from which I have drawn: the practice of criticism. Critics have the formidable task of making sense of some of the most complicated and subtle works that humans have created—works of art. Their professional task is to talk about, say, a painting by Willem de Kooning or a sonata by Beethoven, a poem by e. e. cummings or a novel by John Updike, in ways that treat works fairly and enable others to experience their qualities and meanings. In this regard I do not consider responses to works of art similar to responses to a Rorschach ink blot. I do not believe that any interpretation, any appraisal of a work of art is as good as any other. If I did, I would not have written this book. Works of art—like classrooms, schools, and teaching—participate in a history and are part of a tradition. They reflect a genre of practice and an ideology. Those who know the tradition, understand the history, are familiar with those genres, and can see what those settings and practices consist of are most likely to have something useful and informed to say about them. Criticism is an art of saying useful things about complex and subtle objects and events so that others less sophisticated, or sophisticated in different ways, can see and understand what they did not see and understand before.

The Enlightened Eye participates in a tradition and history populated by those who have attempted to become both perceptive and articulate about what they have encountered. In this sense, educational critics and critics of the arts share a common aim: to help others see and understand.

To achieve this aim, one must be able to use language to reveal what, paradoxically, words can never say. This means that voice must be heard in the text, alliteration allowed, and cadences encouraged. Relevant allusions should be employed, and metaphor that adumbrates by suggestion used. All of these devices and more are as much a part of the tool kit of those conducting qualitative inquiry as analysis of variance is for those working in conventional quantitative research modes.

A word about voice. I have tried in this book, as in all of my writing, to keep a sense of voice present. I want readers to know that this author is a human being and not some disembodied abstraction who is depersonalized through linguistic conventions that hide his signature. This approach is more honest. Hence, I make no apology for the personal tone that I hope comes through on these pages. Although my words were prepared on a computer, they were created by a person. I want that to show.

The reason for emphasizing voice and other tropes is not to gussy up language so that it is "humanistic" or "artsy"; it is to serve epistemological interests. What we look for, as well as what we see and say, is influenced by the tools we know how to use and believe to be appropriate. The language of propositions, that language fundamental to the empirical sciences, Langer (1942) tells us, cannot take the impress of the life of feeling. For feeling to be conveyed, the "language" of the arts must be used, because it is through the form a symbol displays that feeling is given virtual life. The point, therefore, of exploiting language fully is to do justice to what has been seen; it is to help readers come to know.

This practice also has a long tradition. Its theoretical forebears are found in Aristotle's *Poetics* and later in the philosophy of Ernst Cassirer and his conception of symbolic form, as well as the work of his student, Susanne Langer, and her views of the cognitive functions of art. It is also rooted in the Dewey of *Art as Experience* and, even earlier, *Philosophy and Civilization*. It comes to us in the work of continental philosophers such as Wilhelm Dilthey and sociologists such as Georg Simmel. More recently, we find similar themes having to do with the multiple ways in which experience is symbolized run through the writings of Rudolf Arnheim, of Nelson Goodman, and, of course, of Michael Polanyi. Arnheim believes that most knowledge is visual in nature and that propositions and visual art are two ways of representing what has been conceptualized. Goodman argues that there are as many worlds as there are ways of describing them and that the worlds we know are the worlds we make. Polanyi talks about tacit knowledge. "We know," he says, "more than we can tell." Indeed we do.

Richard Rorty and the later Stephen Toulmin are also among those who recognize the multiple ways of knowing; each has "given up" as a mistaken ambition the aspiration to achieve *episteme*—true and certain knowledge. Belief, says Toulmin, is about as good as we can ever get.

These scholars are not household names in the American educational research community. Indeed, philosophy is often regarded as an academic distraction in programs preparing researchers in the social sciences. Philosophy is nagging, it cajoles students into asking questions about basic assumptions, it generates doubts and uncertainties, and, it is said, it keeps people from getting their work done. Many appear to believe that it is better to leave the unanswerable questions and unsolvable problems alone and get down to brass tacks. I regard such attitudes as short-sighted. Core concepts in the social sciences are philosophical in nature: Objectivity, Validity, Truth, Fact, Theory, Structure. Why neglect to examine them, even if their examination will never yield a single unassailable meaning?

One concept that needs attention in research circles is that of the 'qualitative'. I have used the terms *qualitative* and *inquiry* in the subtitle of this book, as well as throughout its chapters, but the terms require some clarification. I considered and rejected several terms before settling on *qualitative*. These other possibilities included *naturalistic, interpretive, practice-guided,* and *ethnographic. Naturalistic,* for example, does not fit well what it is that teachers do when they teach. *Interpretive* inquiry suggests that those who conduct conventional, quantitative research do not interpret. I do not believe this to be the case, even in the most apparently non-interpretive activities. To count the number of times a teacher raises a high-order question depends not simply on numbers, but what counts as a high-order question, and deciding that requires interpretation. *Practice-guided* inquiry is a felicitous phrase, but too limited. One may very well be interested in the qualitative features of a textbook, a school building, or a body of teaching materials—but these are hardly "practices." *Ethnographic* describes work within the field of cultural anthropology, and the subject this book addresses is wider than ethnography.

If these terms have their limitations, so too does *qualitative.* The term *qualitative* suggests its opposite, *quantitative,* and implies that qualitative inquiry makes no use of quantification. This is not the case. For some aspects of education, quantification may be the most appropriate means for describing what one needs to say. *Qualitative* also implies that other forms of inquiry—the scientific experiment, for example—have nothing to do with qualities. Nothing could be further from the truth. All empirical phenomena are qualitative. The difference between "qualitative inquiry" and "quantitative research" pertains mainly to the forms of representation that are emphasized in presenting a body of work. The difference is not that one addresses qualities and the other does not.

Why then, given these caveats, did I use the term *qualitative*? There are three reasons. First, *qualitative* is sufficiently general to encompass not only teaching and other forms of human activity, but also objects such as buildings and books. Qualitative considerations are taken into account in composing sonnets, songs, and scenarios. They are employed in teaching, in leading armies, and in constructing theories. Qualitative considerations are used in telling a story and in making love, in sustaining a friendship and in selling a car. In short, qualitative thought is ubiquitous in human affairs. It is not some exotic form of doing or making, but a pervasive aspect of daily life. For that reason and for others it is useful.

Second, the term *qualitative* has established a firm foothold in the educational research community. It participates in a general universe of discourse in education, and I believe it is better to try to refine that discourse by developing a more critical and analytical approach to it than to coin a new term.

A third reason for using the term *qualitative* is related to the arts. The arts are paradigm cases of qualitative intelligence in action. Qualitative considerations must be employed in composing the qualities that constitute works of art. Since I believe that the qualities composed in art inform, and since I want to convey the potential of the arts as vehicles for revealing the social world, *qualitative inquiry* seems to me to have the appropriate ring.

A word about the term *inquiry*. I used *inquiry* rather than *research and evaluation* because I wish to include within the realm to which this book is addressed efforts to reveal not only the qualities of classrooms and schools, but also the processes of teaching; teaching is a form of qualitative inquiry. In addition, inquiry is a broader concept than either research or evaluation. Research and evaluation are examples of inquiry, but not all inquiry is an example of research or evaluation. By opening up the realm to which qualitative thought is applied, I hope its more general manifestations will be recognized.

One last comment about terminology. The major focus of this book is on a particular species of qualitative inquiry called educational connoisseurship and educational criticism. Sometimes I will be talking about qualitative inquiry to make a general point about its features. At other times I will specifically refer to educational connoisseurship and educational criticism. I mean to address both the general issues and the particular form of qualitative inquiry that has characterized my own work over the past fifteen years. From the context of my writing I hope readers will be able to determine when the focus of my remarks is general and when it is specific.

The word *connoisseurship* comes from the Latin *cognoscere*, to know. In the visual arts, to know depends upon the ability to see, not merely to look. *Criticism* refers to the process of enabling others to see the qualities that a work of art possesses. Effective criticism functions as a midwife to perception. It helps it come into being, then later refines it and helps it become more acute. Both connoisseurship and criticism are applicable to social and educational phenomena as well as to the world of art. They can be applied to schools, classrooms, and teaching, and to the perception and analysis of instructional resources. Examples of their application can be found in the fifteen Ph.D. dissertations my students at Stanford University have completed using educational connoisseurship and criticism.

Both connoisseurship and criticism are focused on qualities. A connoisseur must be conscious of qualities in order to produce useful criticism, although one does not need to be a critic in order to be a connoisseur. Connoisseurship and criticism also reflect my interest in bringing to the world of education frames of reference from the arts and humanities. As terms, however, they, like *qualitative*, have problematic features.

Connoisseurship tends to conjure up something effete or elite. I have no intention that it do so; anyone who is highly perceptive in some domain—a piano tuner, for example—is a connoisseur in that domain. *Criticism* suffers from its association with negativism. Unfortunately many people think of negative commentary when they hear or read the word *criticism*. But this too is not a necessary or intended meaning. Criticism of art, music, literature, poetry, or social affairs does not impose an obligation to make derogatory comments. Criticism can be laudatory. Its aim is to illuminate a situation or object so that it can be seen or appreciated. We appreciate virtues as well as vices.

There are few terms that do not possess some conceptual liabilities with respect to the way in which they might be interpreted. I recognize the potential liabilities of the terms I have chosen to use and express here the hope that readers will work with the terms I have chosen in the ways that I have elected to use them.

The chapter titles of *The Enlightened Eye* suggest what I consider to be among the major issues in qualitative inquiry: generalization, objectivity, ethics, the preparation of qualitative researchers, validity, and so forth. These issues have occupied my mind for the past two decades, and I hope they will occupy my readers' minds as well. I do not believe in "last words" in human affairs, only better conversations. I hope the contents of the chapters help deepen educators' conversations and make the educational world richer and more complex.

This book is based on several premises, which I wish to make explicit at the outset. Some of these premises are more debatable than others, but I am prepared to defend them all. Indeed, this book may be regarded as an argument in support of each of the following:

1. There are multiple ways in which the world can be known: Artists, writers, and dancers, as well as scientists, have important things to tell about the world.

2. Human knowledge is a constructed form of experience and therefore a reflection of mind as well as nature: Knowledge is made, not simply discovered.

3. The forms through which humans represent their conception of the world have a major influence on what they are able to say about it.

4. The effective use of any form through which the world is known and represented requires the use of intelligence.

5. The selection of a form through which the world is to be represented not only influences what we can say, it also influences what we are likely to experience.

6. Educational inquiry will be more complete and informative as we increase the range of ways we describe, interpret, and evaluate the educational world.

7. Which particular forms of representation become acceptable in the educational research community is as much a political matter as an epistemological one. New forms of representation, when acceptable, will require new competencies.

Books, like lectures and lessons, often do both more and less than the author intends. If I were to distill what I hope my book will do, I would say that first, I hope it will establish connections between qualitative inquiry in our daily lives and its functions in both the practice and study of education. Second, I hope it will broaden our understanding of the ways in which humans come to know the world; my aim is to expand what we regard as legitimate modes of inquiry into social affairs. Third, I hope that the book will broaden the already growing interest in conducting qualitative research in education and that it will enable those with interests in such work to do it well.

In a paper that I gave at the American Educational Research Association meeting in 1975 titled "The Perceptive Eye: Toward a Reformation in Educational Evaluation," I expressed a hope that one day there would be journals devoted to qualitative inquiry and programs that prepared people to do such work. I'm happy to say that a decade later some of my hopes have been realized. Stanford University's School of Education now has a sequence of courses in qualitative methods for doctoral students and, in 1988, gave birth to a doctoral concentration in research and evaluation methodology in which qualitative methods play a central role. Similarly, as of 1988, the field has a new journal, *The International Journal of Qualitative Studies in Education*. It provides further testimony that methodological interests in education have expanded. I believe this expansion will continue.

Finally, and for me most important, I hope *The Enlightened Eye* will contribute to the improvement of educational practice by giving us a fuller, more complex understanding of what makes schools and classrooms tick. We shall see.

Chapter I

Qualitative Thought and Human Understanding

A painter takes the sun and makes it into a yellow spot. An artist takes a yellow spot and makes it into a sun.

Pablo Picasso

The Current Scene

Almost everyone in the United States is concerned about the state of American education. We are told by the press that one out of five young Americans leaves school functionally illiterate. We are told by the armed forces that recruits have so hard a time reading technical manuals that they find it extremely difficult to operate their equipment. We are told by the business community that the schools have not prepared students who can do even the simplest calculations and that they, the corporations, have to provide remedial education. We are told by federally appointed commissions that the state of schooling in America is so problematic that unless it is improved, we might lose not only our competitive edge, but our nation.[1]

To those who have worked in the field of education for more than a few years, these concerns are not new. In the mid-1950s American schools were considered an educational wasteland (Bestor, 1985). In the late 1950s we lost the space race to the Soviet Union, a loss that stimulated the U.S. Congress to provide hundreds of millions of dollars for curriculum reform. In the 1970s we bemoaned the drop in Scholastic Aptitude Test (SAT) scores and were worried that grade inflation would further erode our standards. In the 1980s we saw the business community step in with its own agenda and the education profession rethink teacher preparation.[2]

Reactions to these states of affairs have come in a variety of forms. There has been much discussion, but no action, about lengthening the number of days students spend in school each year. However, forty-one states have toughened the curriculum by increasing the number of carnegie units required for graduation, and nineteen states now test students for minimum competency in order to graduate (Digest of Educational Statistics, 1989).

9

The public, too, has expressed concern and demanded public accountability: in many states standardized achievement test scores on a school-by-grade basis are published in the local press. Levels of student performance are displayed for all to see, usually without interpretation. When legal requirements and public scrutiny of test scores are not sufficient to increase performance, money is used as an incentive. In California, cash for academic achievement was until recently standing policy of the state Department of Education.[3] At the national level, President Bush has proposed a plan to reward outstanding schools with payments for excellence.

Those with a more academic bent look toward research. The U.S. Office of Education under former Secretary of Education William Bennett published a booklet titled *What Works* (1987). Presumably it provides schools with research-proven ways to improve school achievement. From researchers we hear of other ways to increase the performance of students. Teachers are urged to increase their students' academic time on task (Rosenshine, 1976). Others (Slavin, 1983) suggest cooperative learning, while still others prescribe a five- or six-step process that they believe constitutes excellence in teaching. While all this is occurring, researchers continue to plug away at the seemingly intractable problem of school improvement, amid headlines that American education is a national disgrace.

Where university schools of education have appeared too esoteric and impractical, the gap has been filled by commercial organizations eager to bring to teachers and school administrators a more useful array of techniques for improving virtually any aspect of practice that can be named. For better teaching there is the Hunter approach (1982). For improved curriculum there is the Dunn method (1978). For the development of mental skills there is the 4Mat System (McCarthy, 1987). For improved classroom discipline there is the aversive discipline approach. There is, it seems, a solution for every problem, and yet the problems remain. Few people seem to be happy with the overall state of our schools, but fewer still seem to know just what to do about them.

The "classical" approach to school improvement looks to universities to provide the research-based knowledge that can be passed along to teachers and other educational practitioners. The aim of the researcher is to discover cause and effect relationships through experimentation, or failing that, through correlational studies that display sufficiently strong relationships to breed confidence that certain variables are consistently related to each other and that manipulation of one might lead to changes in the other. Much educational research is predicated on the assumption that the knowledge secured as a result of careful study can be conveyed to practitioners through university course offerings, in-service education, journals, conferences, and the educational equivalent of agricultural extension workers: people who know and who can carry the message to others. The classical approach has been largely from the top down.[4]

Although I believe "basic" research in education can be important, the educational world has changed during the past decade or so, and conventional assumptions about research and the researcher's role in the improvement of schooling have been questioned. One result is the turn toward what has come to be known as qualitative inquiry.

It does not seem particularly revolutionary to say that it is important to try to understand how teachers and classrooms function before handing out recommendations for change. Yet so much of what is suggested to teachers and school administrators is said independent of context and often by those ignorant of the practices they wish to improve. If qualitative inquiry in education is about anything, it is about trying to understand what teachers and children do in the settings in which they work. To achieve this aim—and there are other aims for qualitative inquiry that are equally important—it is necessary to "get in touch" with the schools and classrooms we care about, to see them, and to use what we see as sources for interpretation and appraisal. Why, for example, do we assume that educational achievement will be fostered by extending the school year, especially when those who wish to extend it complain that schools are not particularly good places for children to be? Why do we believe that more time on task is an educational virtue? Does it not depend on the kinds of tasks in which students are engaged? And if students are engaged in daydreaming or finding more interesting things to think about than what is occurring in the classroom, is not such behavior a testimony to their good judgment? Why do we believe that raising standards is likely to be useful in fostering educational achievement or that more math or science will improve the quality of students' education? What kind of math? What kind of science? What opportunity costs are paid? We ask teachers to take on more and more responsibilities each year: a few years ago it was values clarification, then parenting education, and nowadays AIDS education. Is it realistic to expect more from teachers without reducing their responsibilities in other areas, or is it the case that teachers have too little to teach?[5]

Questions like these are not to be answered by examining new methods of instruction or by scrutinizing achievement test scores. They require an intimacy with what goes on in schools. Schooling needs to be "known" in the Old Testament biblical sense: by direct, intimate contact.

The results of such contact can tell us much that we need to know about how individual schools and classrooms work. Studies of individual cases can generalize, an idea that I will discuss in chapter 8. In addition, the qualitative study of *particular* classrooms and *particular* teachers in *particular* schools makes it possible to provide feedback to teachers that is fundamentally different from the kind of information that they are given in in-service education programs or through journal publications.

In-service programs are typically provided by individuals who have something to say about curriculum, the teaching process, or classroom organization, but who have not actually observed the teaching of the teachers to whom they are speaking. As a result, they offer advice that is so general that it cannot take into account the particular strengths and weaknesses of the individual teachers they address. It is as though a wealthy but tight-fisted owner of a basketball team, trying to save some money, were to hire a coach for her team on a one-day-a-month basis. The team would go to the coach for advice one day a month, but the coach would give his advice without ever having seen the team play. In-service programs are seldom provided as often as one day a month, and few such programs are taught by people who have observed the teachers in action. The instructors would need to be clairvoyant to know what advice might be appropriate for individual teachers.[6]

Qualitative inquiry—in this case the study of schools or classrooms—can provide the double advantage of learning about schools and classrooms in ways that are useful for understanding other schools and classrooms *and* learning about individual classrooms and particular teachers in ways that are useful to them. The beginnings of such work in schools go back to Matthew Arnold, the English school inspector who wrote with brilliant insight about nineteenth-century schools in England (1968). The kind of work that Arnold did has been carried on in exemplary fashion by Her Majesty's Inspectors, an elite group of British school inspectors, appointed by the Queen, no less, to observe schools and teachers and to report to the Queen and the British Department of Education and Science on their strengths and weaknesses. In America, the closest thing we have to the HMIs are subject-matter consultants and county school inspectors, but the record is nowhere near as impressive. American models of supervision have been rooted in the industrial world. The cult of efficiency, as Callahan (1962) reminds us, was America's early effort to reduce teaching to a practical routine. The task of the supervisor, like that of a boss on an assembly line, was to see to it that the job was done right, and this meant according to specifications. Time and motion study became the method through which school productivity could be increased, since it was believed to optimize the workers' (teachers') efficiency by eliminating wasted motion.

We have come a long way from the time-and-motion orientation that characterized much of American education during the first two decades of the twentieth century. The legacy of this period was a hyperrationalized conception of schooling as a kind of educational machine that could be made more productive through research and scientific management. Finding the best method has been a long-held aspiration for both practitioners and researchers in education.[7]

The kind of work that Matthew Arnold did in England has had no equal in the United States. Our research tradition is more in keeping with Taylorism, the scientific management of human behavior, than with interpretive or qualitative orientations to the improvement of teaching. In the mid-1960s the situation began to change.

Although Willard Waller, an American sociologist, studied schools in the 1930s (1932), his work, as well as that of other sociologists such as the Lynds (1937), did not capture the eye of educational researchers. The American educational research tradition emanates from the work of Edward L. Thorndike. It is specific, focused on individuals, and concerned with learning and the shaping of behavior. It is oriented more toward control and less toward interpretation.

In the 1960s, Philip Jackson's *Life in Classrooms* (1968) was published. Jackson had spent a year observing classes in the Laboratory School at the University of Chicago, the same school that John Dewey had founded in 1896. What resulted from Jackson's observations was an insightful, artistically crafted book remembered more for its metaphors and insight than for the nods Jackson gave to the quantitative data he presents in its second half.

Jackson's book was soon followed by Louis Smith and William Geoffrey's *Complexities of an Urban Classroom* (1968). Smith, like Jackson, had been trained as a psychologist, and a hard-nosed one at that, and Geoffrey was the teacher in the classroom where the study was done. Both *Life in Classrooms* and *Complexities of an Urban Classroom* were very important studies, not only—perhaps not even primarily—for their insights, although these were significant, but because of their method: getting into the school and looking to see what was there. Smith followed up his study with *Anatomy of Educational Innovations* (1971). Gradually, others began to reflect on schooling and developed work on the basis of their observations. Although some of the most important work done on schooling in the 1950s and 1960s was within the educational academy, much of it was created by people who had no strong position within educational scholarship, but who nevertheless had important comments to make. I speak, for example, of Paul Goodman, whose *Growing up Absurd* (1960) is a trenchant and incisive account of the Eisenhower generation; with its goals of two cars in every garage, two chickens in every pot, and a house in suburbia. Later, Paul Goodman's *Compulsory Miseducation* (1966) told about the school's role in the diminution of intelligence, and Jonathan Kozol's *Death at an Early Age* (1968) painted a particularly moving portrait of the indignities and inequities conferred upon young black children in the academic citadel of the United States, the city of Boston.

The authors of these books were not making efforts to be self-consciously respectable as scholars. Indeed, many educational scholars today, I believe, would dismiss their work as "romantic" and insufficiently "rigorous." Yet I believe that what they had to say was often authentic and "right." They certainly were widely read. What all of these works displayed was another way of trying to understand the world of education, or, if not the *world* of education, some small part of it. As this approach began to develop, methodological issues loomed large. Could one really regard *Death at an Early Age* as *research*? How could the validity of such a work be tested? How could its reliability be judged? How should its subjectivity be regarded? After all, could research be a matter of opinion, and is opinion the same as knowledge?

Casual perusal of the *Educational Researcher*, the house organ of the American Educational Research Association (AERA), reveals the major features of the controversy. Are qualitative research and evaluation really different in nature from research that is conventional or quantitative in character? Can generalizations be derived from the study of individual cases? Does it make sense to distinguish between qualitative and quantitative research? Answers to these questions differ widely.[8] Smith and Heshusius (1986) worry about closing down the conversation in an effort to ameliorate differences. In an article published in 1982 (Eisner, 1982), I said the difference between conventional research and what has been called qualitative research is a difference between doing art and doing science. Phillips (1987) believes that the term *knowledge* should be limited to the products of science and that *artistic knowledge* is an oxymoron. Lincoln and Guba (1989) believe that the "fight" for legitimacy is a battle between competing paradigms and that the side that has dominated the field of education since the turn of the century is not only largely irrelevant to the problems of teaching and learning, but has caused more problems than it has solved. Miles and Huberman (1984), however, have made a valiant effort to try to treat qualitative data "rigorously"—by their lights—so that the results of such work can be trusted.

Debate on the issues continues while more and more scholars in the field of education are being attracted to the kinds of understandings that qualitative inquiry yields.

For example, Connelly and Clandinin (1988) make extensive use of teacher narratives to understand the experience of teachers as they plan curricula and engage in teaching. These narratives are qualitative materials through which Connelly and Clandinin gain access to the character of the teacher's experience, which they then reveal through their own narratives. Concern for experience in terms that are largely phenomenological is found in Pinar's (1988) work and in the leadership he has provided in reconceptualizing curriculum theory. Other scholars, such as Maxine Greene (1988) and Madeleine Grumet (1988), have had a long-standing interest in the qualitative aspects of educational practice, particularly in its phenomenological features.

It should not be surprising that initial efforts to legitimate qualitative inquiry within the American educational research community identify such inquiry with ethnography. Cultural anthropology, of which ethnography is one part, is after all a member of the family of the social sciences, as are psychology and sociology. It has a research tradition, and it is concerned with field work. Furthermore, researchers need not give up their claim to be doing science if their work is anthropological. Although anthropologically trained scholars in education such as Harry Wolcott (1975) point out that much of what passes for educational ethnography at present is not anthropological at all, ethnography is still appealed to as a model.

I believe that another factor has supported the anthropological turn in education: it is expressed in a classic article written by one of America's leading anthropologists, Clifford Geertz (1973). Geertz's "thick description" focuses on the nature of method and the aims of ethnography. Geertz himself has been influenced by aestheticians such as Susanne Langer and calls into question the tidy positivism that has significantly influenced his own field. Thick description is an effort aimed at interpretation, at getting below the surface to that most enigmatic aspect of the human condition: the construction of meaning. Behaviorists, like positivists, were not much concerned with meaning. The problem, in their eyes, was figuring out how to get people to perform particular tasks. Reinforcement theory and operant conditioning were developed largely in laboratory settings, often with animals, and applied to schools where, given the industrial model we have been using, they seemed not only plausible but appropriate. Geertz is concerned with deeper issues; in fact, many of his concerns are consonant with the aims of Paul Goodman, John Holt, and Jonathan Kozol. All four are concerned with the kinds of meaning that people have in their lives. Geertz's widely read chapter on thick description is linguistically elegant and conceptually insightful, and helped foster the kind of research that was beginning to emerge in the 1970s.

I suggested earlier that the move towards ethnography as a way of doing legitimate qualitative research in education is understandable. As a part of the social sciences, ethnography is a member of the same family. But qualitative research and, more broadly, qualitative inquiry, are far wider than ethnography. Political scientists, historians, sociologists, and clinical psychologists also conduct qualitative inquiry. Indeed, qualitative inquiry infuses the ordinary events of daily life. Qualitative inquiry, and even more generally, qualitative thinking, is not some form of exotic activity reserved for those of special talent or for those who have been properly initiated into special forms of cultural anthropology. It pervades our day-to-day judgments and provides a basis for our most important decisions: whom one chooses for a mate, where one chooses to live, the kind of career one chooses to pursue, how one relates to family and friends. Such decisions are guided by qualitative considerations. The rites and rituals of the church and synagogue, the public celebrations in which we participate, indeed, the way we set a table in preparation for our friends and family are the results of qualitative inquiry.

The roots of such ideas can be found in one of John Dewey's last major works. Dewey was seventy-four when he was invited to Harvard University to deliver a series of public lectures. The topic he chose was art, and the book that came of those lectures was *Art as Experience* (1934). Although this, his last major opus, is all but neglected in schools of education, it provides a view of mind, meaning, and method that could serve well those interested, as I am, in broadening the ways in which we think about inquiry. For Dewey, art is not limited to objects that hang in museums or performances that occur in concert halls. In fact, esoteric concepts of art often interfere, he believed, with our appreciation of its extensive role in our ordinary life. Dewey reminds us that art is fundamentally a special quality of experience, and that the process through which art is lived is dependent on the use of qualitative thinking. This mode of thinking constitutes one of the ways in which human intelligence is manifested. Dewey (1934) writes:

> Any idea that ignores the necessary role of intelligence in production of works of art is based upon identification of thinking with use of one special kind of material, verbal signs and words. To think effectively in terms of relations of qualities is as severe a demand upon thought as to think in terms of symbols, verbal and mathematical. Indeed, since words are easily manipulated in mechanical ways, the production of a work of genuine art probably demands more intelligence than does most of the so-called thinking that goes on among those who pride themselves on being "intellectuals." (p. 46)

The lesson Dewey teaches is that art is the offspring of human intelligence, that it is not limited to objects in museums, that it permeates our daily life, and that the ability to have the form of experience that Dewey calls "art" is something that culture in general and schools in particular can foster.[9] Analogous conditions apply to qualitative inquiry in education: qualitative inquiry is not limited to what research journals normally publish, it is a product of intelligence, and the ability to do such inquiry can be fostered through education.

To state as I have done that qualitative thinking permeates our daily life is to make an assertion. The problem I must confront and with which my readers must deal is one of understanding where and how this occurs. To limit qualitative inquiry to the conduct of research or evaluation is to miss the fundamental role it plays in the generation of consciousness. Because this point is so central to my thesis, I must illustrate its presence in the prosaic and the profound aspects of our lives. To take this journey we must begin with experience.

Experience as Transaction and Achievement

Experience has its genesis in our transaction with the qualities of which our environment consists. By qualities I mean those features of our environment that can be experienced through any of our senses. Well before we are able to assign words to those qualities we call blue, hot, tall, loud, or prickly, we experience them in their nameless state. As long as our sensory system is unimpaired, we are able to perceive the multitude of qualities within our purview.

Our capacity to experience qualities is, from one perspective, well developed when we enter the world. Well-developed fetuses, in fact, are sensitive to sound and may even experience movement before they are born.[10] As children mature their sensory systems become increasingly differentiated. As a result, they are able to experience more and more of their environment.[11] Indeed, experience—our consciousness of some aspect of the world—is an achievement and, to my mind, it is a cognitive achievement. We *learn* to see, or at least we learn to see those aspects of the world that are subtle and complex. When we think about people we regard as expert in some field—a radiologist examining an x-ray, a gemologist inspecting a diamond, a conductor directing an orchestra, a clinical psychologist listening to a client—it is clear that they hear and see more than we do. They also know more about the history and background of the objects and people they attend to, but before they can deal with these matters they must be able to notice their qualities. The inability to experience these qualities leaves no grounds for further reflection. We can only appraise and interpret what we have been able to experience. At the most sophisticated level we call these people "connoisseurs," a concept central to this book.

One other point regarding the perception of qualities. We often tend to experience qualities as labeled objects: "tree," "chair," "classroom," "teacher," and so forth. That is, we move almost instantaneously from the qualities we are able to see to their classification and labeling. We categorize. Of course, categorization is useful: by categorizing we know the "species" of our experience. But categorization can also be a liability when it forecloses, as it often does, the exploration of the qualities that constitute *this* classroom, *that* student, *this* particular school. If our perceptual experience is aborted for the sake of classification, our experience is attenuated; we do not experience all that we can. Dewey (1934) distinguishes between two modes of attention. The process of categorization he called *recognition*. The process of visual exploration he called *perception*.

Art, like science, is one of the tools we use to help us keep our perception alive.

The qualitative aspects of experience are not only secured in attending to qualities out there, but also are manifest in the things we do and make. Painters make qualitative judgments about what they create on canvas, composers think qualitatively as their musical imagination generates those patterned sounds that culminate in a musical score, choreographers design ballets thinking in terms of space and movement. Although manifestations of qualitative thought reach their apotheosis in the fine arts, their roots are, as I said, in the ordinary tasks of daily life.

Consider the creation of a salad. Salads are typically taken for granted—saying that one *creates* a salad or that one can be creative in salad making is not a common locution. Most salads are modeled after cultural stereotypes—other salads we have known. Yet, in fact, the possibilities are infinite. In our imagination we can visualize new gustatory possibilities, we can conceive of what might be, but is not yet. We can also consider the ingredients we have at hand and those that we can acquire. Within the interplay of image and reality we go to work. The options available are multiple. We can decide not only what to use, but how to prepare what we decide to use. How shall the vegetables be sliced? What proportion of each ingredient should be included? How should the ingredients be arranged—mixed, layered, arrayed on a flat tray? And what about the dressing—what kind, how much, and should it be served directly on the vegetables or on the side? Each image of the desirable requires that we attend to, reflect upon, and speculate on the qualities of alternative potential salads. The prosaic salad is now not simply the product of a known recipe, but a creative invention intended to delight our senses: taste, sight, tactility, and smell. We perceive and imagine, we compare and contrast. We estimate the time and cost of each alternative. We act, monitor, and appraise. In the end, our salad reflects our culinary ambitions, the degree to which our skills make our ambitions realizable, and the extent to which our imagination and our sensibilities allow us to innovate and to monitor what we have done. Thus, our humble salad can exemplify sophisticated qualitative problem solving. The qualities of what we have made reflect the extent to which we have succeeded.

Salads are things one makes that require attention to qualities. Another such "thing" is conversation, and conversation is close to teaching. Being good at the art of conversation means knowing when to be still and what to emphasize when speaking, knowing how to hear what one listens to, and seeing expression in body, voice, and gesture. It requires paying close attention to the various qualitative cues that people provide and, in return, being able to convey in similar terms those qualities that keep the conversation alive and interesting.

The good conversationalist—and the good teacher—know how to experience and respond to a wide array of meanings, many of them nonverbal. After all, almost any phrase—such as "Did you do that?"—can take on a very wide array of meanings depending upon which words are emphasized. Emphasis is a matter of controlling qualities. "*Did* you do that?" "Did *you* do that?" "Did you *do* that?" "Did you do *that*?" Any written transcript of classroom discourse that omits such emphasis is likely to miscommunicate. Only one part of the meaning of any set of words resides in their so-called literal meaning. To understand what goes on in schools and classrooms requires sensitivity to how something is said and done, not only to what is said and done. Indeed, the what may very well depend upon the how.

Those most skilled in the qualitative treatment of language are writers. When their skill is great, they give us material that helps us understand, paradoxically, what words cannot express. Consider the words of Elie Wiesel. A child during World War II, Wiesel (1969, 1970, 1972, 1978) spent four years of his life in Buchenwald, a Nazi death camp in which two million people were systematically gassed to death and their corpses burned in ovens. How shall we come to know these events? They are past. How shall we—or can we—relive what those who found themselves there experienced? Through what means can we participate, if only vicariously, in their reality and thus know even vaguely what they felt? Elie Wiesel's words have lessons to teach to those of us interested in the qualitative portrayal of schools and other institutions. Listen to Wiesel as he writes:

> Never shall I forget that night, the first night in camp, which has turned my life into one long night, seven times cursed and seven times sealed. Never shall I forget that smoke. Never shall I forget the little faces of the children, whose bodies I saw turned into wreaths of smoke beneath a silent blue sky.
>
> Never shall I forget those flames which consumed my faith forever.
>
> Never shall I forget that nocturnal silence which deprived me, for all eternity, of the desire to live. Never shall I forget those moments which murdered my God and my soul and turned my dreams to dust. Never shall I forget these things, even if I am condemned to live as long as God Himself. Never.
>
> The barracks we had been made to go into was very long. In the roof were some blue-tinged skylights. The antechamber of Hell must look like this. So many crazed men, so many cries, so much bestial brutality!
>
> There were dozens of prisoners to receive us, truncheons in their hands, striking out anywhere, at anyone, without reason. Orders:
>
> "Strip! Fast! *Los*! Keep only your belts and shoes in your hands. . . ."

We had to throw our clothes at one end of the barracks. There was already a great heap there. New suits and old, torn coats, rags. For us, this was the true equality: nakedness. Shivering with the cold.

Some SS officers moved about in the room, looking for strong men. If they were so keen on strength, perhaps one should try and pass oneself off as sturdy? My father thought the reverse. It was better not to draw attention to oneself. Our fate would then be the same as the others. (Later, we were to learn that he was right. Those who were selected that day were enlisted in the Sonder-Kommando, the unit which worked in the crematories. Bela Katz—son of a big tradesman from our town—had arrived at Birkenau with the first transport, a week before us. When he heard of our arrival, he managed to get word to us that, having been chosen for his strength, he had himself put his father's body into the crematory oven.)

Blows continued to rain down.

"To the barber!"

Belt and shoes in hand, I let myself be dragged off to the barbers. They took our hair off with clippers, and shaved off all the hair on our bodies. The same thought buzzed all the time in my head—not to be separated from my father.

Freed from the hands of the barbers, we began to wander in the crowd, meeting friends and acquaintances. These meetings filled us with joy—yes, joy—"Thank God! You're still alive!"

But others were crying. They used all their remaining strength in weeping. Why had they let themselves be brought here? Why couldn't they have died in their beds? Sobs choked their voices.

Suddenly, someone threw his arms round my neck in an embrace: Yechiel, brother of the rabbi of Sighet. He was sobbing bitterly. I thought he was weeping with joy at still being alive. (Wiesel, 1969, pp. 44–46)

In these few paragraphs Wiesel creates a text that allows us to visualize and feel the desperation that characterized his arrival in Buchenwald. The phrase "never shall I forget. . ." seven times repeated creates a cadence that supports the meaning of "never," an unending sense, an emphatic recapitulation designed to heighten the intensity of an already intense moment. Through the pace of the language, the picture of the barracks and of the nakedness of their bodies, the prisoners' vulnerability is made palpable. Cadence, image, and innuendo, even in these few paragraphs, grab and hold us and provide the images through which we can enter into the scene vicariously. What we have here is a kind of portrait, painted in text, that generates the powerful visual image of a nightmare.

The creation of such a portrait depends upon the writer's ability to experience the qualities of place, to conceptualize their relationships, to experience the shifting pervasive qualities that permeate those relationships, and, not least, to imagine and render them through the text. The episode as lived has passed; the text as written lives. Thus the qualitative is used in two senses. The first is the ability to experience a particular state of affairs; to grasp how it was. The second is its representation, in Wiesel's case through text.

It might seem strange to be reading a book on qualitative inquiry in education in which the first topics given attention are salad making and a death camp operated by the Nazis during World War II. I have two reasons for using these examples. First, I wish to show that writers who attempt to enable their readers to enter into an event, even one as repulsive as a death camp, must somehow create a text that makes such vicarious participation possible. The experience of the camp and the form of the text must have some experiential congruence. Second, as I indicated earlier, I wish to show that qualitative considerations in human affairs are limited to neither the horrendous nor the exotic. They are a ubiquitous part of life and manifest themselves whenever we experience the qualities of the environment, even something as simple as a salad. Qualities are candidates for experience. Experience is what we achieve as those qualities come to be known. It is through qualitative inquiry, the intelligent apprehension of the qualitative world, that we *make sense*.

Features of Qualitative Inquiry

My discussion thus far has explored a number of issues. It would be helpful, I think, to distill and recapitulate the most important of these and then to indicate specifically what qualitative inquiry means in the context of education.

First, our sensory system is the instrument through which we experience the qualities that constitute the environment in which we live. For experience to be secured, qualities must be present, either in the environment or through an active imagination.

Second, the ability to experience qualities requires more than their presence. Experience is a form of human achievement, and as such it depends upon an act of mind; qualitative experience depends on qualitative forms of inquiry. We *learn* to see, hear, and feel. This process depends upon perceptual differentiation, and, in educational matters as in other forms of content, the ability to see what is subtle but significant is crucial. Those who are able to do so we often refer to as perceptive.

Third, qualitative inquiry is not only directed towards those aspects of the world "out there," it is also directed to objects and events that we are able to create. Salads, symphonies, and conversations require the exercise of qualitative thought. Because the selection and organization of qualities demand qualitative judgment, teaching and textbooks, school architecture and classroom layout are all influenced by qualitative considerations. Becoming smart about qualitative matters requires the ability to experience or create qualities worth experiencing. At their best we call such experience art.

Fourth, one of the most useful forms of qualitative inquiry, for my purposes, is found in literature. Writers display the ability to transform their own experience into a public form called text, which, when artfully crafted, allows us to participate in a way of life. We come to know a scene by virtue of what the writer has made. Thus, the writer starts with qualities and ends with words. The reader starts with words and ends with qualities.

Finally, texts can take different forms: literally written text can do what the figurative treatment of language cannot; poetry can say what prose cannot convey, and vice versa. Cultures throughout the world have provided their inhabitants with the resources necessary to transform experience into a public form so that it can be experienced by others. Although no two experiences can ever be identical, the kind of text one creates makes the difference, and that difference is epistemic. We come to know the world, in part, by virtue of the text we read, the images we see, and the songs we sing.

What do salads and the Holocaust have to do with inquiry into education? Just this. The problems that beset our schools are typically addressed by policy makers who have little first-hand knowledge about them. As a result, we are offered "solutions" to those problems that do not work. We are told that by lengthening the school day and school year, we will increase levels of achievement. We are told that by raising expectations, the performance of students will be raised. We are told that our country's place in the world is being threatened because our students do not score high enough on standardized achievement tests compared to students in other countries. We are told that if parents can choose the schools their children attend, competition among schools will raise the quality of schooling.

To know if more time in school is a good thing for children, we need to know what goes on in schools. If schools are really poor places for children to be, the last thing we want to do is to have them spend more time there. To know what schools are like, their strengths and their weaknesses, we need to be able to *see* what occurs in them, and we need to be able to tell others what we have seen in ways that are vivid and insightful. We need to achieve a critic's level of educational connoisseurship to recognize what counts, and we need to create a form of educational criticism to make what we see clear to those who have a stake in our schools. Raising test scores on multiple-choice tests might indeed be possible. But what, from an educational perspective, does it mean? Only by assessing the quality of teaching and the significance of the content being taught can we be in a position to make such judgments. This requires appraising education in ways akin to those in which critics appraise novels, films, poetry, and art. It requires judgment. A body of scholarship is not determined by counting the number of pages in an article or the number of articles a scholar publishes. Qualitative judgments must be made, and such judgments depend upon connoisseurship in the field in which the work is done.

When we are told that teachers should raise their expectations for students, we need to know if at present their expectations are too low. One way to find out is to ask teachers what they expect. A better way is to watch them teach. To *see* what we watch, we need to be able to attend to the implicit cues as well as to the explicit cues teachers provide. Such seeing depends upon qualitative forms of thought. Those who cannot see anything except what is most obvious are likely to be of little help in determining what schools are about, how classrooms function, or how teachers teach. Are teachers' expectations too low? At present we do not know.

The connection among schools, death camps, and salads is found in the attention that is paid to the qualities of the material or situation about which we want to speak or write. Qualitative thought is employed in teaching as well as in making salads. It occurs in the relationships we form with others, as well as in the environment we create for our children. To create telling prose, skilled teaching, and constructive relationships, we need to pay attention to the qualities that collectively constitute them. This attention furthers understanding. In the case of education, it provides the kind of understanding we need in order to create better schools and to evaluate the results of our efforts. Not everything can be said in a test score; for some things we need literary forms. This book is about the process of securing such understanding by building upon an existing tradition in the arts and humanities, a tradition that has generally been neglected as a way of understanding and enhancing educational practice. Our next step is to ask about the features of such work. Just what is it that makes a study qualitative? We now turn to that topic.

Notes

1. The concerns that I describe appear weekly in local newspapers and in periodicals published throughout the United States. Dozens of national reports proclaiming the unfortunate state of American education have been published since the early 1980s. See, for example, D. I. Commons (1985), *Who Will Teach Our Children?*; L. M. Branscomb (1986), *A Nation Prepared: Teachers for the 21st Century;* W. J. Bennett (1986), *First Lessons: A Report on Elementary Education in America;* and L. Alexander (1986), *Time for Results: The Governor's 1991 Report on Education.*

2. See, for example, the California Business Roundtable Report (1988), *Restructuring California Education: A Design for Public Education in the Twenty-First Century.*

3. This program is called "Cash for CAPS." *CAPS* refers to the California Assessment Program.

4. The utilization of knowledge produced by basic research in education has often been likened to the way in which farmers receive information from agricultural extension workers who have received information from basic researchers. The idea is that basic researchers in education will hand on their findings to extension workers in education, who will then pass on research conclusions to teachers in the field through in-service education. This orientation to research utilization significantly underestimates the differences between agriculture and education and puts teachers in a passive, receptive role. For a critical review of such procedures and the assumptions on which they rest, see H. Broudy (1976), "The Search for a Science of Education."

5. One of the distressing features in the educational arena is the rapidity with which ideas about ways to improve practice come and go. Every three or four years, it seems, a new "solution" is found for seemingly intractable educational problems. When these nostrums appear, teachers expected to follow the new lead. Eventually veteran teachers learn to ignore and ride out the new fad and continue on their own doing largely what they have always done. Having little stake in what is being offered and having had little success in what has been offered in the past, they have learned that passive resistance is an effective way to deal with changing fancies in education.

6. The recent reemergence of interest in *action research*, the idea that teachers themselves should be given an opportunity to define research problems and attempt to deal with them, is among the more promising of recent ideas concerning school improvement. For this to be successful, in my view, the teacher's role will need to be diversified so that the teachers interested in such work will have the opportunity, as a part of their normal work day, to pursue such endeavors. Such pursuits cannot be effectively undertaken if they are added to an already heavy teaching load. For an insightful discussion of this matter, see J. M. Atkin (1989), "Can Educational Research Keep Pace with Education Reform?"

7. For an illuminating discussion of the efforts by American educationists to create a uniform and effective system, see D. Tyack (1974), *The One Best System*. Also relevant to this general topic is L. Cuban (1988), *The Managerial Imperative*.

8. For examples of these debates, see E. W. Eisner and A. Peshkin (1990), *Qualitative Inquiry in Education: The Continuing Debate*.

9. There is a general tendency among lay people and even some educationists to regard performance in the arts as something other than the result of thinking. The association of art with emotion has been so powerful that the arts are often seen as the offshoot of emotion, and emotion has been regarded as the antithesis of thinking. Dewey's early recognition of the intelligent character of artistic thought serves as a precursor to some of the current views concerning various types of human intelligence. See, for example, J. Dewey (1931), "Qualitative Thought," in *Philosophy and Civilization*.

10. The well-developed fetus's sensitivity to sensory stimuli is discussed in detail in M. C. Robeck (1978), *Infants and Children: Their Development and Learning*.

11. Gestalt psychologists in particular have emphasized the process of perceptual differentiation, a process through which increasingly refined distinctions among qualities of the world are perceived. See, for example, the work of R. Arnheim (1954), *Art and Visual Perception*.

Chapter II

What Makes a Study Qualitative?

Artistic form is congruent with the dynamic forms of our direct sensuous life; works of art are projections of "felt life," as Henry James called it, into spatial, temporal, and poetic structures. They are images of feeling that formulate it for our conception.

Susanne Langer

The Primacy of Experience

All *empirical* inquiry is referenced in qualities. Even inquiry in the most quantitative of the sciences results in claims that refer to qualities. The truth or falsity of the claims one makes are determined by relating them to the qualities to which they purportedly refer. These qualities and the meaning we assign to them constitute the content of our experience. The word *empirical* is derived from Latin, *empericus,* which comes from Greek *emperikos,* "experience." Neither science nor art can exist outside of experience, and experience requires a subject matter. That subject matter is qualitative.

But if the matter were left there, there would be no difference between studies we refer to as quantitative and those we regard as qualitative. Yet, we know, both in our bones and in our heads, that they are not the same. The aim of this chapter is to describe the features of qualitative research. To do so in a principled way requires building an argument from the ground up. The first step is the idea that experience depends upon qualities and that all empirical inquiry is, at base, rooted in them.

The consequence of this observation is not only that knowledge of the empirical world is qualitative, but also that we confront the formidable task of trying to represent what we have come to know through some medium. The most common medium we use is language. One feature of a medium is that it mediates and anything that mediates changes what it conveys; the map is not the territory and the text is not the event. We learn to write and to draw, to dance and to sing, in order to *re*-present the world as we know it.[1]

What we are able to represent depends on two key factors. First is the form of representation we wish to use. The world we are able to create in text is a different world from the one we can present in a photograph. Second, the conceptual framework we employ directs our attention in particular ways and, therefore, what we experience is shaped by that framework. Thus, the questions we ask, the categories we employ, the theories we use guide our inquiry; indeed, what we come to know about the world is influenced by the tools we have available. An important but subtle point here is that language, like all other forms of representation, is constitutive of experience, it is not merely a conveyor of it. Language shapes, focuses, and directs our attention; it transforms our experience in the process of making it public.

The implication of these ideas is that the decision to study and describe the educational world through, say, sociology, influences what we study. It does this in a variety of ways. First, it shapes the content of experience by providing the categories and theories that define what is of interest. Sociologists are concerned with many aspects of human groups, but not all. Second, the decision to study education through sociology shapes the ways in which experience is to be represented because the form used to convey sociological understanding is linguistic in character. Third, it shapes both focus and message because it typically embraces a particular epistemology and therefore tends to neglect what will not meet conventional criteria for acceptable work within the sociological community. Method and medium are not passive instruments in making a message.

Further, just as sociological forms of inquiry (the example I have used merely for convenience) influence the content of experience, so do the other social sciences. Political scientists are interested in power, coalition, and exchange; psychologists in reinforcement, ego, and schema; sociologists in affiliation, status, and role; anthropologists in kinship, culture, and ritual, and so it goes. Each discipline defines its own interests, employs its own categories, specifies its own aims, and in so doing, creates its own world (Goodman, 1978). They have in common, however, their use of qualitative methods. Qualitative inquiry is not the property of any one discipline.

Although all of the social sciences, as well as history and literature, use language to describe the world, they use it in particular ways. One form of language is propositional. Propositional discourse consists of assertions having noun-predicate relations. In conventional approaches to research and evaluation, such discourse emphasizes the denotative use of language and literal meaning as ideal. The operational definition—defining terms with respect to the ways in which they can be measured—is one important means of achieving precision. Indeed, some regard mathematical language as the epitome of precision in representation.

Another way of achieving precision in language is to diminish its affective and personal features. Some social sciences still emphasize the importance of neutralizing voice in writing research reports. The presence of voice is thought to be a liability. This attitude manifests itself in the admonition (fortunately less prominent than it was) to use third-person singular or first-person plural in scientific writing, to refer to the people studied as subjects or "Ss," and to avoid metaphor and simile. I shall return to such matters when I address issues of subjectivity and objectivity in research, but for now the point is that the portrayal of the world that the social sciences study must eventually be made public through some form of representation. Language constitutes one such form, and the ways language can be used are multiple.

Novelists, playwrights, and poets, for example, also use language to describe and interpret what they have experienced. Yet their use of language is seldom mainly literal. Novelists, for example, use plot, metaphor, cadence, and innuendo as means through which to tell their stories. Their reasons have to do with the special functions that these linguistic devices perform. The potential of language to describe a setting and to convey the content of human experience is tremendous, as long as one is not restricted to a narrow set of linguistic conventions. Consider the ways in which language functions in the following:

> The village of Holcomb stands on the high wheat plains of western Kansas, a lonesome area that other Kansans call "out there." Some seventy miles east of the Colorado border, the countryside, with its hard blue skies and desert-clear air, has an atmosphere that is rather more Far West than Middle West. The local accent is barbed with a prairie twang, a ranch-hand nasalness, and the men, many of them, wear narrow frontier trousers, Stetsons, and high-heeled boots with pointed toes. The land is flat, and the views are awesomely extensive; horses, herds of cattle, a white cluster of grain elevators rising as gracefully as Greek temples are visible long before a traveler reaches them.
>
> Holcomb, too, can be seen from great distances. Not that there is much to see—simply an aimless congregation of buildings divided in the center by the main-line tracks of the Santa Fe Railroad, a haphazard hamlet bounded on the south by a brown stretch of the Arkansas (pronounced "Ar-kan-sas") River, on the north by a highway, Route 50, and on the east and west by prairie lands and wheat fields. After rain, or when snowfalls thaw, the streets, unnamed, unshaded, unpaved, turn from the thickest dust into the direst mud. At one end of the town stands a stark old stucco structure, the roof of which supports an electric sign—DANCE—but the dancing has ceased and the advertisement has been dark for several years. Nearby is another building with an irrelevant sign, this one in flaking gold on a dirty window—HOLCOMB BANK. The bank closed in 1933, and its former counting rooms have been converted into apartments. It is one of the

town's two "apartment houses," the second being a ramshackle mansion known, because a good part of the local school's faculty lives there, as the Teacherage. But the majority of Holcomb's homes are one-story frame affairs, with front porches.

Down by the depot, the postmistress, a gaunt woman who wears a rawhide jacket and denims and cowboy boots, presides over a falling-apart post office. The depot itself, with its peeling sulphur-colored paint, is equally melancholy; the Chief, the Super-Chief, the El Capitan go by every day, but these celebrated expresses never pause there. No passenger trains do—only an occasional freight. Up on the highway, there are two filling stations, one of which doubles as a meagerly supplied grocery store, while the other does extra duty as a cafe—Hartman's Cafe, where Mrs. Hartman, the proprietress, dispenses sandwiches, coffee, soft drinks, and 3.2 beer. Holcomb, like all the rest of Kansas, is "dry."

And that, really, is all. (Capote, 1965, p. 3–4)

It should be noted that Truman Capote's *In Cold Blood* is a true story. He depicts, with a certain literary license, what occurred "one morning in mid-November of 1959." It is what some critics have called "literary journalism" (Wolfe, 1973). My point here, however, is not one of classifying genre, but of displaying how a writer sets a stage that allows the reader to get a sense of the scene and mood in which, in Capote's case, a murder will be committed.

Schools also have moods, and they too display scenes of high drama that those who make policy and who seek to improve practice should know. The means through which such knowledge is made possible are the enlightened eye—the scene is seen—and the ability to craft text so that what the observer has experienced can be shared by those who were not there.

The ideas just expressed have several implications. First, it is in principle possible to write a text, even one born of imagination, that illustrates or exemplifies some important aspect of the world. Through imagination the writer creates a novel, for example, that conveys an intimate portrait of events that did not in fact occur, but could have occurred. Or the writer creates a text that portrays events that did not actually occur to the writer, but did occur to others. Then there are writers who, like Capote, write with artistic license about events that did in fact occur, but were reconstructed after the fact. And then there are those who select particular situations to study and who do so through premeditated means that allow others to replicate what they have to say about these events. The most systematic example of such a procedure is found in the laboratory experiment. Thus, there is a kind of continuum that moves from the fictional that is "true"—the novel for example—to the highly controlled and quantitatively described scientific experiment. Work at either end of this continuum has the capacity to inform significantly. Qualitative research and evaluation are located toward the fictive end of the continuum without being fictional in the narrow sense of the term.

Stating versus Expressing Meaning

Aesthetically oriented philosophers have attended to the ways in which qualitative, artistically crafted form can convey meaning. One of these is John Dewey. Dewey makes an important distinction between forms that state meaning and those that express them. Writing in *Art as Experience* (1934) he says:

> The problem in hand may be approached by drawing a distinction between expression and statement. Science states meanings; art expresses them. Statement sets forth the conditions under which an experience of an object or situation may be had. It is a good, that is, effective, statement in the degree in which these conditions are stated in such a way that they can be used as directions by which one may arrive at the experience.
>
> The poetic as distinct from the prosaic, esthetic art as distinct from scientific, expression as distinct from statement, does something different from leading to an experience. It constitutes one. (p. 84)

Dewey's point here is echoed by Susanne Langer in her distinction between *representational symbols* and *presentational symbols*. For Langer (1942), representational symbols, like Dewey's stated meanings, are symbols that *point to* the meanings they are intended to convey. Propositional discourse, a prime example, directs readers' or listeners' attention to its referents. The sentence "The cat is on the couch" is, in a sense, a set of directions that tell one what to anticipate if one used the statement as a guide. The words themselves do not express "catness," "on-ness," or "couchness." For such meanings to be expressed, as contrasted with stated, a form must be created that presents directly the quality of the experience the author or speaker wishes to convey; here the task becomes an artistic one. Thus when Dewey says that science states meanings and art expresses them, he means, using Langer's terminology, that the symbols used in science are representational while those used in art are presentational. Representational symbols are, so to speak, transparent. We move through them to their referents. Artistic symbols are opaque. We do not use them to move to their referents, but secure from them directly the meanings they display. An illustration of this may be seen in the graphic treatments of the word cat on the following page.

In the first version the word *cat* is strictly denotative and conventional. Although Bodoni type face has, in fact, an expressive quality, this typeface is so prevalent that we tend to neglect its form and deal with the

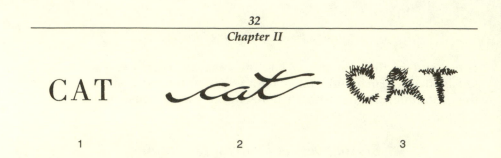

word's denotative meaning rather than with the interaction between denotation and form. In version one, the word *cat* is a cue whose referent we can imagine without difficulty.

Version two presents a different state of affairs. Here the letters *C-A-T* are still quite legible. From a literal perspective there is no difference between versions one and two. But, the form used to spell *cat* in version two is quite different from version one. In version two, we experience some of the sleek and feline qualities of cats. This version of *cat* depicts or expresses one aspect of the cat's "catness." Words, or more precisely the treatment of letters within a word, say as much as the letters considered from a literal perspective.

Version three also possesses expressive features, but the pervasive quality of these features is wholly different from those exemplified in versions one and two. Although both the letters and the word remain identical, the way each version has been treated conveys a different meaning. Version three presents to us a very different cat—or, at least, aspect of "catness"—from version two.

Six Features of Qualitative Study

I turn now to the enumeration and description of the features that make a study qualitative. There are six such features, each of which contributes in different ways to the overall character of a qualitative study.

First, qualitative studies tend to be *field focused*. In education, those conducting qualitative research go out to schools, visit classrooms, and observe teachers. They might observe school boards in action, watch children as they play, hang out at the local park in order to get the material they need. But the field focus that I describe is not limited to places in which humans interact, it also includes the study of inanimate objects: school architecture, textbooks, classroom design, the location of trophy cases in schools, and the design of lunchrooms. In short, anything that has import for education is a potential subject matter of qualitative study.

Reflect for a moment on the women's movement and its concern with sexist language in textbooks, with the proportion of attention devoted to men and women on textbook pages, with the visual illustrations used. All these and more are the proper objects of qualitative study. Vallance (1975) made social studies textbooks the objects of her qualitative study. She was interested in the ways in which texts employed aesthetic features to convey their messages. Such matters are not marginal because how books are written, how buildings are designed, how classrooms are organized tell us as much about how people are supposed to behave and what they are supposed to learn as anything else can. It is not for nothing that banks have made such a heavy use of Doric columns and neoclassical architecture. Rationality and reliability inhere in Greek architecture; the message is unmistakable.

As a part of a field focus, the qualitative study is usually nonmanipulative, that is, it tends to study situations and objects intact: as Lincoln and Guba (1978) say, it is "naturalistic." This feature is close to anthropologists' desire to appear invisible to the individuals in the cultures they study, although some anthropologists have begun to explore the significance of intervention within the cultures in which they work (Scheper-Hughes, 1979). On the whole, however, qualitative researchers observe, interview, record, describe, interpret, and appraise settings as they are.

In emphasizing the typical features of qualitative studies, I do not want to preclude studies that do examine educational change. In a qualitative study undertaken by Decker Walker and myself (Eisner & Walker, 1989), we provided a private foundation with information on the extent to which funds allocated for curriculum change in four school districts located in three states resulted in successful changes. Our charge from the foundation was to study the process of change, to determine the extent to which it was occurring, and to make judgments about the quality of the program that was being implemented in relation to the program's goals. To do this we observed teachers in action, visited classrooms in each of the districts, interviewed school administrators and school board members, as well as teachers, and appraised the curriculum materials that each of the districts was using. In this situation change (indeed improvement) was the ultimate subject matter of our interests, but we were not the ones who were manipulating change, though we were observing it. Since the process of change was under the control of each district, there was no reason why self-generated change should not be studied in qualitative ways. Indeed, many school districts are engaged in educational experimentation that begs for qualitative study: magnet schools, cooperative learning, restructuring, uses of mentor teachers, peer coaching, computer-assisted instruction, and the like. Opportunities for qualitative research abound in school districts throughout the country.

A second characteristic of qualitative studies relates to *the self as an instrument*. I have made much of the importance of sensibility and perceptivity in the context of qualitative research. My emphasis is due to the fact that the features that count in a setting do not wear their labels on their sleeves: they do not announce themselves. Researchers must see what is to be seen, given some frame of reference and some set of intentions. The self is the instrument that engages the situation and makes sense of it. This is done most often without the aid of an observation schedule; it is not a matter of checking behaviors, but rather of perceiving their presence and interpreting their significance.

The ability to see what counts is one of the features that differentiates novices from experts. According to Berliner (1988), novice teachers tend to describe virtually everything they can in a classroom when they are asked to say what is going on there. The expert knows what to neglect. Knowing what to neglect means having a sense for the significant and possessing a framework that makes the search for the significant efficient. In the 1940s, de Groot (1946) demonstrated that the visual memory of grand masters in chess was no more sophisticated or well-developed than their not-so-grand chess counterparts. The difference between experts and those less expert was that grand masters possessed a wider array of schemata with which to sort out the configurations on the board. Their visual memory was specific to chess. Meaning was the source of their perception.

We have here, when applied to the study of classrooms and schools, the interplay of sensibility and schema. Both sensibility and schema provide the means through which we make sense of a complex qualitative array. Sensibility alerts us to nuanced qualities and the schema relevant to a domain, the significance of what to seek and see. Without sensibility the subtleties of the social world go unexperienced. Without a schema no sorting into significance is possible.[2]

Related to the self as instrument is the positive exploitation of our own subjectivity (Peshkin, 1988). As I have intimated in the foregoing, each person's history, and hence world, is unlike anyone else's. This means that the way in which we see and respond to a situation, and how we interpret what we see, will bear our own signature. This unique signature is not a liability but a way of providing individual insight into a situation. In conventional research, conformity to a standard criterion applied uniformly by a clutch of judges whose scores can be correlated to determine the level of consensus is characteristic. The operational question is, "Do the judgments of the judges correlate at a level significantly beyond chance?" To achieve high levels of interjudge agreement, judges are trained to apply prespecified criteria on sample cases until differences among the judgments are diminished. When ratings are sufficiently uniform among judges, the actual judging begins.

In that form of qualitative inquiry called educational criticism, the picture and the assumptions in qualitative research are different. Although critics can be trained to make common appraisals, even common interpretations of classrooms, prespecifications suppress or neglect those uniquely astute observations and interpretations that are the hallmarks of perceptive educational critics. Rather than regarding uniformity and standardization as the summmum bonum, educational criticism views unique insight as the higher good.

This appreciation for personal insight as a source of meaning does not provide a license for freedom.[3] Educational critics must provide evidence and reasons. But they reject the assumption that unique interpretation is a conceptual liability in understanding, and they see the insights secured from multiple views as more attractive than the comforts provided by a belief in a single right one.

A third feature that makes a study qualitative is its *interpretive character*. In the context of qualitative inquiry, the term *interpretive* has two meanings. First, it means that inquirers try to *account for* what they have given an *account of*. Why does this teacher respond to the class in this way? What accounts for the use of these kinds of incentives in this classroom? How has a new educational policy influenced the way teachers teach? What kinds of assumptions about intellect are reflected in new curriculum requirements? What kinds of messages does the allocation of time to subject matter send to students about the importance of what they study? In short, one meaning of *interpretation* pertains to the ability to explain why something is taking place. This requires, at times, the use of constructs from the social sciences. At other times it requires the creation of new theory.

A second meaning of *interpretation* pertains to what experience holds for those in the situation studied. As I indicated earlier, qualitative research is concerned with matters of meaning. *Meaning* is an elusive term, and one way to treat such elusive matters is to neglect them entirely. Behaviorism took this road. What matters most in behaviorism is what people or animals do, not what the doing means to them. For qualitative researchers and evaluators meaning, though elusive, still counts. In this sense qualitative researchers are interested in matters of motive and in the quality of experience undergone by those in the situation studied. Just what does motivate Jimmy to do his work in math? How does Jane feel when asked to organize a mural for the forthcoming play? How does an announcement on the public address system affect fourth graders when it interrupts a lively discussion of a poem that they have just been reading?

It is certainly true that attention to behavior is necessary, but observation and description do not end with behavior. Qualitative inquiry penetrates the surface. Qualitative inquirers seek what Geertz (1973) has called "thick description." They aim beneath manifest behavior to the meaning events have for those who experience them. Elie Wiesel (1969) helped us understand a bit of that deep structure in the few paragraphs of his text on the Holocaust quoted in chapter 1; he wished to render not just manifest behavior, but image and its import.

The terms within which matters of meaning are made public depend in large measure on the theoretical structures or frames of reference that are brought to bear upon the scene. Earlier I said that both sensibility and schema gave import to observation. The kind of import that emerges in any portrayal of a situation is shaped by the kind of schema that is employed. If anthropologists study a village, the traditions, habits, and theoretical constraints within the brand of anthropology they practice will provide the windows for perception and the terms within which meanings are made. Rite, ritual, kinship, and the like are likely to be salient schema for providing focus. If the village is encountered by political scientists, another story, no less real, will be told. Historians will pay attention to other matters, painters still others. And so it goes. Meanings are construed, and the shape they take is due, in part, to the tools people know how to use. Different disciplines employ different tools. Thus which meanings become salient is a function not only of the qualities "out there," but of which tools people bring to them.

Conceptual tools, immediately at hand, are not the only factors that influence the meanings we secure from what we observe. Our appreciation for antecedent factors is another. The historical antecedents of a context provide a background against which particular episodes acquire meaning. Humans learn; they bring with them memories and interpretations of past events. What they experience is, in part, shaped by their personal history. For example, whether a school superintendent takes risks or does not may be related to her perception of the history of the district and its implications for her and the district in the present. Billiard balls in motion are all cause and effect. To my knowledge they participate in no cultural legacy and possess no memory. Here, history is unimportant. Not so in classrooms, schools, or school districts. Where has the community come from? How has it changed? In which direction does it appear to be tending? And what about this particular ten-year-old child? Is his parents' marriage still intact? What does a shaky home life mean for his ability to deal with criticism? Do I need to be extra supportive? Such questions are relevant in qualitative research.

A fourth feature that qualitative studies display, particularly educational criticism, is one I have already discussed: *the use of expressive language* and the presence of voice in text. The kind of detachment that some journals prize—the neutralization of voice, the aversion to metaphor and to adjectives, the absence of the first person singular—is seldom a feature of qualitative studies. We display our signatures. Our signature makes it clear that a person, not a machine, was behind the words. The rhetorical devices that are used in some social science journals in order to mask the fact that a person did the work reported is ironic; the need for objectivity leads to camouflage. "I" becomes "we" or "the researcher." How such magic occurs is not clear, but what is clear is that such locutions are deceptive.

The presence of voice and the use of expressive language are also important in furthering human understanding. German psychologists call it *einfuhlung*. In English, it is called "empathy."

Empathy is the ability to don the shoes of another human being. One experiences this in reading Elie Wiesel or Truman Capote. Good writers put you there. Empathy pertains to feeling or to emotion, and emotion, interestingly, is often regarded as the enemy of cognition. I reject such a view. To read about people or places or events that are emotionally powerful and to receive an eviscerated account is to read something of a lie. Why take the heart out of the situations we are trying to help readers understand?

A lovely discussion of the way in which scientific language transforms experience into symbols bereft of feeling is that of Eddington (1929), the great physicist of the first half of the twentieth century.

> Let us examine the kind of knowledge which is handled by exact science. If we search the examination papers in physics and natural philosophy for the more intelligible questions we may come across one beginning something like this: "An elephant slides down a grassy hillside. . ." The experienced candidate knows that he need not pay much attention to this; it is only put in to give an impression of realism. He reads on: "The mass of the elephant is two tons." Now we are getting down to business; the elephant fades out of the problem and a mass of two tons takes its place. What exactly is the two tons, the real subject-matter of the problem? It refers to some property or condition which we vaguely describe as "ponderosity" occurring in a particular region of the external world. But we shall not get much further that way; the nature of the external world is inscrutable, and we shall only plunge into a quagmire of indescribables. Never mind what two tons *refers* to; what *is* it? How has it actually entered in so definite a way into our experience? Two tons *is* the reading of the pointer when the elephant was placed on a weighing machine. Let us pass on. "The slope of the hill is 60°." Now the hillside fades out of the problem and an angle of 60° takes its place. What is 60°? There is no need to struggle with mystical conceptions of direction; 60° *is* the reading of a plumb-line against the divisions of a protractor. Similarly for the other data of the problem. The softly yielding turf on which the elephant slid is replaced by a coefficient of friction, which though perhaps not directly a pointer reading is of a kindred nature. No doubt there are more roundabout ways used in practice for determining the weights of elephants and the slopes of hills, but these are justified because it is known that they give the same results as direct pointer readings.
>
> . . .And so we see that the poetry fades out of the problem, and by the time the serious application of exact science begins we are left with only pointer readings. If then only pointer readings or their equivalents are put into the machine of scientific calculation, how can we grind out anything but pointer readings? But that is just what we do grind out. The question presumably was to find the time of descent of

the elephant, and the answer is a pointer reading on the seconds' dial of our watch. (pp. 251–53)

Now it should be said that for the aims of physics, transforming information into measured forces is appropriate. It is inappropriate if one is trying to help readers understand what other people experience. To model inquiry in education after inquiry in physics might serve some small purpose, but I do not believe physics can provide an adequate model for educational research. Feeling the heat on the seat of one's pants as one slides down a slope is not at all like reading a gauge that measures velocity and friction. Good qualitative writing helps readers experience the heat—vicariously, of course.

A fifth feature of qualitative studies is their *attention to particulars*. Conventional social science uses particulars to arrive at general statements. It does this through the use of sampling procedures and inferential statistics. For statistical procedures to be used, data have to be created. The form data take to be statistically treated is numerical. When this transformation occurs the uniqueness of particular features is lost. What emerges is a description of relationships, almost disconnected from the particulars from which the data were originally secured.

This transformation of qualities into their quantitative "equivalents"—they are never equivalent—is one of the contributions of post-Galilean science. In *The Quest for Certainty*, Dewey (1929) discusses this transformation.

> The work of Galileo was not a development, but a revolution. It marked a change from the qualitative to the quantitative or metric; from the heterogeneous to the homogeneous; from intrinsic forms to relations; from esthetic harmonies to mathematical formulae; from contemplative enjoyment to active manipulation and control; from rest to change; from eternal objects to temporal sequence. (pp. 94–95)

It can, of course, be useful to transform particular qualitative features into generic statements; aggregation is possible through this process, and through aggregation, a kind of conceptual economy. At the same time, the flavor of the particular situation, individual, event, or object is lost. Qualitative studies tend to provide that flavor. This is done, first of all, by sensitivity to what might legitimately be called the aesthetic features of the case. The most sophisticated manifestations of such perception are located in the fine arts. Connoisseurs of the fine arts are able to make very fine-grained distinctions among the works of art they attend to. In fact, the best are able to detect fakes and forgeries that would fool their somewhat less sophisticated peers. Revelation of the particular situation requires, first, awareness of its distinctiveness. Perception is still central, but beyond that, the ability to render those distinctive features through text is required. When reading a finely honed case study using educational criticism, readers gain a feeling for the distinctive characteristics of the case. The classroom, the school, the teacher are not lost to abstraction. Again, in the cases of Holcomb and Buchenwald, Capote and Wiesel do this for us. At the same time, particulars exemplify more than they describe directly. In the particular is located a general theme.

I will address this issue in chapter 8. For the present, the point is that qualitative studies provide a sense of the uniqueness of the case; the best make the case palpable.

A sixth feature of qualitative studies pertains to the criteria for judging their success. Qualitative research becomes believable because of its *coherence, insight,* and *instrumental utility.*

Unlike the experiment that demonstrates relations of cause and effect or correlations that statistically describe the strength of association, qualitative studies typically employ multiple forms of evidence, and they persuade by reason. The term *persuasion* might seem at first inappropriate for an enterprise aimed at furthering human understanding. We usually seek to discover truth, to dig up the facts, to come to know things objectively. This conception of knowledge tends to discount its social nature and the influence that framework and perspective have upon the ways in which we make what we know. Qualitative inquiry, like conventional quantitative approaches to research, is ultimately a matter of persuasion, of seeing things in a way that satisfies, or is useful for the purposes we embrace. The evidence employed in qualitative studies comes from multiple sources. We are persuaded by its "weight," by the coherence of the case, by the cogency of the interpretation. We try out our perspective and attempt to see if it seems "right" (Goodman, 1978). In qualitative research there is no statistical test of significance to determine if results "count"; in the end, what counts is a matter of judgment.

The entire character of the enterprise has a strong rational and often aesthetic spirit. It is an approach to the social world that accepts its dynamic and living quality. We acknowledge that what we believe to be the case enjoys only a temporary status. Social situations are in a state of flux. This does not mean that conclusions drawn about schools, classrooms, teachers, or students have only a brief and fugitive life. It does mean that qualitative inquirers do not seek those universal, invariable, and eternal natural laws represented by the aims of physicists. Ours is a "softer," more malleable universe—or a collection of them.

The practical implication of the foregoing is that judgment will play a larger role than is often the case when the results of an inquiry appear "incontrovertible." In qualitative inquiry, judgment is alive and well, and hence the arena for debate and difference is always open. In qualitative research the facts never speak for themselves.

There is, of course, a model for such work, not only in literature and anthropology, but in a field whose conclusions have profound social and individual consequences. The field I speak of is law. Courts of law are the theaters in which cases are made or lost, and the means for the making is arguments based upon reasons that appeal most often to evidence of various kinds, but that seldom lead unambiguously to a single conclusion. There are always ambiguities, circumstances, alternative positions, other ways to interpret the evidence, and other evidence. The attorney in court tries to make her case by mustering evidence that will persuade a jury that the evidence calls for an innocent verdict. Her adversary seeks the opposite. In many ways qualitative research is similar in its effort to persuade.

I want to make it clear that I am not suggesting that conventional research, particularly in the field of education, is not similarly engaged. It is. However, it typically does not couch its efforts in these terms. *Persuasion* has a subjective ring, for some the ring of the huckster. Yet how studies are designed, the kind of instruments used, the settings studied, the statistics employed, and the way data are interpreted are all ultimately intended to yield a persuasive case that will withstand the doubts of skeptics and the attacks of those whose values lead them to see the situation differently. Perspectivism is not an attractive idea to those who believe a nature exists and that it can be known as it really is.

Finally, it should be recognized that the features I have described are present to varying degrees in any particular study. Studies can be qualitative by degree.[4] The formalized, quantitatively described experiment in the psychological laboratory will have few of the features I have described. A study of schools of the kind that Sarah Lawrence Lightfoot (1983) or Tom Barone (1978) creates will have many of the features. It is possible to find examples all along the way. Some studies explicitly combine qualitative and quantitative material and do so effectively (Sternberg, 1978). My point here is to make it clear that when I talk about what makes a study qualitative, I am not referring to a notion of class inclusion, class exclusion—the idea that something must be one thing *or* another. Human works can be located on a continuum. *Hamlet* resides at one end of the continuum, Duncan Luce's (1960) work in mathematical psychology at the other.

One of the major concerns of those who reflect upon the methodological issues in qualitative research centers upon questions of subjectivity and objectivity. Can we trust subjective accounts? Chapter 3 addresses this and related questions.

Notes

1. The concept of representation should not be interpreted in this book to mean the creation of an image isomorphic with the perceived world. The process of *re*-presentation is a process of construal, a reconstruction, and as such it

reconstitutes the experience from which it originates. We have no mirror for nature.

2. For a lucid and useful discussion for the role of schemata in cognition, see U. Neisser (1976), *Cognition and Reality: Principles and Implications of Cognitive Psychology.*

3. The charge that "anything goes" is prevalent in qualitative research and is often made by individuals who require a strict standard or criterion for determining the meaning and value of claims or who simply do not understand the features of qualitative inquiry. As training in qualitative methods continues to grow in schools of education and elsewhere, I expect that we will be hearing less about "anything goes."

4. Not only can studies be qualitative by degree—that is, some qualitative studies may be extremely figurative and literary while others more literal in the use of language—they can employ both literary and quantitative forms of representation. There is no reason why several forms of representation, including the quantitative, cannot be combined in the conduct of a study that is dominantly qualitative in character, or vice versa.

Chapter III

Objectivity and Subjectivity in Qualitative Research and Evaluation

Man is an animal suspended in webs of significance that he himself has spun.

Clifford Geertz

The Search for What is Real

In American culture at large, but especially within the educational research community, the search for an objective view of things remains an elusive ideal. Whatever else we may want in our efforts to understand the world, objectivity is surely among the most cherished ideals. But what is objectivity, and what makes it so important? And how do we attain it?

This chapter will address these questions. My analysis will be built upon a distinction between what Newell (1986) calls *ontological* and *procedural objectivity*. I hope to persuade readers that ontological objectivity cannot, in principle, provide what we hope for and that procedural objectivity provides less than we think. I will then provide a conception that I believe does not suffer from the unrealizable expectations that we have held for an objective view of things. I hope that by reconceptualizing the way in which we create and relate to the worlds in which we participate, we will be able to secure a more reasonable and useful way of thinking about the status of our empirical beliefs.

Objectivity usually means seeing things the way they are. To be objective is to experience a state of affairs in a way that reveals its actual features. To see things the way they are is to experience or know them in their ontological state. This is called *ontological objectivity*, or *veridicality*. In the best of all worlds, we seek veridicality in both perception and understanding. What we wish to see and know is not some subjective, make-believe world created through fantasy, ideology, or desire, but what is really out there. Like Sergeant Friday, we want to know the "facts, ma'am, just the facts." Veridicality implies an isomorphic relationship between claim and reality.[1]

Those familiar with epistemology will know that veridicality as an ideal is predicated upon a correspondence theory of truth. The aim of epistemology, as the Greeks had it, was to achieve true and certain knowledge. This was what differentiated knowledge from belief. Knowledge was *episteme*, belief was *doxa*. Thus, whatever we *knew* was, by definition, true. If it were not true, we could not know it. We could *believe* it to be true, but belief and knowledge were then, and are today, different states of being. This orientation to knowledge regards knowledge as a matter of discovery. Thus, we say that scientists *discover* the laws that govern the universe and that they unearth the facts. We seek an objective world objectively known.

It should also be noted that as an ideal, correspondence between the world and inquirers not only refers to what inquirers perceive, but also to what they have to say about the world. In other words, correspondence is to occur not only in perception and understanding, but also in representation. At its best, such representation provides, as Richard Rorty (1979) chided, a mirror to nature.

Procedural objectivity is the development and use of a method that eliminates, or aspires to eliminate, the scope for personal judgment in the description and appraisal of a state of affairs. One of the commonest examples of such a method is the objectively scored achievement test. Once the test has been constructed, identifying a correct or incorrect response does not require interpretation. Although there are interpretive issues at stake at the level of test construction, at the level of scoring, the optical scanner will do. Since scoring requires no judgment, it is procedurally objective—hence, we say that we have an objective test or an objective method for scoring responses.

Operational definitions are also procedurally objective. Defining a concept or skill by how it is measured means employing a set of procedures that others can also use. Furthermore, when such procedures are used, they are expected to yield identical results as long as the procedures are followed and as long as the phenomenon that was measured does not itself change. Tests or procedures that depend upon personal judgment, are referred to as subjective, and as most researchers have come to believe, subjective judgments cannot be trusted. The aim of the research enterprise, from a methodological perspective, is to use a procedurally objective set of methods in order to gain an ontologically objective understanding of the events and objects under study.

Procedural objectivity is also secured by training judges to make identical judgments about the objects of their judgment. This is done by specifying the criteria that are to be employed and by assigning numbers to qualities along a continuum displaying excellence on each criterion. When judges are successfully trained in the application of the criteria, correlations among the judges' scores will be high; ideally, they will be uniform. In such circumstances, even when measurement is not used in a literal sense, we say that the judges have used objective or nearly objective scoring procedures. We believe that judges at the Olympic Games are not making merely subjective judgments about the quality of the dives they score. As differences among judges' scores increase, our confidence in the judges' judgment decreases. Consensus breeds confidence in the objectivity of the judgments rendered.

Subjectivity is such a troublesome notion in the educational research community that we have created language norms to reduce its presence.[2] We refer to ourselves as *the researcher* or use the first-person plural. Until quite recently the first-person singular,—*I, me, my*— was proscribed in research reports. We talk about *subjects*, not about people, or, even more remotely, we use the letter *S* to refer to them. In short, we formalize our language as much as possible in order to depersonalize our presence in the works we create. Personalization undermines objectivity; that is, we fear that it will suggest that what we have to say about the world will reflect more about ourselves than about the world as it is. Our discourse traditions are intended to create the illusion that we have provided an ontologically objective mirror image of what is really out there.

The problems with ontological objectivity and procedural objectivity are important, both because they lead to certain practical problems in the conduct of empirical research (we often tend, for example, to avoid studying what we cannot measure) and because they reinforce a view of knowledge that is itself problematic. Consider, for example, the correspondence theory of truth upon which an ontological objectivity rests.

How can we ever know if our views of reality match or correspond to it? To know that we have a correspondence between our views of reality and reality itself, we would need to know two things. We would need to know reality, as well as our views of it. But if we knew reality as it really is, we would not need to have a view of it. Conversely, since we cannot have knowledge of reality as it is, we cannot know if our view corresponds to it.

Some argue that a "true" view of reality allows us to predict or control events. When we are able to do this, our view of reality may be said to correspond with reality itself. But our ability to predict or control events does not entitle us to conclude that the views we hold about the world correspond to the world as it really is. Faith healers have for years achieved "miraculous" results from their ministrations. The fact that their ministrations sometimes work does not mean that their beliefs about the source of their effects are true—or that our views are. Using prediction and control as criteria for verifying belief is an instance of affirming the consequent, a procedure that is not logically justified, as Popper (1959) and others have pointed out. Indeed, Popper's view is that we can never verify the truth of a claim, we can only refute it, and even then, never completely. Popper is a fallibilist, not a verificationist.

Related to the impossibility of knowing the world in its pristine state—a kind of immaculate perception—is the framework-dependent character of perception. Perception of the world is influenced by skill, point of view, focus, language, and framework. The eye is not only a part of the brain, it is a part of tradition. How shall teaching be perceived? It depends upon what I think counts. If I am interested in "wait time," then I will look for it. The clarity of language, the teacher's relationship and rapport with students, the significance of the ideas presented, and the teacher's personal style, warmth, and enthusiasm are all candidates for attention. Which to choose depends upon framework. To paraphrase Kant, percepts without frameworks are empty, and frameworks without percepts are blind. We secure frameworks through socialization, professional and otherwise. What we come to see depends upon what we seek, and what we seek depends, as Gombrich has pointed out, on what we know how to say. Artists, Gombrich reminds us, do not paint what they see, they see what they are able to paint. An empty mind sees nothing. Bruner, Neisser, Goodman, Arnheim, and Geertz have all pointed out that mind mediates the world and because it does, perception itself is a cognitive event.

There is, of course, a further complication regarding ontological objectivity. That complication deals with the limitations inherent in representation. Any report of the world has to take some form and be carried by some symbol system. Some systems, such as language, describe. Others, such as visual art, depict. Some languages describe literally, others metaphorically. Some visual systems depict visually, but appeal basically to our emotions—as in expressionism. Others depict visually, but appeal to our imagination—as in surrealism. Still others depict visually, but appeal to our optical experience—the work of Josef Albers and color field painting come to mind. Within a single symbol system there are unique constraints and unique possibilities. Because any symbol system both reveals and conceals, its use provides, of necessity, a partial view of the reality it is intended to describe or depict. In fact, the form we select is constitutive of the understanding we acquire: the medium is a part of the message.

To complicate matters further, the schemata we use themselves structure perception. These schemata may be thought of as *structures of appropriation*. They define the contours through which our perception and comprehension of the world are created. In this sense, Goodman's point (1978) about the world-making nature of symbol systems becomes especially cogent: To prolife activists, a fertilized egg is a child and its destruction murder. To the prochoice population, it is an unviable protoplasm that has not yet achieved the status of a person. Each group creates its own world through the schemata of the human that it uses.

Given these considerations, the prospects for achieving ontological objectivity—the pristine, unmediated grasp of the world as it is—seem to fade. For many, I suspect, the absence of what Goodman (1978, p. 96) has called "something stolid underneath" is a problem. Without an anchor, how can we maintain our stability? The need for such an anchor creates the motivation to find it, to assure ourselves that it is there, and that with adequate effort and ingenuity, it will be found. The quest, as Dewey lamented, is a quest for certainty.

As for procedural objectivity, the creation of procedures that eliminate judgment is certainly possible. The ubiquity of hermetically sealed, plastic-wrapped achievement tests that open with a poof, answered by filling in blanks with graphite so that they can be scored by machines that are untouched by human hands provides testimony to the attractiveness of such procedures. They are politically safe (exercising judgment on high-stake tests can be dangerous) and also efficient. Yet consensus provides no purchase on reality, it merely demonstrates that people can agree. Agreement can be facilitated in several ways. One is to simplify the object or qualities judged so that they require no interpretation or subtlety of perception; this is called low-inference data. The other is to create a set of restrictions that limit the scope for judgment so that its use is unnecessary, and even impossible. When the constraints are very great, the scope for choice is very limited. Bank tellers, for example, often are placed in such circumstances.[3] Consensus as a criterion for procedural objectivity is informative about consensus, not necessarily about the world as it is. Thus, what procedural objectivity tells us is that people agree: we hope they do so for good reasons. That may be all we can ever have, but we ought to recognize it for what it is.

On Solipsism and the Tower of Babel

Does the view presented here, that of framework-dependent knowledge, lead to solipsism? Do we deny the existence or contributions of the world out there? In what sense is qualitative inquiry possible if the only qualities we can refer to are those located in our heads? In short, when we reject ontological objectivity, do we slip into radical subjectivism and hence lose any basis whatsoever for making rational choices? Do we, as Denis Phillips has claimed (1983), proceed to a Tower of Babel in which our capacity to communicate or to determine whether we have made a mistake is relinquished? If we wish to avoid a Tower of Babel, must we agree upon a single, official language?

I do not think so. To deny that we can have ontologically objective knowledge is to say that whatever we come to know about the world will be known through our experience. Our experience, in turn, is mediated by prior experience. Our prior experience is shaped by culture, by language, by our needs, and by all of the ideas, practices, and events that make us human. It is also shaped by our genetic capacities, those particular aptitudes or dispositions that constitute our intellectual thumbprint and distinguish us from the rest of humanity. To recognize our uniqueness and to appreciate our culture and its contribution to our way of seeing things is not to be driven to the Tower of Babel that Phillips claims to be our inevitable destination. Our ability to communicate, to get on with each other, to accommodate differences in perspective, to accept different interpretations of experience, and indeed to change our minds provides ample evidence that the predicted catastrophe that some warn us of is basically a rhetorical device or a scare tactic to motivate us to accept a certain epistemology. Indeed, I believe it is far more liberating to live in a world with many different paradigms and procedures than in one with a single official version of the truth or how to find it. Verificationists are right to worry about the validity of claims; they are wrong to claim that the road to truth is the sole property of their party.

The Virtues of Subjectivity and Multiple Perspectives

Are there virtues to subjectivity? Is subjectivity one or many? In an interesting article on virtuous subjectivity, Peshkin (1985) writes:

> My subjectivity is functional and the results it produces are rational. But if they are rational only to me and no one else, not now or ever, then I have spawned illusions and my views are bound to be ignored. When I disclose what I have seen, my results invite other researchers to look where I did and see what I saw. My ideas are candidates for others to entertain, not necessarily as truth, let alone Truth, but as positions about the nature and meaning of a phenomenon that may fit their sensibility and shape their thinking about their own inquiries. If, somehow, all researchers were alike, we would all tell the same story (insofar as its non-denotable aspects are concerned) about the same phenomenon. By virtue of subjectivity, I tell the story I am moved to tell. Reserve my subjectivity and I do not become a value-free participant observer, merely an empty-headed one. . . .(p.280)

One of Peshkin's points is that personal biographies and unique modes of thinking make it possible for individuals to experience the world in unique ways. These unique ways of experiencing make possible new forms of knowledge that keep culture viable. These new forms then become candidates for shaping the experience of others, who in turn can use them to create even newer forms, which in turn. . .and so forth.

Peshkin also points out that our subjective self views new situations in terms relevant to it and different from the selves of others, and that we have many subjective selves. Which one of the many selves comes to the fore depends upon the situation in which we find ourselves. This subjective self can be viewed as a single self if the range of selves possessed by any individual is regarded as one; or it can be regarded as many, if each self is regarded as one. Whether one or many, the point is that perspectives alter, and those we choose or are compelled to use are related to the features of the context at the time.

There is another sense in which selves may be said to be plural. That sense has to do with our ability to see a situation from several points of view. In some ways formal schooling is intended to develop the ability to shift perspectives (Hirst, 1974). We can learn how to regard a state of affairs from an economic perspective, a psychological perspective, a biological perspective, and so forth. That is, we can learn to alter our frame of reference. Each frame of reference provides a different view and a different interpretation of a state of affairs.[4] A brief story illustrates this point.

A group of college students was told that in the state in which they lived, a state blessed with lush green forests, hunting season was about to begin. They were also told that in the hunting season ahead it was certain that many deer were going to die. The question posed to them was: Why were the deer to die?

One student said that the deer would die because the hunters in the state were good shots and were skilled at tracking deer. Another said the deer would die from blood loss and a consequent shortage of oxygen to the brain. Another said the real reason the deer would die was that humans had an innate need to express their aggressive instincts and found a legal outlet in killing deer. Another said the real reason the deer would die was that the state legislature was pressed by the National Rifle Association to permit the hunting of deer.

Each of these explanations is in some ways plausible. No one of them is necessarily truer than another; it depends upon the perspective one takes. As one's ability to take different perspectives grows, what is considered relevant shifts. The data one seeks change. The interpretation that is appropriate alters. Taking various perspectives is a way of examining situations from different angles. It is not so much a matter of ultimately achieving a coherent integration among the many perspectives, as one of being intellectually versatile or theoretically eclectic (Schwab, 1969). It is a matter of being able to handle several ways of seeing as a series of differing views rather than reducing all views to a single correct one.

The Self as Instrument

Before proceeding to a conception that I believe better serves our aim—the enhancement of educational practice—let me recite the concerns that objectivists have about the threats to objectivity from qualitative research and evaluation.

1. Unless procedures are specified and the scope for personal judgment reduced, conclusions say as much about the observers as the observed.

2. Nonpropositional language, the use of metaphor or figurative language, for example, undermines the possibility of verification.

3. The use of frameworks that are logically incommensurable means that one can then have contradictory conclusions without being able to find a resolution.

4. Knowledge is best conceived of as the product of scientific inquiry, and art, poetry, and literature are essentially irrelevant to such matters.

5. Truth exceeds belief, because there may be high degrees of consensus on beliefs that are not true.

6. Ontological objectivity should be the ideal toward which all research should strive.

Another View: A Transactive Account

Each of the concerns and beliefs enumerated above is at odds with the views developed in this chapter. The belief that only through a standard prescribed procedure can a useful description, interpretation, or evaluation of the world be secured dismisses what novelists, film makers, historians, and anthropologists have provided through their works. The most important work in these fields depends upon personal insight and interpretation, not simply upon following a set of replicable procedures.

Regarding nonpropositional language, the *rightness* of fiction is not the *truth* of physics. To say a work of fiction is "right" or "true to life" is to say that it captures and illuminates some aspect of reality. This reality is a function of the writer's ability to use a form we call literature to disclose something about the world that he or she has experienced and that we find believable. Scientific truth tests are as relevant to testing fictional truth as knowledge of chemistry is relevant to making souffles. To dismiss the ways in which literature or poetry inform because they cannot be scientifically tested is to make a category mistake. We can live with many versions of rightness, truth being one.

As far as the incommensurability of frameworks is concerned, objectivists will sometimes say of qualitative research that it is adequate as a reconnaissance, but that real knowledge is secured through experiment. This view reflects their commitment to experimental science. Experiments are good ways to understand, but they are not the only ways. As Cassirer (1961–64), Polanyi (1958), and Langer (1942) have said, propositions will not take the impress of all that humans have come to know and wish to express. Language in any of its forms is not the same as the experience those forms are intended to represent. That is one of the reasons why veridicality fails as a criterion for objectivity or truth. No proposition can stand in a one-to-one relationship to the qualities it seeks to describe. Propositions can contradict other propositions, but not qualities.

The idea that truth exceeds belief is itself a belief in the possibility of an ontological objectivity. Yet all that we can ever know is the product of an active mind in commerce with a world. To seek more than what *ultimately* is referenced to our own beliefs *after using criteria appropriate for holding them* is to appeal to a higher authority or to seek a main line that bypasses minds' mediation of nature. Both, as far as I can tell, are unlikely. Stephen Toulmin, one of America's leading philosophers of science, makes this point:

> All of our scientific explanations and critical readings start from, embody, and imply some interpretive standpoint, conceptual frame-work, or theoretical perspective. The relevance and adequacy of our explanations can never be demonstrated with Platonic rigor or geomet-rical necessity. (Not to mince matters, *episteme* was always too much to ask.) Instead, the operative question is, Which of our positions are rationally warranted, reasonable, or defensible—that is, well founded rather than groundless opinions, sound *doxai* rather than shaky ones? (1982, p. 115)

What concerns those who believe in ontological objectivity is the introduction into the community engaged in research and evaluation of paradigms, norms, and methods that undermine the possibility of *episteme*. They worry about cognitive pluralism and even more about relativism, and they worry about losing rationality because of an approach to inquiry that has no way of knowing if its claims are true.

The prescription of method is, at base, not only epistemological, but also political (Eisner, 1988). Methods or perspectives that deviate from accepted norms are often regarded as mistakes; they threaten competence and conventional lore. If new criteria are needed to appraise new forms of inquiry, if *how* things are said is relevant for understanding the meanings of a message, one needs to be able to "read" these meanings and understand the forms that convey them. What is needed is interpretation and exegesis—in a word, rationality.

By rationality I mean the exercise of intelligence in the creation or perception of elements as they relate to the whole in which they participate. I do not restrict rationality to discursively mediated thought or limit it to the application of logic. Human rationality is displayed whenever relationships among elements are skillfully crafted or insightfully per-ceived. Poets as well as physicists, painters as well as philosophers, actors and teachers as well as mathematicians and astronomers function rationally. The root of the term rationality is related to ratio—order of relationship. Thus, teachers planning a lesson, evaluators assessing a classroom, and administrators providing leadership to a faculty are all rational actors.

In my view logic, in its more narrowly-defined sense, pertains to the practice of drawing defensible conclusions from a set of premises: To be logical is to exercise reason with respect to the inferences or deductions necessary for consistency to be achieved. But logic itself is narrower than rationality: It is one of its subsets. To function logically is to function rationally, but to function rationally does not require one to function logically.

The import of this distinction is to recognize rationality as a virtue of intellect that supersedes logic. It includes under its umbrella a wide array of activities whose intelligent pursuit does not depend upon the application of logic. A second implication pertains to the ends of education. Insofar as rationality is a prime intellectual virtue, its refinement in the wide variety of spheres in which it can be exercised ought to be a major educational aim.

Turning to Transaction

Is there a way to avoid the dichotomy that the concepts *objective* and *subjective* suggest? I should like to propose an alternative arrangement, one derived from Dewey's work (1938). Consider the three concepts presented here:

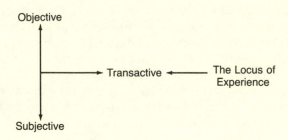

Here the *transactive* is conceived of as the locus of human experience. It is the product of the interaction of two *postulated* entities, the objective and the subjective. Since what we can know about the world is always a result of inquiry, it is mediated by mind. Since it is mediated by mind, the world cannot be known in its ontologically objective state. An objective world is postulated both as a general and as a particular entity. Since what we know about the world is a product of the transaction of our subjective life *and* a postulated objective world, these worlds cannot be separated. To separate them would require the exercise of mind, and since mind would need to be employed to make the separation, anything "separated" as a result of its use would reflect mind as well as what was "separated" from it. Hence what we have is experience—a transaction, rather than independent subjective and objective entities.

Where does this leave us? If we cannot have a purely objective view and refuse to trust a subjective one, how do we know when to trust a transactive account? I now turn to that issue.

Criteria for Appraising Transactive Accounts

What we trust ultimately depends upon the features of the text we read and what those features enable us to understand, see, or anticipate. There are no operationally defined truth tests to apply to qualitative research and evaluation, but there are questions to ask and features to look for and appraise. Recognizing that neither pristine objectivity nor pure subjectivity is possible, recognizing that all experience derived from text is transactive, we can ask what it is about text that is likely to make it believable. I believe the following features to be relevant: (1) *coherence*, (2) *consensus*, and (3) *instrumental utility*.

Coherence

One criterion through which the believability of a qualitative narrative is determined is the coherence or tightness of the argument it presents. Does the story make sense? How have conclusions been supported? To what extent have multiple data sources been used to give credence to the interpretation that has been made? Are the observations congruent with the rest of the study? Are there anomalies that cannot be reconciled? Are there other credible interpretations? If so, what leads one to accept the interpretation offered? How well does the study relate to what one already knows?

Permeating coherence are aesthetic features. When we say that a study or rendition "rings true," we mean, I think, that it coheres and makes sense. When we talk about the "weight of evidence," we use a metaphor to describe the sense of facticity that we experience after having heard or read a rendition of the way things are. When we say something does not "feel right," we make judgments based upon criteria that we may not be able to describe, but which, nevertheless, we trust.

Coherence pertains to *Gestalt* qualities. In one sense the Law of *Prägnanz*—the good fit—is relevant to our assessment of the coherence of the interpretation or appraisal. When we say an argument is "watertight," we mean that we can "find no holes in it." We scrutinize the argument by looking for inconsistencies, lapses of logic, things that just don't fit.

Coherence also is related to what Nelson Goodman has called

"rightness" (1978). Speaking of depictions and exemplifications, Goodman argues that asking whether a poem, painting, novel, or play is true is to ask the wrong question. We ought, he says, to ask whether it is right. For example, a piece of fiction is not literally true in the sense that the fictional character corresponds to a real character. There may not be an actual Willy Loman, or Blanche Dubois, or Hamlet. Yet, though referring to no one in particular, the fictional characters refer to all who share similar dilemmas, conundrums, and travails. The stories in which these characters appear are "right," even if they are not literally true. That is, they are not true in the sense in which a scientific assertion might be said to be true. Goodman writes:

> Such matters aside, a statement is true, and a description or representation right, for a world it fits. And a fictional version, verbal or pictorial, may if metaphorically construed fit and be right for a world. Rather than attempting to subsume descriptive and representational rightness under truth, we shall do better, I think, to subsume truth along with these under the general notion of rightness of fit. (1978, p.132)

Goodman offers us a conception of rightness that transcends truth. In his terms, truth is a subset of rightness of fit. At the same time, it would be a mistake to say that the Willy Lomans of the world do not live and that therefore what Arthur Miller has to say about them is not illuminating, useful, informative, or revealing. To say that a qualitative study produces a work that is not literally true is not to say that the work is not right or useful.

Coherence, although important as a criterion in the assessment of qualitative research and evaluation, can mislead. As Geertz (1973) points out, nothing is as coherent as a swindler's story. Coherence can be constructed out of whole cloth. Investigators may leave out evidence that might weaken or challenge their case. The data might have been sweetened. Words can be shaded for meaning to convince subtly. In short, we can be misled by those who have a need to convince—and even by those who don't. It is possible to be so committed to a preconceived conclusion or a particular way of seeing things that we unwittingly focus only on those aspects of the situation or story that supports our preconceptions.

One of the virtues of operational definitions and optically scored standardized tests is that through them the possibility of replication is increased.[5] The data, when secured this way at least, are "untouched by human hands." In qualitative research the observer or researcher is the major instrument; one can unknowingly overlook what does not conform to one's values or expectations.

We have a trade-off. If we rely upon standardized test instruments or observation schedules to describe states of affairs, we have no assurance that the particular instruments used will be sensitive or appropriate to what the instrument maker could not anticipate, namely, the unique features of a particular classroom. For those features of a classroom for which the instrument is relevant, however, we can secure greater reliability. The need for replicability is a need for reliability. The need for relevance is the need for validity. There is now and has been a classic tension between what is reliable and what is valid.

Related to coherence as a criterion for assessing qualitative research and evaluation is *structural corroboration* (Eisner, 1986). Structural corroboration is the term I use to describe the confluence of multiple sources of evidence or the recurrence of instances that support a conclusion. In many evaluation circles it is called *triangulation* (Webb et al., 1966; Mathison, 1988). For a study to be structurally corroborated, one needs to put together a constellation of bits and pieces of evidence that substantiate the conclusions one wants to draw. In the field of law, circumstantial evidence can be used to convict someone of a crime for which there was no eyewitness. The test is one of reasonable doubt; where there is no basis for reasonable doubt, the verdict is regarded as justifiable.

In American jurisprudence, the kind of evidence necessary for conviction depends upon whether the case at hand falls under criminal or civil law. In criminal cases a verdict for conviction must meet a higher standard than under civil law. For a criminal case, the verdict depends upon evidence beyond a reasonable doubt. For a civil case the less severe criterion of preponderance of evidence must be met. The differences in criteria reflect appropriately the different situations for which verdicts are to be issued. Such a practice is, in my view, appropriate for educational inquiry as well.

In educational studies Peshkin's (1986) numerous examples of the ways in which evangelical Christian schools promote Christian values—their virtual control of the lives of the students under their care, prohibition of certain kinds of music, rules about relationships between males and females, emphasis on the infallibility of the Bible, incorporation of scripture into course content—provide a plethora of data upon which conclusions about the characters of these schools are structurally corroborated.

Even short-term observations of schools, such as those made by Jackson (1981 a, b, c) and Lightfoot (1981 a, b, c), provide numerous instances in which a community of upper-middle-class parents conveys to teachers and school administrators alike the importance of academic achievement—almost at any price. When Lightfoot mentions "grade grubbing" at Highland Park High, it does not come out of the blue; it fits the educational climate she has described. When David Elkind (1988) describes "the hurried child," he provides dozens of examples of the ways in which ambitious parents pressure their children. When he expresses concerns about the potential costs of such behavior, we are ready to take those concerns seriously. Indeed, when we hear about school districts that are attempting to "academicize" the kindergarten, we recognize such efforts as examples of the hurried child syndrome that Elkind has written about.

The use of multiple data sources is one of the ways conclusions can be structurally corroborated. As different kinds of data converge or support each other, the picture, like the image in a puzzle, becomes more distinct. In the best of circumstances the interpretation appears inescapable.

It is always possible to introduce competing interpretations to any analysis: what constitutes compelling evidence for a Freudian is not likely to convince a behaviorist. Furthermore, there is no supratheory that can resolve differences, no higher court of appeals to sort out interpretations and to decide which one is right. Paradigm differences are often differences in starting points. In the end, one might not satisfy every skeptic, regardless of how tight the corroboration had become. Researchers strive to make their conclusions and interpretations as credible as possible *within the framework they choose to use*. Once they have met that difficult criterion, their readers are free to make their own choices.

Consensus

Consensus is the condition in which investigators or readers of a work concur that the findings and/or interpretations reported by the investigator are consistent with their own experience or with the evidence presented. *Consensus*, a term derived from the Latin verb *consentive*, "to agree," is a form of multiplicative corroboration. With respect to qualitative research and evaluation, affirmative consensus confirms the researcher's conclusions. How does one gain consensus in qualitative research and evaluation?

Some of the features previously described regarding coherence and structural corroboration are important for securing consensus. Consensus is, after all, a matter of agreement, and agreement is ultimately a matter of persuasion. What some find persuasive others may find unpersuasive. For some, research that does not result in measured variables, ipso facto, can have no credibility. Socialization has been so powerful and their methodological commitments so strong that anything that does not fit their image of research has no place in the pantheon of knowledge. The power of commitment and image has been likened by Kenneth Boulding to religious conviction. In an incisive and provocative book called *The Image*, Boulding writes:

> A devout Moslem, for instance, whose whole life has been built around
> the observance of the precepts of the Koran will resist vigorously any

message which tends to throw doubt on the authority of his sacred
work. The resistance may take the form of simply ignoring the
message, or it may take the form of emotive response: anger, hostility,
indignation. In the same way, a "devout" psychologist will resist
strongly any evidence presented in favor of extrasensory perception,
because to accept it would overthrow his whole image of the universe.
If the resistances are very strong, it may take very strong, or often
repeated messages to penetrate them, and when they are penetrated,
the effect is a realignment or reorganization of the whole knowledge
structure. (1956, p. 12)

For those with strong resistances, the likelihood of change is small.
For those willing to consider evidence other than measured variables,
probability coefficients, and confidence intervals, the possibility of change
is good.

As I have already indicated, achieving consensus is simple if one
attends to the obvious. Educational sophistication is not required in order
to count the number of times a teacher clears his throat in the classroom,
or to compute wait time as the time elapsed between a teacher's question
and the student's response.

When it comes to more subtle matters, those that require interpretation, achieving consensus can be a formidable task. Readers may infer from
these arguments that the extent to which meaningful consensus has been
achieved is not unrelated to the subtlety and complexity of what is being
described and interpreted. We might reasonably expect near-perfect
consensus on cleared throats, perhaps somewhat less consensus on wait
time, and considerably less on the extent to which the students' comments
were incisive. We should not expect the same degree of precision in all
matters. Aristotle said it best in the *Ethics* (McKeon, 1941):

> For it is the mark of an educated man to look for precision in each class
> of things just so far as the nature of the subject admits; it is evidentially
> equally foolish to accept probable reasoning from a mathematician and
> to demand from a rhetorician scientific proofs. (p. 936)

There are other considerations as well. How much consensus we
need before we act depends upon the significance of the decision we need
to make and the potential costs of action. If a decision pertains to firing a
teacher, for example, we would want to be almost certain we had a level of
consensus adequate to justify such action. If we wanted to help a
beginning teacher, we might act on evidence for which there was
substantially less consensus. In short, what level of consensus is considered adequate will depend on what we are judging and how significant the
consequences of our action will be.

Consensus is concurrence as a result of evidence deemed relevant to
the description, interpretation, and evaluation of some state of affairs.

Consensus does not imply "truth." Many of the greatest works of art and science were initially rejected; they secured consensus all right, but it was negative. These same works today—Galileo's investigation of free fall, van Gogh's paintings, Stravinsky's music, for example—all enjoy substantial consensus, but today they receive encomiums, not rejection.

We should also remember that those who held opinions about these works when they were created were as certain then of the validity of their judgments as those who hold opposite opinions today. Indeed, in both situations there is consensus. The moral here is simply that it is important to try to get consensus on one's work, but having gotten it, one should not think one has cornered Truth. What one has cornered is agreement.

Instrumental Utility

The most important test of any qualitative study is its usefulness. Usefulness is of several kinds. First, there is the usefulness of comprehension. A good qualitative study can help us understand a situation that would otherwise be enigmatic or confusing. One reads a narrative, reflects on its contents, and puts the pieces together. For example, one might read a new history—say, a revisionist history of American industrialism—and experience, for the first time, a ring of truth that one did not have before; for the first time the relationship between trade unions and American capitalism makes sense. Things fall into place.

Much of political science consists of interpretations of political events that give order and structure to what otherwise would be little more than disarray; one feels one now understands the motives and interests of the major players.

In both history and political science the possibilities of experimental trials are remote; it is very difficult to manipulate experimentally the political behavior of foreign powers and impossible to replay the politics of Renaissance Italy. Yet analyses of the politics of the NATO alliance or of the Medici can be enlightening. One instrumental utility of comprehension is satisfaction, even when nothing might be done as a result.

A second kind of usefulness is anticipation. Those who write about educational matters are often interested in more than revealing the unique features of a comparatively minor part of the world. Most teachers and school administrators do not have the historical stature of an Abraham Lincoln or a Martin Luther King, Jr., and studies of their lives are likely to be of little moment. Yet individual teachers might be studied, as Tracy Kidder (1989) has done, and individual schools analyzed as samples or exemplars of larger types. The usefulness of studies of particulars, whether schools or people, is located in descriptions and interpretations that go beyond the information given about them. The need to anticipate the future, indeed the ability to do so, is primary. Qualitative studies can make an important contribution in that direction.

The anticipation of the future occurs in three related but different ways. One kind of anticipation is reflected in prediction. We can get probability coefficients from meteorologists about the likelihood of rain tomorrow. Qualitative research and evaluation seldom provide information of this kind.

A second kind of anticipation is provided by maps. Maps are scaled portrayals of terrain. They are designed to enable the traveler to anticipate (and to secure or avoid) particular encounters on the journey. We expect the map to have a congruent and scaled relationship with the territory it describes. Maps can portray space, height, temperature, ocean depth, topology, and flora and fauna—virtually anything that can be symbolized. Maps help us get to where we want to be.

Qualitative research and evaluation can serve as a map, but they are more likely to function as a guide, a third type of usefulness. Guides, more than maps, are closely associated with the utilities of qualitative studies. Unlike maps, qualitative studies are general, they are not mathematically scaled to match the territory, and they are more interpretive and narrative. Their function is to highlight, to explain, to provide directions the reader can take into account. Guides call to our attention aspects of the situation or place we might otherwise miss. They are typically prepared by people who have visited a place before and know a great deal about it. If the guide is useful, we are likely to experience what we otherwise might have missed, and we may understand more than we would have without benefit of the guide. The good guide deepens and broadens our experience and helps us understand what we are looking at.

An example of the utility of what might be called a "qualitative guide" is found in Tracy Kidder's description of Mrs. Zajac in his book *Among Schoolchildren* (1988). Kidder leaves no doubt that Mrs. Zajac cares about her students and that she not only feeds them, but is fed by them. He also leaves no doubt that Mrs. Zajac can be tough when she needs to be and soft and warm when this is required. In fact, the ability to lay down the rules, to enforce them, and to keep expectations consistent is one of the keys to her success as a teacher. Although at times her best-intentioned efforts backfire, for the most part they work.

By creating a vivid portrait of an elementary school teacher, Kidder helps us understand something of the personal as well as the professional tension that such a role can generate. By understanding the teacher's life through his book, we come to understand aspects of teaching that hardly ever show up in descriptions of "productive schools" or excellent teachers. Kidder, by putting a human face on the teacher, invites us into a part of her inner life. As a result, we come away from *Among Schoolchildren* with an awareness of the pedagogical terrain that we might not have had before we turned its pages.

In this chapter I have tried to avoid the pitfalls of objectivity and subjectivity by emphasizing the idea that we cannot secure an ontologically objective view of the world, that mind and matter transact, and that our experience of the world is a function not only of its features, but of what we bring to them. We are always in a constructive position. We *make* our experience, not simply *have* it.

This constructivist view recognizes that the resources we use to construe the world not only guide our attention to it, but when used to represent it, both constrain and make possible what we are able to convey. Knowledge is thus mediated in two ways. First, it is mediated by what we bring to the world as we achieve experience. Second, it is mediated by what we use to convey our experience once it is secured. Furthermore, a purely subjective view would be uninfluenced by objective conditions and a purely objective view would be uninfluenced by subjective ones. Neither is possible. I believe, with Dewey, that a transactional orientation to the process of knowing allows us to avoid the dualisms—objective and subjective—that have led to so much mischief in the methodology of educational research.

Notes

1. The most widespread belief concerning the relationship between perception and the world we inhabit is that it is possible to secure a perception and an understanding of the world that accurately reflect the world's true features. We speak of people as being sober-minded, cool, detached, and clear-eyed. Both emotion and imagination are often regarded as antithetical to such qualities. Hence, most people believe that the world can be known as it really is and that the aim of understanding is to secure a veridical or isomorphic relationship between reality and our conception of it.

2. Language is a powerful vehicle for expressing and suppressing particular values. The conventional language used in writing research reports is one that creates the illusion of detachment by attempting to diminish the presence of the researcher in the research. It is interesting (and distressing) to note how far we go to convince ourselves of our own conceptual neutrality.

3. One virtue of using procedurally objective methods is that such methods tend to make uniform the ways in which individuals function. For institutions interested in controlling variance in human performance, the use of such methods is important. The cost, of course, is that individuals subject to such methods relinquish their ability to exercise judgment. In the long term, such individuals may be said to be deskilled.

4. The phrase "state of affairs" is not exactly correct. When different frames of reference are employed to address the world, the world addressed is not identical to the one revealed by a different frame of reference. Thus, each

framework provides for a different world. For an elaboration of this view, see N. Goodman, (1978), *Ways of Worldmaking*.

5. *Operational definitions* are definitions that define by the way in which something is measured. Thus, someone's intelligence is operationally defined by the procedures employed to secure his or her score on a Stanford-Binet Intelligence Test.

Chapter IV

Educational Connoisseurship

Reality is an infinite succession of steps [and] levels of perception. A lily is more real to a naturalist than it is to the ordinary person. But it is still more real to the botanist. And yet another stage of reality is reached with that botanist who is a specialist in lilies.

Vladimir Nabokov

The Meaning of Connoisseurship

The preceding chapters assigned to perception a central role in our knowledge of the world. Perception manifests itself in experience and is a function of the transactions between the qualities of the environment and what we bring to those qualities.[1] The character of that experience is in large measure influenced by our ability to differentiate among the qualities we attend to.

The ability to make fine-grained discriminations among complex and subtle qualities is an instance of what I have called *connoisseurship* (Eisner, 1976, 1985b). Connoisseurship is the art of appreciation. It can be displayed in any realm in which the character, import, or value of objects, situations, and performances is distributed and variable, including educational practice.

The focus of this chapter is upon connoisseurship as it applies to teaching, curriculum, and schooling generally. But before addressing educational matters, I will examine connoisseurship as a process. For this purpose there is no better subject than the connoisseurship of wine.

Again, I must beg readers' patience in what might seem like a tangent into an unrelated area. This book is built upon methods that pay close attention to the subtleties of qualitative experience, and wine serves well to illustrate these methods. I hope that understanding how connoisseurship applies to wine will help build a foundation for understanding its role in the perception of educational practice.

What is it to be a wine connoisseur? Certain requirements appear obvious. First, one needs access to wine and the ability to taste it. But tasting wine—by which I mean experiencing its visual, olfactory, and gustatory qualities—is not simply a matter of putting some wine into one's mouth. It is a matter of noticing, and noticing requires perceptivity. *Perceptivity* is the ability to differentiate and to experience the relationships between, say, one gustatory quality in the wine and others. Like the interplay of sounds in a symphonic score, to experience wine is to experience an interplay of qualitative relationships.

Second, wine connoisseurship requires an awareness of not only qualities of taste but also qualities of appearance and smell. The color at the edge of a red wine when the glass is tipped is indicative of its age; the browner it is, the older. The way in which its "legs" hang on the inside of the glass says something about its body. The perfume or nose of a wine is another quality that counts. These qualities and others constitute the features of wine that provide potential experience. I say "potential" because whether we can in fact experience the wine's perfume, for example, depends on *both* the presence of perfume in the wine *and* our ability to notice it. Experiencing this transaction is a manifestation of qualitative intelligence (Ecker, 1963). Connoisseurship depends on high levels of qualitative intelligence in the domain in which it operates.

Third, wine connoisseurship depends upon the ability to experience those qualities as a sample of a larger set of qualities; it is not "simply" a matter of sensory differentiation.

One kind of tasting focuses upon the quality of qualities per se. We taste a certain sweetness or flintiness in a white wine. We experience its qualities. We *know* what experience it yields. We notice its effects on the inside of our mouth—we might describe one white wine as round, full, and buttery, another as sharp, light, and dry. What we know through the qualitative distinctions we are able to make pertains to qualities experienced. What we may or may not know is that one wine is a Sauternes while the other is a Chardonnay. If we know that one is a Sauternes and the other a Chardonnay, we know more than the qualities of each wine—we also know that each is a sample of a larger class.

Because wines (like children) are never identical, we are able to place each wine within the class it represents, and also to assign it a position among the wines within that class. To do so we need a concept of what Sauternes and Chardonnay, in general, taste like; further, we need to remember the differences among particular Sauternes and Chardonnays we have tasted. We need a gustatory memory. The ability to differentiate and remember enables us to form the gustatory concepts to which the words *Sauternes* and *Chardonnay* refer.

The Utilities of Antecedent Knowledge

Our connoisseurship of wine is influenced by more than our ability to differentiate the subtle and complex qualities of wine we taste and to compare them in our sensory memory with other wines tasted. It is also influenced by our understanding of the conditions that give rise to these qualities. Knowing how a Sauternes is made—the kind of grapes used, the time at which the grapes are harvested, the manner in which the grapes are pressed and processed—contributes to our ability to experience the nuances of wine. Every wine manifests its history. Knowledge of that history can have a bearing on our ability to experience its qualities. Tokay grapes have a presence and character that Concord grapes do not possess. French oak barrels impart a flavor that can be discerned from that of stainless steel vats. The Sauternes wines of France possess a style that differs from those of California. The point is that true connoisseurship includes the ability not only to experience qualities, but to experience qualities as a case or a symptom of factors that have a bearing upon the qualities of the wine experienced. Put another way, antecedent factors are relevant for making sense of the wine. Any wine can be treated as a symptom or exemplification of those antecedent factors—a wine can illustrate the effects of using stainless steel in wine making. Knowledge of antecedent factors can serve as a guide for searching for the qualities of the wine to be experienced. Which of these we emphasize depends upon what we wish to use the experience for.

The development of the palate is fostered in other ways as well. Knowing that coopers use different kinds of wood in the construction of barrels alerts one to taste for the qualities that different woods confer upon the wine. Coopers also "toast" the inside of the barrel with a small fire. The extent to which the barrel has been toasted—light, medium, dark—influences the taste of the wine. Connoisseurs of wine can note these differences, and wine makers bring such factors under control in the wine-making process. Furthermore, connoisseurship enables wine makers to adjust that process on the basis of anticipated taste. That is, wine makers are interested in the wine's taste potential, and they judge this potential on the basis of what the wine tastes like before it is ready to drink.

One final point regarding the art of wine making and its relationship to connoisseurship in general. Enologists now are highly trained in the chemistry and science of making wine, yet in the end, the making of wine is an art. It is an art because the quality of wine depends on someone's being able to (1) experience the qualitative nuances of wine and (2) make judgments about the virtue of the qualities experienced. Even a recipe or a formula has its ultimate test in the qualities experienced when the wine is tasted. In the end, a qualitative experience is the "measure" of wine quality, and not the formula.

There is no foolproof recipe that can be used to reproduce what has been produced before. Wine grapes, like children, do not come in standard forms. The amount of sugar in grapes varies from season to season, from location to location. Differences in the raw material due to difference in climate from year to year must be taken into account in deciding what to do.

So far, the main focus of this discussion of connoisseurship has been on the appreciation of qualities. In virtually every domain the qualities that participate in some class are varied. The more complex the subject, the wider the array of information we must use. Classrooms are probably one of the most complex subjects of connoisseurship. In classrooms, knowing the history of the situation, something about the teacher and the school, and the values that are regarded as important in the community can help us to notice and to interpret what we have noticed. What we might see and say about a first-year teacher would probably differ considerably from what we would see and say if we knew the teacher was a fifteen-year veteran. If we knew the students in the class had a measured mean IQ of 140, our knowledge would influence what we would look for and how we would regard what we had seen. The point here is not difficult to grasp: it is that our perception and interpretation of events are influenced by a wide range of knowledge we believe to be germane to that classroom or situation. Our ideas about something make a difference in how we regard it (Rosenthal, 1986).

What is germane to a particular classroom is not necessarily limited to knowledge secured solely through observation. Our understanding of theories of teaching and learning, our views of what is important in the educational process, and our image of acceptable teacher-pupil relationships all come to bear upon what we are likely to notice and how we interpret it. The kind of knowledge relevant to the observation of classrooms derives from general knowledge about educational theory *and* classroom-specific knowledge. In general, as these domains of knowledge expand our awareness of the situation, our experience is likely to be increasingly differentiated.

Readers will note that in the previous sentence I qualified my remarks by the phrase "in general." That is because just as knowledge relevant to a situation can provide a new window through which it can be perceived, knowledge can limit perception as well.

The Liability of Antecedent Knowledge

One of the built-in dilemmas of acculturation is the fact that the language we acquire, our expectations, and the norms that permeate our culture all provide cues that are useful for negotiating the world in which we live. We learn a language that is categorical, and categories frame our perception in particular ways. These categories, moreover, are value laden. We learn to look for those qualities that are labeled, but especially for ones that have particular value for us. If the qualities of snow affect skiing, we develop categories for describing snow that are relevant to skiing. Thus, our aims influence our language, and our language influences our perception. We teach the young to look for certain qualities by giving these qualities names, thus making it easier to remember them. Mnemonic devices perform similar functions, for by virtue of these devices we can remember an array of qualities that we would otherwise find difficult to store and retrieve (Hintzman, 1978).

Practitioners of the social sciences acquire terms such as *social mobility, adaptation, ethnocentricity, defense mechanism, reinforcement,* and *cognitive dissonance,* and then learn the meaning of these terms by encountering examples. The terms themselves originally were developed from the perception of qualities that were conceptualized and then labeled: The labels followed the experience, so to speak. In professional socialization, the experience usually follows the label. As one moves from labels to relationships among labels and from there to explanations for the covariability among the qualities the labels designate, one acquires theory. Theories are complex explanatory structures designed to satisfy human rationality, need for order, and desire to anticipate the future—if not always to control it. Labels and theories, says Jerome Bruner (1964), are among the most useful "technologies of mind."

Yet labels and theories are not without their costs. The very order that they provide engenders expectations that often impede fresh perception. Labels and theories provide a way of seeing. But a way of seeing is also a way of not seeing. There are stock responses, and there are also stock perceptions. What we see is frequently influenced by what we know. This influence is graphically illustrated in learning to draw.

Artists in training must learn to disregard what they logically know, for example, about the length of a model's arm in order to render a foreshortened view of the arm convincingly. Some drawing teachers ask students to copy a photograph that has been turned upside down in order to minimize the effects of "cognitive" knowledge on the students' perception of form (Edwards, 1979). In this case, what is real is the visual relationship as it *appears,* not as it is measured, for measurement distorts.

There is a tendency in American culture to treat the visual world as data to be labeled rather than as qualities to be explored. We treat qualities most often as means rather than as ends; that is, we use qualities to do something else, to get to some other place, to predict what will happen. We see only as much of the facade of our house as we need to, in order to know that we are home. If you doubt this, try drawing the front of your house from memory, and then compare your drawing to the actual house. Matters of proportion, details, and even major features are likely to be ill-treated. In a culture with a penchant for efficiency, we seldom devote much attention to allocentric forms of perception (Schactel, 1959).

The result of such inclinations is inattention to nuance and detail: a diminution of connoisseurship. Not having time to attend carefully, we simply do not see what we have no immediate use for. When our labels and our aims jointly shape our modes of perception, their effects upon perception can become especially limiting. We begin to do the kinds of things we can do with the labels and the theories we know how to use. The more we use these labels and theories, the more we are likely to use them. Familiarity breeds comfort, and the theories we know and use provide a coherent and consistent structure for our relationship to the world.

Epistemic Seeing

The processes of connoisseurship I have described can be regarded as examples of epistemic seeing[2] (Dretske, 1969). *Episteme* refers to knowledge, and epistemic seeing is the kind of knowledge secured through sight. My emphasis on seeing should be regarded as a shorthand way of referring to all of the senses and the qualities to which they are sensitive. Classrooms, like wine, are known by their smell and tactile qualities as well as by their sight. As Jackson (1968) remarked, the smells of chalkdust and stale milk are almost certain signs of an elementary school classroom.

We have seen that awareness of qualities is a primary means of epistemic seeing; indeed, it is foundational. We must become conscious of qualities before other considerations can be taken into account. Thus, awareness of the qualities of voice, manner, movement, and visual environment, at the very minimum, provides knowledge of those qualities per se. But as I have indicated, those qualities can also be regarded as samples of a larger class. We see something "as." The lecture is not only a lecture, it is an example of lecturing. By seeing the lecture as belonging to a class, and by seeing the class as a varied array of examples, we can situate any particular lecture in that array. *Primary* epistemic seeing depends upon awareness of the particular. *Secondary* epistemic seeing refers to seeing the particular as a member of a larger set.

It is important to note that the term *knowledge* as I use it here is not limited to true propositions, but includes awareness of an array of qualities. We need not make a statement or claim to know what is before us. And during the course of most of our lives we do not. We not only know more than we can tell, as Polanyi (1967) has said, we tell far less than we know. Our knowing does not depend upon our telling. Our telling is a way of making public what we have come to know. Connoisseurship is the means through which we come to know the complexities, nuances, and subtleties of aspects of the world in which we have a special interest.

One aspect of connoisseurship is subject to misinterpretation. I said earlier that connoisseurship is the art of appreciation. *Appreciation* is a term that unfortunately is conflated with "a liking for." There is no necessary relationship between appreciating something and liking it. To appreciate the qualities of a wine, a book, or a school means to experience the qualities that constitute each and to understand something about them. It also includes making judgments about their value. One can appreciate the weakness of an argument, a teacher, or a poem as well as their strengths. Nothing in connoisseurship as a form of appreciation *requires* that our judgments be positive. What is required (or desired) is that our experience be complex, subtle, and informed.

To some degree all people have some degree of connoisseurship in some areas of life. In virtually all cases, however, the level of their connoisseurship can be raised through tuition. Teachers of literature can help people learn how to read a novel, indeed to learn the several ways in which a novel can be read. Coaches help players learn how to read a field of play in motion so that their performance in the game can be more effective. Critics of film and painting help others learn to see what they might otherwise not notice and in the process increase their level of connoisseurship. Members of groups concerned with gender and minority discrimination have helped others appreciate the subtle but significant forms of sexism and racism found in books, newspapers, laws, and other seemingly neutral materials. In the process, people's consciousness is raised, and they become more able to notice and respond to such material. To appreciate a racist comment is not to say that one likes it, but rather to recognize it. Again, the seeing is epistemic.

In its customary mode connoisseurship is concerned with matters of quality, in the sense of value.[3] Connoisseurs of wine, of art, of cabinetry are typically those who can discern the value of what they attend to. They can often provide reasons for their judgments.

Concern with the value of student and teacher performance in educational settings has been important and strong. We want to know about the quality (value) of education that children are receiving.

Judgments concerning quality depend upon memory or what Broudy (1987) has called our "imagic store." Refined sensibilities allow us to make fine-grained discriminations from which concepts may be formed. These concepts are images that are construed from our experience with qualities. For example, we have an auditory image of Baroque music that allows us to distinguish it from Romantic music. We have an image of Gothic architecture that allows us to distinguish it from Georgian architecture. We have an image of cocker spaniels that allows us to distinguish them from Great Danes, and so forth. Within any of these images we have a further array of examples that we can order with respect to quality. Dog connoisseurs can distinguish not only between cocker spaniels and Great Danes, but between cocker spaniels whose features are regarded as excellent and those regarded as mediocre.

Similarly, we have images of forms of teaching, kinds of classroom life, and types of student activity that allow us to distinguish between degrees of excellence in each. In fact, in a complex act like teaching, there are many, many varieties or genres. What constitutes excellence in one is likely to be different from what makes for excellence in another. The qualities that constitute excellence in a lecture are not identical to those that make for excellence in a discussion. In short, we possess a multitude of images from which we select in order to identify and appraise what we experience. Connoisseurship requires the appropriate application of criteria to the instance. In the field of education, the criteria are far more complex than those employed in judging either works of art or cocker spaniels.

Consider a fairly straightforward example—judging the quality of diving at the Olympics. Here five judges assign a score to the diving performances of a number of divers. The judges know which dive the divers are to perform—say, a half-gainer with a full twist. To perform their role, judges must be able to do three things. First, the judges must *see* the dive. This requires making a fine-grained visual discrimination. Second, they must place what they have seen within a range of diving performances remembered, one end of which represents the perfect example of a half-gainer with a full twist. Third, the judges must assign to each dive a score on a ten-point scale that signifies the quality of the diver's performance within that distribution. It is in principle possible for each of the ten scores to be referenced in a judge's visual memory of a particular level of performance; in short, each judge may know beforehand what constitutes a 1, 2, 3, 4, or 5 performance and so on. The judges' task is essentially one of seeing and matching.

Compared to the assessment of teaching, even the judgment of Olympic diving performances is simple. First, there is no single ideal to which a teaching performance can be assigned. The varieties of excellence are numerous, and they relate to differences in form, and to differences with respect to what is valued. Different conceptions of educational virtue lead to different conceptions of virtuous teaching. Further, who is being taught counts in judging how well someone is teaching.

Second, in the Olympics each diver dives into the same water, from the same height, and from the same board. This is not the case in teaching, where virtually everything differs from teacher to teacher. When one considers the antecedent factors that ought to be taken into account in judging teaching, the greater complexities of judging teaching compared to judging diving become especially clear. Furthermore, in evaluating teaching we are seldom concerned with single isolated performances. We are not typically interested in a single group discussion or a one-shot lecture, but in performance within a range of situations over a period of time. Unlike diving, it's not a matter of split-second action. Thus our judgments must take into account not only contingencies related to particular classrooms, but also a series of performances that unfolds during an extended period. Educational connoisseurs have more, and more complex, factors to consider, than their counterparts on the Olympic diving competition.

What Educational Connoisseurs Consider

I have tended to describe educational connoisseurship as if its exclusive focus were upon the teacher. Although teaching is clearly a prime focus for educational connoisseurship, it is far from the only one. In fact, educational connoisseurs attend to everything—almost. That is, they must attend to everything that is relevant either for satisfying a specific educational aim or for illuminating the educational state of affairs in general. For example, textbooks and instructional materials are important candidates for the attention of educational connoisseurs. Since decisions about content inclusion and exclusion are related to what students have an opportunity to learn (Walker & Schaffarzick, 1972), the examination of the content and form of instructional materials is important. Texts that pose interesting questions, convey a sense of excitement about the subject matter being taught, are *appropriately* easy to read, and stimulate imagination are likely to be better than materials that do not have these features. To determine that some materials possess these features while others do not is to call upon educational connoisseurship (Vallance, 1975).

Seeing what appears obvious is not always easy. For years textbooks were published that assigned women to roles as nurses, but never as doctors, gave to men the responsibility for important decisions, and to women responsibility for keeping their husbands happy. We now are able to see what in earlier periods we apparently could not see or had no interest in seeing. At present, states like California scrutinize school texts to make sure such muted messages are not among those that children get from state-adopted texts.

How school buildings are designed, we have come to realize, affects how people behave in them. To what extent does the design of a school—or a classroom—facilitate or impede the attainment of the school's aims? How are classrooms laid out, and what about the design and placement of furniture? Are these conducive to the image of schooling and of the child that the faculty embraces?

In a compelling article, Getzels (1974) points out that the shifts in classroom layout were due, in large measure, to shifts in the image of the learner. Consider the change from screwed-down desks to movable ones.

> The vision of the learner as an empty organism was transformed into a vision of the learner as an active organism. Learning was conceived of not only as a connective process but as a dynamic cognitive and affective process as well. From this point of view, the learner—not the

teacher—became the center of the learning process. It was the learner rather than the teacher who determined both the stimulus—what was to be learned—and the response—what was learned. Experimentation in the learning laboratory became concerned with the relation between the learner's personality and his learning, and the teacher in the classroom with the learner's needs and his adjustment in the learning situation.

It was no accident that the image of the ideal classroom took on a new conformation. The teacher-centered classroom became the pupil-centered classroom. The teacher's desk was moved from the front of the room to the side, and the pupils' rigid chairs in straight rows, which had seemed so sensible and practical from the older point of view, became quaint if not primitive objects and were replaced by movable chairs that could be shifted at will according not only to the requirements of the teacher but, even more important, to the needs of the pupil. (p. 532)

Getzel's points are well taken. For our purposes they explain the importance of discerning how physical features (and organizational ones as well) can affect what we are trying to accomplish. The nineteenth-century classroom with its raised platform upon which the teacher sat behind a large wooden desk and looked down upon pupils, who in turn looked up at the teacher, conveys both symbolically and practically a set of values. The image of the classroom as a series of desks lined up in rows, six across and eight deep, into which children are pinned like butterflies conveys a very different sense of life and of students' role than a classroom in which desks are clustered, where students face each other, and in which desks are unevenly distributed throughout the room. Since matters such as these count, educational connoisseurs can acquire knowledge of classrooms by marking the ways in which space is used in them.

School buildings can be designed as egg crates or as large living rooms. The spaces can be regular or irregular. The surfaces can be mechanical or organic. The environment can include growing plants and living animals or can be furnished to meet janitorial needs. "What is it like to be here?" is a nontrivial question that educational connoisseurs might very well ask.

Some Major Dimensions of Schooling

One way to think about the subject matters of educational connoisseurship is to consider the following five dimensions that I believe contribute to what I have called the ecology of schooling (Eisner, 1988). These dimensions are: (1) the intentional, (2) the structural, (3) the curricular, (4) the pedagogical, and (5) the evaluative. Each of these dimensions can be examined from the standpoint of educational connoisseurship. First, I will describe each dimension and then provide an example of how it might be addressed.

The Intentional Dimension

The *intentional dimension* deals with goals or aims that are formulated for the school or a classroom. The term *intentions* designates aims or goals that are explicitly advocated and publicly announced as well as those that are actually employed in the classroom. These aims or goals may be general or specific, and may focus on a wide range of outcomes or on a few. They may deal with sophisticated modes of cognition or be based upon recall, they may attend to or neglect affective or attitudinal aspects of student behavior, they may be educationally trivial or significant. What school districts, schools, or teachers attempt to accomplish and what they actually do are important matters, ones that can be the subject of educational connoisseurship. Indeed, the notion of the "hidden curriculum" is predicated on the importance of the muted messages children receive. Further, appropriate goals depend on a host of considerations, some of which I identified earlier in discussing antecedent factors pertaining to judgments about classrooms.

First, there are the questions of who the students are and what is in their long-term best interest. On such matters there will always be more than one view (Adler, 1982; Apple, 1982). Then there are matters of value—abstract values pertaining to general educational goals, and values that pertain specifically to the various legitimate aims of any subject area. (There are at least a dozen aims, not just one, for the social studies. Even math, a subject that is often thought of as relatively standardized, has more than one defensible version.) Further, there are matters of proportion. How much attention ought to be devoted to, say, cognitive aims, and how much to so-called noncognitive aims? Given an aim, how well is it being achieved? If the aim is educationally questionable or problematic, does it matter if it is being achieved? Why worry about doing what's not worth doing?

The difference between intended aims and operationalized aims in a classroom is of particular importance. A teacher or a school district may endorse one kind of outcome, but in practice emphasize quite another (Eisner, 1986). What occurs in practice may be far better than what the curriculum guide prescribes, or even what the teachers say they aim to achieve. It can also be worse. The point is that there is often a discrepancy between what educators say they want to achieve and what they do when working with students. Students themselves may not understand clearly what their teachers want to achieve and may have very different goals in mind. Indeed, a student might know quite well that the teacher's aim was to get him to understand and enjoy physics, while the student's aim was to be accepted into a selective college. Success at the latter would not necessarily mean achieving the former.

There are numerous ways to think about goals or intentions. One of these pertains to the degree to which they are achieved. Another is whether they are of value. One need not endorse the goals that a teacher values in order to recognize that they are being realized. At the same time, because students attain the goals that a teacher has set does not mean that an educational process has taken place. A painter who sets out to produce a third-rate painting and who succeeds has been successful in doing third-rate work.

The Structural Dimension

A second major area that can be considered by the educational connoisseur is the *structural dimension*. Dreeben (1968), Apple (1982), and others have pointed out how the organizational forms of schools—how the school day is divided and how subjects are assigned to time blocks—influence what students learn. The educational connoisseur might ask, What are the effects of dividing a school day into nine equal periods of fifty minutes each? Although this form of organizational structure is common in secondary schools, there are other ways to organize time.

The structure of an organization typically has persistent features. Unlike the topics that students study, which can change within days or weeks, the school's organizational structure is encountered daily for years. Because the structures people operate within influence many aspects of their lives, their importance can be profound. Roger Barker's work in ecological psychology (1968) is especially articulate in making this point.

Consider the way in which we organize high schools. It seems rational to divide the high school day into equal units, and to assign teachers, subjects, and students to each unit. The day is uniformly ordered so that at any given time one can know just who is where doing what. Yet this order has other consequences as well. Students in high school move every fifty minutes, seven times a day. They have about six minutes to get from one location to another. When a secondary school has fifteen hundred or more students, the movement between classes is reminiscent of a game of musical chairs or a moving conveyor belt. Punctuality is important. It becomes necessary for students to turn their attention on and off on the basis of clock time, rather than psychological time. Shifting cognitive gears from math to history, from history to science, from science to art, from art to French, from French to physical education is something that students must learn to do—or at least to appear to do.

Not all of these requirements, which are a function of the way in which we have decided to organize schools, are deleterious. An educational connoisseur can note which are and are not conducive to the attainment of a given set of educational values. What does such an organizational scheme mean for teachers' preparation? How does it affect their ability to get to know the students they teach? What does it imply for the planning of lessons? What does it mean for building relationships across subject areas? Must schools be organized into such time blocks? What are the alternatives? Must students move? Why not have teachers move and students remain stable, rather than the other way around?

Understanding the influence of an organizational structure in schools provides a basis for considering its utilities and liabilities, its benefits and costs. It allows us to consider other ways of doing things.

Another organizational structure that has had an important influence on schools, as Goodlad and Anderson point out (1959), is the graded structure of elementary schools. If schools have grades and if each grade has a content to be taught and learned, then a student who already knows the content of the next grade should be "double promoted," a practice that has been widely employed in American schools. Conversely, a student who has not learned the content of the grade by the end of a school year should repeat the grade, another practice widely employed in American schools. Are these practices, which appear to flow logically from a graded school structure, consistent with what is known about the variability of children's development? What does a graded school structure do to both students' and teachers' conceptions of educational progress? Is education mainly concerned with teaching students a graded body of content? What happens to children who repeat grades? Do they prosper?

Educational connoisseurs focused upon the structural aspects of schooling would note how the organizational envelopes we have designed affect how education occurs. Schools, like hospitals, factories, and prisons, have a unique virtue they seek to attain. In what ways does the organizational structure of our schools and our classrooms facilitate their attainment?

The Curricular Dimension

The *curricular dimension* is another important area for the educational connoisseur to consider. One of the most important aspects of connoisseurship focuses upon the quality of the curriculum's content and goals and the activities employed to engage students in it. To make judgments about the significance of content, one must know the content being taught *and* the alternatives to that content within the field. Is this content up-to-date? From a disciplinary perspective, is it important? How is it being interpreted by the teacher and understood by the students? And what about the means through which this content is encountered? Do the activities engage students? Do they elicit higher order thinking? Is the content being taught and learned in ways that enable students to apply it or to perceive its relevance to matters outside the subject?

What is the connection between this subject and other subjects? Put another way, what is the degree of *boundary strength* (Bernstein, 1971) between subjects? Is this curriculum, as the British sociologist Basil Bernstein (1971) would say, an *integrated* or a *collection type* curriculum? Who *frames* the activities: the teacher, the student, the curriculum guide? And is there continuity between activities? Is the curriculum a series of individual events and activities, or are relationships drawn among the content areas students study? Does this curriculum afford students opportunities to practice the skills they have learned, or are these skills left to atrophy after they have been introduced?

Decisions about curriculum teach students many important things besides the content. For instance, students learn quickly what adults believe is important for them to learn. This message is conveyed in several ways; among the most important is the amount of time allocated to subjects. We assign time to what is regarded as important (Bernstein, 1971). Another is grading practices. What is graded counts—for both teachers and students. "Minor" subjects receive less time and are less likely to be graded or tested. As these allocations are made, a sociology of knowledge emerges in the school. The curriculum becomes both a means for developing modes of thought *and* a symbolic structure that defines a hierarchy of values for the young. What does this hierarchy teach the young? What kinds of thinking does the curriculum evoke and practice? What does it neglect? And what, if anything, does such neglect mean for the kinds of minds children are likely to develop? What will they have knowledge of, and what is likely to be outside their ken? In what cultural resources will they be able to participate, and which shall be other people's pleasures?

Consider also the manner in which learning is fostered. Is children's encounter with the curriculum viewed as one in which children travel alone on their own tracks, pursuing an individualized but personally isolated journey, or as one in which they have opportunities to work with others? Put another way, are the activities used to foster learning mainly individual or cooperative? To what extent is this a one-person race?

The terms I have used—*cooperative, race, isolated*—are value laden. The values that they imply are not embraced by everyone. I am not suggesting that these particular values should be the ones through which the curriculum is viewed. I do suggest that the value implications of the curriculum should be considered. Which values are used remains with educational connoisseurs.

It is important to remember that the features of the curriculum I have described manifest themselves in qualities we can perceive. These qualities, once experienced, can be interpreted. Without consciousness of, say, the boundary strength of a subject, we cannot consider boundary strength or examine its effects. Learning to see what we have learned not to notice remains one of the most critical and difficult tasks of educational connoisseurs. Everything else rests on it.

The Pedagogical Dimension

The *pedagogical dimension* is the fourth major area of schooling that can be the focus of educational connoisseurs. It is the one that has received the greatest degree of attention so far. Two points about teaching are particularly relevant to educational connoisseurship. First, virtually all curricula are mediated by a teacher. How that mediation occurs has a substantial bearing on what is being taught and learned. One of the most insistent outcomes of research on teaching is that the "same" curriculum is taught in different ways by different teachers, so that how students experience the curriculum is inextricably related to the way in which it is taught (McCutcheon, 1976; Rubinek, 1982; Hawthorne, 1987). In *this* sense, the distinction between curriculum and teaching is artificial. One cannot teach nothing to someone. One cannot teach someone nothing.

Second, what students learn in the classroom is never limited to what teachers intend to teach or to curriculum content. As Dewey put it, "it is one of the greatest of educational fallacies to assume that children learn only what they are being taught at the time" (Dewey, 1938). Teachers teach by example, by covert cues, by emphasizing some aspects of content more than others, by rewarding students directly and indirectly, by the animation and excitement they display in class, by the level of affection they provide to students, by the clarity of their explanations, and more. Teachers teach by relying on illustration, using metaphor, employing diagrams and maps, organizing discussions, lecturing, assigning projects, posing questions. Furthermore, these means or resources are used in idiosyncratic ways by individual teachers. The features of their teaching convey their own messages. Educational connoisseurship can address the very qualities of teaching that typically elude standardized observation schedules and standardized achievement tests.

I will make two final comments about educational connoisseurship as applied to teaching, one concerning the importance of the teacher's aims and the relevance of the context in making judgments about what has been seen, the other concerning seeing an instance of teaching as an example of a teaching genre.

First, it is easy to be hard on teachers if one tries to appraise an act of teaching by comparing it to its ideal case. Under these circumstances almost any teacher will fall short. It is more reasonable not to relinquish ideals, but to moderate them by considering the context in which the teaching occurs and the aims the teacher embraces. Teaching, like life, is filled with trade-offs. Assessing the quality of the teaching, on balance, considering trade-offs, is more realistic than attempting to match actuality to its ideal. An experienced teacher working with a "difficult" class might have to use approaches that from one perspective might be questionable in another type of class. A new teacher might make choices that would be troublesome if made by a veteran. A lesson that had low-level, short-term aims might be acceptable if seen as a small part of a more significant enterprise. What is the context, who is the teacher, who are the students, with what other demands must a teacher cope, what are the teacher's aims—these are all relevant considerations in attempting to see and appraise teaching. Educational connoisseurship is enhanced and perception made more acute as the context is known. Since the perception of qualities in school situations is almost always interpreted, knowing the features of the context is likely to make the interpretation more defensible and more equitable.

Second, much research on teaching has been predicated on the assumption that there is a "best" system or method which could, in principle, be discovered and which would lead to high levels of student achievement (Tyack, 1974). Experimental studies of teaching are often designed to identify and convey those best methods. In some ways the effort can be regarded as the search for laws, as an effort to find cause-effect relationships that work. By discovering "what works,"[4] teachers could then reproduce their successes, something like getting teaching down to a science. Although some also realize that teaching is an art (Gage, 1978), the search for its scientific basis has dominated research on teaching.

If we take a leaf from the arts and apply what we can learn from them to the study of teaching, we would expect excellence in teaching, as in art, to be of many kinds. That is, we would expect to find different kinds of excellence rooted in different genres of teaching. Music, painting, and poetry contain a multitude of genres. The qualities that command admiration in Flemish painting of the sixteenth century are not those that command admiration in twentieth-century cubism. What constitutes excellence in jazz differs from excellence in Gregorian chant. One mark of a connoisseur is to understand the genre and to employ criteria from that genre to the work or performance encountered.

Teaching also has genres of performance. Even one genre, such as lecturing, can take many forms. A lecture that is systematic, specific, logical, and clear has important virtues. But a lecture that is speculative, sometimes halting, one that gives students a sense of a teacher trying to deal with ideas that are not fully resolved, but which continue to be interesting, has other educational virtues. It is not necessary to appraise the merits of one by using criteria that are appropriate to the other. We need to recognize the general style in which an example of teaching participates and to assess its quality by "rules" that are appropriate to it. In Plato's *Republic,* Socrates teaches Glaucon through a dialectic procedure. The dialogues often wander and circle back to points made earlier. They seldom follow a straight line. Aristotle, however, teaches through an analytically developed hierarchical order whose logic is meticulous. Both Plato and Aristotle are excellent teachers, but their excellence is based on different genres of teaching. Recognizing these genres is a mark of a sophisticated connoisseur. In simpler terms, one predefined observation schedule *will not* fit all teaching situations.

It is easy to distinguish between lecturing and discussing or between individual consultation and small group instruction. It is patently clear that the criteria appropriate for assessing skill in leading a discussion differ from the criteria needed to assess or perceive the qualities of a lecture. What is more difficult to see and assess is the teacher's personal signature. Both Monet and Renoir are impressionists, but their work is different. Renoir would not be a better painter if he became more like Monet in his work, or vice versa. Educational connoisseurs recognize the signature that individual teachers give to their work. These are, so to speak, styles within genres. We need to recognize the pervasive qualities of teaching as they are displayed in some form and a judgment—one that is difficult to make—of how the teaching might be enhanced.

There is almost a teleological character to this kind of assessment—can teaching become more of what it is trying to be? Looked at from a different perspective, we can ask how the coherence of the teaching can be increased. The task in coaching teachers is not to try to transform the pedagogical signature of a teacher into another form, but to help the teacher develop the strengths that "come naturally." This is not an argument for "biological determinism" in teaching—rather, it is a plea to enhance what is personally distinctive about teaching. The cultivation of productive idiosyncrasy in the art of teaching is as important as in the art of painting.

This attitude toward teaching runs counter to what is sometimes put forward as a technology of teaching seeking to get teaching, as they say, "down to a science"; the latter implies finding or trying to find, as Frederick Taylor tried to find, the most effective and efficient *standardized* way to effectuate a complex human performance (Callahan, 1962). The vision put forward here, in contrast to Taylorism, celebrates productive diversity rather than standard uniformity.

The Evaluative Dimension

The fifth major dimension that can serve as a focus for educational connoisseurship is the *evaluative dimension*. In this discussion I will focus on the ways in which evaluation practices, especially those embodied in tests, influence the students' outlook.

Testing has been and is being used extensively in American schools in our effort to secure reliable and valid information about school productivity. Through state departments of education, an educationally anxious public worried about its schools relies upon a battery of tests to monitor their effects. From one perspective, testing students to determine their academic achievement appears to be a reasonable way to identify student accomplishment and school effectiveness. Why not "sample" and make inferences about school productivity from the scores students achieve? Further, why not reward teachers on the basis of their students' academic achievement? Why not compare schools on the basis of their test scores? The higher the scores a teacher or a school achieves, the better the teacher or the school.

Educational connoisseurs would examine the effects of such assumptions as they manifest themselves in practice. What, if any, are the consequences of testing for teachers and pupils? Does testing influence what is taught? Does it shape teaching methods? Does it convey messages to students that support the values the faculty and community embrace? Does it create a status hierarchy among subjects that children study? In short, educational connoisseurs whose attention was devoted to evaluation would be concerned not only with the technical adequacy of the tests employed—do the tests have content validity, are they relevant to the curriculum, are they statistically reliable, and so forth—but also with what, besides academic achievement, they might engender, and what the subtext of the testing program might be.

Consider the fact that in many school districts children are tested in May or June in order to assess their levels of academic achievement for that academic year. By the time the tests have been scored and student performance scores reported, their teachers have been assigned a new class of students, so that it is impossible for them to use the test results to do anything differently with the students who have been tested. Clearly there is a trade-off regarding the timing of a testing program, but consideration of the costs and benefits of such a trade-off might very well be one of the considerations that educational connoisseurs would take into account in reflecting on what they had seen.

Connoisseurship in the evaluative arena is not limited to testing, since evaluation does not necessarily require the use of tests. Evaluation concerns the making of value judgments about the quality of some object, situation, or process. Evaluation practices permeate classrooms because of the ways in which teachers appraise students' comments, their social behavior, and their academic work. These evaluative messages are constant in the life of schooling. Tone of voice, facial expression, and messages of support and enthusiasm are part of classroom culture. These, too, are appropriate events for educational connoisseurs to appraise. Indeed, one could argue that the culture of evaluation is so pervasive in schools that manifestations of this culture are collectively more powerful in shaping the day-to-day priorities of schools than those special moments devoted to formal testing.

Evaluation occurs everywhere: when teachers listen to children read, when children hand in what they have written, when students respond to teachers' questions, and so forth. Because schools are designed to be places in which the tasks children encounter are always somewhat out of reach, some schools almost continuously create settings in which children are at the edge of failure. Relatively little time is provided to students to practice or relish their newly acquired skills; more complex skills are seldom far ahead. When one considers further that districtwide expectations for students are typically standardized rather than individualized, the evaluative dimension is seen to have even greater impact. Because of a common evaluative format, children can compare their position in a pecking order defined by the performance of other children competing in the same race. Educational connoisseurs not only would notice the effects of teaching on the culture of schooling, but also they would interpret what they had come to appreciate.

One final comment: evaluation practices within schools, including those used in testing, are among the most powerful forces influencing the priorities and climate of schools. Evaluation practices, particularly testing practices, operationalize the school's values. More than what educators say, more than what they write in curriculum guides, evaluation practices tell both students and teachers what counts. How these practices are employed, what they address and what they neglect, and the form in which they occur speak forcefully to students about what adults believe is important. Because of the importance of evaluation, it is a critical subject for educational connoisseurship. I believe no effort to change schools can succeed without designing an approach to evaluation that is consistent with the aims of the desired change.

Data Sources for Connoisseurship

The data sources for educational connoisseurship are many. The most important is undoubtedly the observation of teachers and classroom life. But insights about teaching and classrooms can be secured by talking with students about their work and asking their views about what is transpiring, as well as by observation. Similarly, interviews with teachers can be a very rich source of information. Educational connoisseurs not only watch and see, they talk to others and listen to what they have to say. The interview is a powerful resource for learning how people perceive the situations in which they work. It is important to remember that connoisseurship is aimed at understanding what is going on. Any source of data that can contribute to that end is an appropriate resource.

Among these resources are instructional materials, student work, teacher-made tests, bulletins from school administrators, homework assignments, and the like. What is the text and the subtext of these message systems, and what do they convey because of their form and content? What kinds of questions are asked of students on their homework assignments? What is the nature of their teachers' responses, and to what extent are the responses elaborated or interpretive, as contrasted with the use of checked-off answers indicating a correct or incorrect response? How soon after they are turned in are homework assignments returned? Again, the problem is to make sense of the situation; anything that allows us to deepen our understanding by using multiple data sources is advantageous (Lincoln & Guba, 1985).

Data sources also include the history of the school or community since it is likely to enhance our ability to interpret what we see. Such data can be secured by perusing local newspapers and by talking to "old-timers" who know the history of the situation. In saying that historical context is a potentially useful resource for deepening connoisseurship, I wish to emphasize the word "potentially." I do not suggest that it is always necessary to situate a school or classroom in its historical context, only that in some cases it may be helpful. Whether it is useful or not will depend upon the nature of the problem that is being addressed and the availability of various resources. My main aim, however, is not to construct a laundry list of potential data sources for educational connoisseurship, but rather to underscore the point that whatever is relevant for seeing more acutely and understanding more deeply is fair game.

Although seeing what transpires in educational contexts is a fundamentally important achievement, seeing is never adequate *if* knowledge is to become social. For that to occur seeing must be transformed into saying. That is the task of criticism, the subject of the next chapter.

Notes

1. The term *quality* has two quite different meanings. The first and most common refers to the value of something, as in "a quality carpet" or "a diamond of good quality." The second meaning refers to the sensory features of something—the quality of redness or the elegance of a move on a dance floor or a basketball court. Although we often use language to stand for the qualities we experience, the language we use is rarely adequate to reveal the character of those qualities. Artistically treated language, as employed in poetry and literature, and interestingly enough in the utterances of preschool children and in some uses of slang, comes close to the creation of an analogue to the experience of qualities

that themselves have no name. When I speak of qualitative research and evaluation, I refer to a form of research and evaluation that not only pays attention to qualities—which, of course, all empirical research must address—but uses representational forms that attempt to render such qualities expressively through the way the form itself has been shaped.

2. It should be pointed out that Fred Dretske's (1969) conception of epistemic seeing, from which I have borrowed the term, is radically different from the conception I offer in this book. Dretske holds that epistemic seeing requires a belief that such and such is the case. In other words, while nonepistemic seeing provides sensation, Dretske believes that only when belief enters the picture does seeing become epistemic.

    I do not embrace this view. I believe seeing becomes epistemic when individuals become aware of a certain array of qualities, whether or not they have beliefs about them. My knowledge of the taste of Coca-Cola, for example, is an example of epistemic "seeing" or epistemic tasting. I do not want to restrict epistemology to matters of belief, but rather to relate it to matters of consciousness.

3. John Dewey points out in *Experience and Education* (1938) that while beefsteak might be good, it's not good for infants. Goodness, without consideration for context, is virtually meaningless. I concur.

4. For an example of the effort to codify "what works" in educational research, see *What Works* (1987).

Chapter V

Educational Criticism

Every critic, like every artist, has a bias, a predilection, that is bound up with the very existence of individuality. It is his task to convert it into an organ of sensitive perception and of intelligent insight, and to do so without surrendering the instinctive preferences from which are derived direction and sincerity.

John Dewey

The Meaning of Criticism

In *Art as Experience,* John Dewey writes, "The aim of criticism is the re-education of the perception of the work of art" (1934, p. 324). It is a conception I embrace, and one that I will examine here as it pertains, not primarily to works of art, but to works of education, particularly to the practice of schooling.

In the previous chapter I discussed the meaning of connoisseurship and its relationship to five dimensions of schooling. Connoisseurship, unlike criticism, is a private act. Its aim is to appreciate the qualities that constitute some object, situation, or event. To be a connoisseur in some domain means to notice or experience the significant and often subtle qualities that constitute an act, work, or object and, typically, to be able to relate these to the contextual and antecedent conditions. But connoisseurship imposes no obligation upon the connoisseur to articulate or justify, to explain or persuade: One can be a connoisseur of fine wine without uttering a word about its quality. One can appreciate an excellent—or not so excellent—teacher in action without writing a report, telling an administrator, or providing feedback to the teacher. Connoisseurship can be and most often is the quiet act of appreciation.

Because connoisseurship is basically private, it has, by itself, little social utility. Of course, those who have high levels of connoisseurship in, say, furniture are more likely to look for and buy what they regard as being of high quality—within the limits of their budget. Nevertheless, the fact that someone is a connoisseur in some domain has relatively little import for those who are not. For connoisseurship to have a public presence, we must turn to criticism, for criticism provides connoisseurship with a public face.

Educational connoisseurship gives access to the complex and subtle aspects of educational phenomena, and it is through such access that educational critics secure the content they need to function as critics. If connoisseurship can be regarded as the art of appreciation, criticism can be thought of as the art of disclosure. The primary function of the critic is educational. By "educational" I mean providing the material through which perception is increased and understanding deepened. To do this the critic must be able to function as a connoisseur. And in educational matters, the critic must function as an educational connoisseur. Criticism depends upon awareness of qualities and their antecedent and contextual conditions for its content: One can be a great connoisseur without being a critic, but one cannot be a critic of any kind without some level of connoisseurship.

The task of the critic is to perform a mysterious feat well: to transform the qualities of a painting, play, novel, poem, classroom or school, or act of teaching and learning into a public form that illuminates, interprets, and appraises the qualities that have been experienced. Since there is no literal linguistic equivalent for qualities per se, the task cannot be simple translation. With no rules of equivalence, there is no one-to-one correspondence of referent to symbol. Thus every act of criticism is a reconstruction. The reconstruction takes the form of an argued narrative, supported by evidence that is never incontestable; there will *always* be alternative interpretations of the "same" play, as the history of criticism so eloquently attests.[1] Further, even the qualities described in any critical account are not necessarily either all that could have been described or those that other critics might have described. In short, selection is always at work in both the perception and the critical portrayal of what has been seen.

The roots of criticism are found in the ordinary activities of daily life. Whenever people make judgments about the qualities of things—food to be purchased, arguments engaged in, music heard, policies and laws enacted, meals eaten, games played or observed—connoisseurship and criticism are present. It is in our self-interest to be able to describe and appraise what we experience: It is a necessary skill in our negotiations with others and in deciding what a situation calls for. Young children acquire such skills as they learn to play with others and as they try to argue their case when inevitable differences of opinion emerge. Indeed, the sports arena remains a bastion of vernacular criticism, not written for the intelligentsia, but for the man or woman in the street. Consider the language in the following description of a sports event.

> It's chaos in the open court. Just the way Knicks guard Gerald Wilkins likes it. The Cavaliers are sprinting back, now turning around and trying to find a man—any man—to guard as Wilkins pushes the ball into his frontcourt with two lefthand dribbles.
>
> Wilkins drives right into the upper part of the lane. Halfway

down the avenue massive Cavs center Brad Daugherty is just starting
to raise his arms into a defensive position as Wilkins, a 6-6 leaper,
plants and then launches himself for the little pull-up jumper, fading
away slightly from the basket. Daugherty, late this time and never a
particularly good jumper, has no chance on the play. But behind him,
screened from Wilkins' view, lurks John "Hot Rod" Williams.

Williams, number 18 in the Cavs' home whites, is crouched down
low, head up, with both arms extended to the sides. At 6-11, 230, he is
one of the skinniest power forwards in the league. He's mostly legs; his
waist happens two-thirds of the way up his body (the knee bend is
one-third marker). The thighs are thick and strong-looking but from
there he narrows, chest not at all deep, all the way to his smallish head.

As Wilkins releases the ball at the top of his jump, Williams
extends, leaping over and across Daugherty. His right arm, a thin
cylinder, seemingly the same diameter from wrist to socket, telescopes
out and swats the shot, catching it a good four feet away from its
release point. (Capouya, 1988, p. 60)

Now compare this sports criticism with a criticism of the work of an
important American painter, Ben Shahn. This art criticism was written for
The New Yorker by the late Harold Rosenberg, who was one of America's
leading art critics and a professor of social thought at the University of
Chicago. The excerpt is extensive because, I believe, it is important to get
a sense of what Rosenberg is doing and the issues he addresses.

For those who respond to them, the paintings of Ben Shahn are
enhanced by a species of moral and social virtue. That the paintings say
the right things makes them look right, regardless of their individual
quality. Shahn is among the most extensively collected artists of the
past forty years: more than sixty private collections and museums are
credited as lenders of the one hundred and eighty paintings, drawings,
prints, posters, and photographs that constitute his retrospective at the
Jewish Museum. Even subjects such as "Stop H Bomb Tests," "Tom
Mooney and His Warden, J.B. Holohan," and "Scabbies Are Welcome"
appear to have been unable to discourage acquisition of Shahns for
living rooms and institutional galleries. The often seen and reproduced
"The Passion of Sacco and Vanzetti" (not in the show) is received as an
emblem of Injustice Recalled, rather than as a tempera painting of a
group of figures in a setting of classical steps and columns. The general
impression left by Shahn's paintings and graphic works is one of an
artist constantly embattled along a line of contemporary history—the
line of issues supported in the nineteen-thirties by the majority of men
and women of good will.

Still, the notion of Shahn preeminently as a painter supporting
social and political causes is only partly correct—even in the thirties,
when his dedication to victims of oppression was at its height, he went
off in directions unconnected with the ideology that seemed central to
his work. In the same year (1931) that he composed "Sacco and
Vanzetti: In the Courtroom Cage," he designed "Haggadah for

Passover," and in that decade, too, he produced such "neutral" works as "Photographer's Window," which is a literal rendering of the display in a neighborhood studio, and "Seurat's Lunch," in which white dots are scattered over a storefront in a comically awkward homage to the celebrated New-Impressionist. In his own view, Shahn represented a humanist, rather than a narrowly political, position. If the humanist artist was sensitive to instances of injustice, past and present—to the Dreyfus case, Sacco and Vanzetti, Tom Mooney, slums, urban and rural poverty, unemployment, strikes, minorities, concentration camps, Nazi brutality, the menace of nuclear bombs—he was also moved by children at play, spring, and the flowering countryside, meditations on man's fate, the Scriptures, and by abstract emotions, such as rage and brotherhood, and metaphysical insights expressed in symbolic terms, as in "Age of Anxiety" and "Everyman" (a clown doing a somersault in the company of two reflective figures with their hands clasped). (Rosenberg, 1985, University of Chicago Press, pp. 90–91)

Criticizing basketball and criticizing a retrospective show of a major American painter have common features. Both require connoisseurship and the skills of the critic to do them well. Both describe and appraise. Both make their subject matter vivid. Both give us material to reflect upon, even if we have not been there.

The Structure of Educational Criticism

In chapter 4, I described five important dimensions that educational connoisseurs could attend to in the study of schooling. These five dimensions provide a structure for perception. But what about a structure for criticism? How might one organize one's criticism of what has been experienced?

Educational criticism can be thought of as having four dimensions: *description, interpretation, evaluation,* and *thematics.* I will discuss each of these in turn. At the outset, however, I want to point out that in identifying these dimensions—what can be regarded as the structure of educational criticism—I risk giving the impression that this structure prescribes a sequence for writing educational criticism or that what one has experienced in a school or classroom can be easily parceled into the four dimensions that I am about to describe. This is not the case. The four dimensions of educational criticism do not prescribe a sequence among the parts of an educational criticism, although they do not prohibit critics from using these dimensions to organize their writing. The four dimensions, further, do not imply that each is wholly independent of the others, although for analytic purposes it might be helpful to make such distinctions. In short, the distinctions I am about to make are intended to have heuristic utility and should not be regarded as prescribing an approach; in fact, the world we experience is a mix that we often try to sort out later, but the mix once sorted is no longer the mix, even if the sorting sheds some light upon it. My message is to treat these distinctions as tools with which to work, not as rules to follow.

Description

Description enables readers to visualize what a place or process is like. It should help them "see" the school or classroom the critic is attempting to help them understand.

Seeing in the mind's eye is not the only important effect of descriptive writing; the text should also enable readers to participate vicariously in the events described. That is, it should enable readers to get a feel for the place or process and, where possible and appropriate, for the experience of those who occupy the situation. We have already seen how Truman Capote enables readers to "see" Holcombe, Kansas, in the opening scene of *In Cold Blood*. And we have experienced the powerful way in which Elie Wiesel recreates for us his experience in a Nazi death camp. Imagine what we would not know about either Holcombe or Buchenwald if they were described in strictly literal form. An emotionally eviscerated account of a death camp would be a partial account at best; it would also be misleading. Schools and classrooms also lend themselves to similar forms of description. To understand the kind of place a school or classroom is, we need to have the kind of account that will enable us to know what it would feel and look like if we were there.

To make vicarious participation possible, educational critics must have access to the qualities the situation displays. This is, of course, a transactive event. The ability to construe a situation with perceptivity—that is, to *make* sense of it—provides the basic content with which critics work. But they must then create in written form a structure that will carry meanings forward through descriptive prose. Doing so requires artistry in the treatment of narrative language, and, as I have already indicated, this achievement means shaping text, hearing its cadences, selecting just the right word or phrase, employing apt metaphor, and on rare occasions creating neologisms that do some epistemological work. The "trick" in writing, often taken for granted, is to create in the public world a structure or form whose features re-present what is experienced in private. The sense of discovery and excitement that pervades a classroom is not simply a set of words; it is a set of qualities, including a sense of energy that must somehow be made palpable through prose. This is what effective writers achieve.

Again, the function of such an achievement is not mere embellishment or ornamentation or making something "literary," it is epistemic. Its aim is to help the reader know. One source of knowing is visualization.

Another is emotion. How a situation feels is not less important than how it looks. The descriptive dimension of educational criticism makes both possible.

In writing educational criticism, particularly the descriptive dimension, the writer always tells an incomplete story. One does not—nor can one—tell it all. In this sense a narrative, like perception, is inherently selective. But selectivity, although partial and framework dependent, is a way of giving point to observations and thereby helping others learn to see. Only the less competent try to attend to everything (Berliner, 1988). The skilled teacher knows what to neglect. The competent student knows what to focus upon. The expert chess player knows what patterns on the board count. Insofar as the writing of criticism is itself an art, and I believe it is, the writer must be selective in both perception and disclosure. The making of a fine meal does not require the use of everything in the pantry.

Selectivity does not cease with writing. There is a line of argument in literary theory that holds that texts are made by readers, not by writers (Fish, 1980). This is, in a trivial sense, true. Readers, like writers, must construe what they read to make it meaningful, but to say this is not to say that the kind of text read makes no difference. What is written and how it is written make a difference; that is the whole point of learning to write.

Let's turn to an example of descriptive writing in educational criticism. It comes from the opening pages of a longer study. I include it here as an example of vivid writing and an illustration of how the scene is viewed.

Where to Park
Peggy Hagberg

Where to park? The cyclone fence–enclosed asphalt parking lot of the 1950ish modern Cox School is now occupied by box car–like portable school rooms. Defying the orderly arrangements of car parking lots (or train yards), the portables seem to have been dropped from high above, as though the School Board had packed them into a huge plane, flown it up high over Cox and dropped the contents onto the school parking lot.

This may be a plus. The former parking lot also serves as the only playground area for the 700 pupils of Cox School. The haphazardly-arranged portables seem to actually provide private, unmonotonously arranged play areas for groups of kids of distinctly different sizes and ages.

Stories of declining enrollments and the auctioning of surplus suburban school buildings must seem like a bad joke to the people of Cox School. It was built to house 400 students.

In 1971, this school was added to Oakland's list of compensatory education schools. Too many of the children were not achieving, were poor, were black. All of the students at Cox are now categorized by the State as "EDY's" (educationally disadvantaged youth). I wonder what six years of extra money and special programs has meant for the students. To get and keep this money the school must have a curriculum that emphasizes D-P-T (diagnosis, prescription and treatment), Individualization of Instruction, basic skill improvement.

Mr. N and I are to meet in the principal's office at 8:45 A.M. N left a good, bright-future-young-executive position to come to California and to teach. He has taught for seven years now; during those years he earned a Master's in counseling, a counseling credential, an administrative credential and was placed on Oakland's Administrative Preferred List. His ambition is to become a school administrator. Six years a junior high teacher, this year he is teaching a combined 5th and 6th grade class—he wants to obtain the breadth of experience that will help him secure an administrative position.

I have trouble keeping up with the long strides of the tall Mr. N as we walk towards his classroom. The wood steps of the portable shake as, amid kids' greeting, "Hi, Mr. N!" and questions, "Who she?" we two adults and twelve children enter the portable.

Six rows of five desks each share the space of the turquoise blue 20 by 40 foot portable classroom with a large free standing space heater, a small teacher's desk, one work table, thirty children and one adult. About 18 inches of space separate the seats of the front row from the front wall black board. How does N, who has one of those "I'd Rather Be Sailing" stickers pasted on the bumper of his vintage Volvo, navigate through and around in the crowded room? Certainly, the students can't move around much.

Blackboards are mounted along one short and one long side of the room. Designed for use by little primary children, they are below the eye levels of these 5th and 6th graders; stooping to write on them must give this teacher a daily backache. Mounted above the boards are large cards, each bearing the name of one student. Tacked below each card is a sample of each child's composition efforts.

8:50—

Five minutes after the final bell rings, 23 children (ten girls and thirteen boys) are in the room; ten have taken seats. In a few more minutes, all but one student has taken an assigned seat—the noise dies down as N tells them the lunch choice for today is a Hoagie or a hot dog. After this critical bit of information has been received, the next order of business is to find out who I am. N tells them my name and what I am doing in their classroom (about ten students appear to listen to this second bit of intelligence). N's voice is obscured by many individual conversations.

N calls for quiet, which he gets—momentarily.

9:00—

N tells the kids: "In ten minutes we will do vocabulary; while I am taking roll do five minutes of math. Do these four problems on the board. Simplify these fractions."

1) $18/30 = /$
2) $9/45 = /$
3) $5/6 = /18$
4) $2/5 = /20$

(I guess the plan is that they spend five minutes doing the problems, five minutes checking their answers. Somehow I get mixed up. How do you simplify $5/6$ with $X/18$ or $2/5$ with $X/20$? Nobody asks.)

While N is taking roll, five students work on the problems, others are generally quiet and conducting private business of their own—talking, checking out each other's outfits, a few are looking at their own materials and books. Something that is to happen several times during the morning occurs: almost as though on cue, as soon as N says "do these four problems" a tall, thin red-jacketed girl arises from her seat at one far corner of the room, walks up one row and down the next. At midpoint of the second row another, taller girl in a pink dress steps behind her and the two proceed down the aisle and cross behind two end desks of rows three and four. At row three, a chubby girl in a too-small denim pants-suit steps up behind the girl in a pink dress. The procession swings around and up row two and it is joined by its final member—the girl in the green granny dress. The four arrive at the pencil sharpener in the corner, carefully sharpen their already-sharp pencils, and without breaking rank retrace their trail back to their seats. The members of this classroom conga-line take soft pokes at some classmates and jive with others as they move along. N says nothing to them.

A sniper has positioned himself on the wall cabinet and takes make-believe pot shots with an umbrella at two of the "sharpeners."

There is a loud banging on the door which is opened by the monitor. A "traffic boy" carrying a load of STOP signs is admitted. He is really small and the signs are big. The signs escape from his arms, hit the floor, wall and door jamb. N orders him to take the signs out. He leaves.

9:15—

N says "Okay, let's go". . .But several students do not permit him to continue—they are demanding pencils. N is calm: "You got some yesterday. This is it—we don't get any more pencils—tomorrow I say no. You can't borrow any." Another cue? The "sharpeners" are up again and making their way to the sharpener. They follow the same route as before. This time they are followed by several other students. N says nothing.

N begins checking the fraction problems. Six students are looking at him and raising their hands. One girl sitting directly in front of him is playing with what appears to be a desk full of deflated balloons. N warns her, Shanna, to put them away. The response comes quickly: a blown-up balloon is pulled out of the desk and released into the air. The action and the noise breaks everybody up. Before the merriment subsides, N reacts: "Okay, that's it! Get out!" Shanna refuses. N grabs her hand and arm and pulls her out the door. She stands outside looking in the window. She is ignored by everyone but me and finally disappears.

For fifteen minutes the fractions are reviewed. N calls on hand-raisers for an answer. If the answer is wrong, he asks for another. Students call out until correct answers are found. $\frac{9}{45}$ is reduced to $\frac{3}{15}$, but is reduced no further. One green plaid-jacketed boy provides a step-by-step explanation of his "reduction" of $\frac{2}{5}$ to $\frac{8}{20}$—which he points out is not a reduction. But his message is lost; no one seems to be listening to him. This procedure continues until the four problems are covered.

(Roll-taking and settling-down activity have taken 32 minutes.)
9:32—

N tells students to take out homework. Amid general noise of desk lid-banging, foot-shuffling, personal conversation and child protestations, (on cue) the March of the Sharpeners begins again.

While the "sharpeners" are traveling, honing pencil points and returning, N delivers an even-toned lecture on the lack of personal discipline indicated by losing or not bringing in homework. His point: done or not, "at least you could have brought the paper back to school to work on." (Then why take it home? I wonder)

Eight students are without homework papers. N tells them to move their desks near others and share. This shift occupies about three minutes—just enough time for one blue-jacketed girl to demonstrate dance steps to a small-but-interested seated audience at the back of the room. N says nothing to her.

The homework paper is a crossword puzzle. Most of the students have become intent on checking answers or filling in the squares as answers are given. N instructs them on the way to handle crosswords: "Look ahead, predict the number of letter spaces to be filled and use starting letters for clues."

Shanna knocks loudly. The monitor opens the door for her. Looking gleefully expectant, she announces to everybody that the Vice Principal said that he is busy with parents and "Mr. N should handle his problems himself." N responds to Shanna (and everybody) with: "No, I will not do that. Shanna, get out!" Shanna smiles and leaves. N picks up the room phone and calls the Vice Principal. The kids have become quiet and are listening attentively. After a minute's wait on the phone, the Vice Principal is reached, N says loudly that he has sent Shanna to the Vice Principal again. He then hangs up.

9:59—

N calls for and gets momentary quiet. He announces that they will break into reading groups. He will meet with the "Kaleidoscopes" first. The other groups should read and answer questions listed for their reading groups on the board.

The Kaleidoscopes pull their desks into a cluster by the space heater. N stands next to the group listening to their oral reading and asking questions.

The Other Children: a few have *Be A Better Reader* open and appear to be reading. Most are still shuffling seats together, going to the pile of readers for a book, talking or otherwise absorbed in their own businesses. N seems to have escaped into his reading group; he pays no attention to the non-Kaleidoscopers.

The monitor opens the door to admit an attractive young woman. N greets Mrs. Johnson. I learn later that she is the parent of a suspended student.

N tells the class to *continue* their reading (hardly anyone is reading) and walks over to and out the door with Mrs. Johnson. He keeps the door slightly ajar with his foot. Before the door has closed over (and on cue?) the "sharpeners" begin another trek. The noise level becomes a din. N appears in the doorway: "Get quiet and get back to work!" (back to work?) N disappears again. (At this point I cannot break years of teacher-habit-response and glare at the worst offenders in some attempt to indicate that I am a responsible adult.)

The noise wave builds again. N enters classroom, demands quiet. The room becomes almost quiet and the "sharpeners" wend their way back to desks. N delivers a lecture on manners: "What impression will—If you were Mrs. Johnson, what would you think about your daughter's class? (*I* wonder what Mrs. Johnson does think.) Are you embarrassed?" The response is silence.

10:15—

N tells them to "Read and answer questions, to look over pages 22, 23, 24 and be ready for questions when I work with your group. I want the Kaleidoscopes." (He doesn't say when he will work with the others.)

The recess bell rings, kids bolt toward the door. N yells: "No! Sit down. The longer it takes to get quiet and orderly, the less recess you're going to get. Now, line up." (Girls form one line, boys another.) They stand quietly.

N dismisses them. (Hagberg, 1975, pp. 1–7)

What follows in the longer report is the author's interpretation of the events she has described. That interpretation will not be provided here. What the excerpt given here illustrates is the way in which one writer makes vivid the events she believes significant in the classroom she observed. It is not difficult in reading her description to generate a picture of those events, to secure a feel for the classroom, to see "the sharpeners" make their way between the aisles to the sharpener, to imagine the sniper taking pot shots at the enemy. The clarity of her writing and the vividness of her images allow us to participate vicariously in the scene. The qualities of experience that such writing makes possible are as important in understanding an inner city classroom as are precise, quantitative descriptions of discourse strategies employed in classrooms in those schools.

Interpretation

If description can be thought of as giving an account *of*, interpretation can be regarded as accounting *for*. Educational critics are interested not only in making vivid what they have experienced, but in explaining its meaning; this goal frequently requires putting what has been described in a context in which its antecedent factors can be identified. It also means illuminating the potential consequences of practices observed and providing reasons that account for what has been seen.

In the social sciences theories are developed to account for relationships. It was believed at one time, and still is in some circles, that the necessary and sufficient conditions in a social situation could be specified to control or predict the occurrence of an event from a set of antecedent conditions. Cronbach (1977) and others have pointed out that there are so many contingencies and interactive relationships among variables in classrooms that it is more reasonable to regard theories as guides to perception than as devices that lead to the tight control or precise prediction of events.

Educational critics can work with a heuristic conception of theory. When critics work with theory, they use it as a tool for purposes of explanation—not to meet the rigorous tests for the "true experiment," but to satisfy rationality, to deepen the conversation, to raise fresh questions. Further, seldom will one theory satisfy all of the dimensions about which critics may wish to speak or write, hence there will be a certain eclecticism in the application of theory. Several theories might be used to account for different (or even the "same") sets of qualities.

Suppose a teacher has planned a science lesson. The children, who are in the third grade, are supposed to learn something about the densities of fluid. Each is given a glass test tube and five bottles containing liquids of different densities. Each density has a specific color. Red is the heaviest density, green the next, then blue, yellow, and orange. The students' task is to determine the density of each fluid by putting fluids in the tube in different orders. In the end they are to have the heaviest density in the tube at the bottom, the next heaviest on top of it and so forth. If they are successful, the color arrangement will be: Red, green, blue, yellow, and orange, although the children do not know this.

The teacher believes that it will require two twenty-minute periods for students to complete the experiment and to record their trials and observations. To the teacher's surprise, most of the students solve the problem in fifteen minutes of the first session. What is the teacher to do? Does he introduce the next lesson in the science curriculum? Does he move to another subject? Near the end of the first class period, a student brings a test tube up to him for inspection and shows that she has found a way to mix colors (and therefore densities) that allows her to create a new sequence of densities, as well as new colors. The teacher is both surprised and delighted and encourages other children to experiment in a similar way. The children do so enthusiastically throughout the second twenty-minute period.

What would an educational critic do with such a situation? How would the critic describe and interpret the event? Here the critic's task is to interpret the teacher's actions and the children's activity and to employ, where applicable, theoretical ideas from the social sciences to account for factors such as the kind of learning in which the children were engaged, and the educational and psychological meaning of the teacher's abrupt shift in tactics during a critical period in the lesson. In discussing the kind of learning in which children were engaged, the critic's attention might be directed not only to the problem the teacher assigned, but to the social arena, to the kind of learning fostered by the social context in which the problem was addressed. Were children helping each other? What kind of problems did they run into, and how did they deal with them? What was their degree of engagement and participation? These and other questions like them would normally be considered in the context of connoisseurship, which would then influence the content of criticism. In short, the context, considered broadly, would be an appropriate candidate for interpretation.

It is important to realize that no theory in the social sciences can encompass a set of particulars within a specific classroom. And for good reasons. Joseph Schwab, an astute student of educational practice, writes:

> Nearly all theories in all the behavioral sciences are marked by the coexistence of competing theories. There is not one theory of personality but many, representing at least six radically different choices of what is relevant and important in human behavior. There is not one theory of groups but several. There is not one theory of learning but half a dozen. All the social and behavioral sciences are marked by "schools," each distinguished by a different choice of principle of enquiry, each of which selects from the intimidating complexities of the subject matter the small fraction of the whole with which it can deal.
>
> The theories which arise from enquiries so directed are, then, radically incomplete, each of them incomplete to the extent that

competing theories take hold of different aspects of the subject of enquiry and treat it in a different way. Further, there is perennial invention of new principles which bring to light new facets of the subject matter, new relations among the facets, and new ways of treating them. In short, there is every reason to suppose that any one of the extant theories of behavior is a pale and incomplete representation of actual behavior. (Schwab, 1969, p. 27)

The idealizations of theory *are* idealizations. Practice is particular and idiosyncratic, hence theory must be treated with flexibility: it must be *shaped* to fit practice.

In writing about connoisseurship I said that awareness of qualities was a fundamental achievement. This is so because what one can interpret depends initially on awareness. Without awareness interpretation is not possible. If one is dealing with nonobjective visual art or symphonic music, the saliency of their qualities might diminish somewhat the need for interpretation, at least compared to the qualities emerging from social interactions. In the situations in which humans interact, however, the need for interpretation is almost always pressing. Things are not always what they seem to be. To understand the covert or implied meanings in a situation, one must penetrate the surface, one must seek what Clifford Geertz (1973) refers to as "thick description": interpretation. Geertz writes:

> If anthropological interpretation is constructing a reading of what happens, then to divorce it from what happens—from what, in this time or that place, specific people say, what they do, what is done to them, from the whole vast business of the world—is to divorce it from its applications and render it vacant. A good interpretation of anything—a poem, a person, a history, a ritual, an institution, a society—takes us into the heart of that of which it is the interpretation. When it does not do that, but leads us instead somewhere else—into an admiration of its own elegance, of its author's cleverness, or of the beauties of Euclidean order—it may have its intrinsic charms; but it is something else than what the task at hand—figuring out what all that rigmarole with the sheep is about—calls for. (1973, p. 60)

There is a difference, sometimes a subtle one, between the description of behavior and its interpretation. Sometimes "straight" description is what one wants; but it is almost never adequate without interpretation, *if* the effort is to understand the import of events or situations for people. Thus in the interpretive frame educational critics must, so to speak, distance themselves from the scene in order to explain its meanings and to account for what has been described. To interpret is to place in context, to explain, to unwrap, to explicate. It is, as some might say, a hermeneutic activity of "decoding" the messages within the system. To be sure, there is no code to crack, at least not in the technical sense. But there is a surface to be penetrated. If description deals with what is, interpretation focuses upon why or how.

The line between description and interpretation is harder to draw than one might like to believe. I have been writing of interpretation in a way that might give the reader the illusion that the four dimensions of educational criticism find their counterparts in life. In fact, much of perception is at its inception interpretive. Geertz (1973), quoting Gilbert Ryle, points out the difference between judging a behavior to be a wink or a blink. A wink implies a message, a blink does not. Much of the time we have more than one possible message. Consider the difference between a smirk and a smile. The lips in each case might have the same concave form, yet we read one as a smile, the other as a smirk. Interpretation, not simply description, is at work. The reasons we might use to justify our interpretation (assuming we know) might have to do with the context in which the smile or the smirk is seen, with recent antecedent conditions, or with messages sent by other parts of the body. The point is that in this case the behavior of the smiler or smirker is not just seen, it is seen "as." It is assigned to a class and interpreted as part of that class.

The interpretation of events in schools and classrooms is seldom the result of single occurrences. The sense we make of social situations, the meanings we assign to action, and the motives we infer from what we see are typically built up over a period of time. They are iterative. Like markers along the way, they plot the past and provide cues to the future. They enable us to anticipate the future by establishing patterns from the past as a guide. Thus if we see a teacher act in a particular way toward a child or handle a lesson in a special manner, and if these ways and manners of relating and teaching appear over and over again, we derive from that pattern a set of expectations. We come to know a person within a particular context. Surprises diminish. Predictability increases.

The creation of patterns derived from observation as a basis for explaining and predicting is both the boon and the bane of observation. Knowing what to look for makes the search more efficient. At the same time, knowing what to look for can make us less likely to see things that were not a part of our expectations. As I indicated in speaking of connoisseurship, our knowledge in one sphere can interfere with the construction of knowledge in another.

Evaluation

Education is a normative enterprise. Its aim is not merely to change students, but to enhance their lives. Because schools are social institutions whose mission is educational, the significance of what transpires in schools is subject to criteria that allow its educational value to be appraised. John Dewey (1938) makes a distinction among three kinds of experience that can occur in schools and in life generally. Experience, for Dewey, is the means through which educational processes work, hence understanding education requires appraisal of the kind of experience individuals have. One kind of experience is what Dewey calls noneducational. Noneducational experience has no effect one way or another on the course of human growth. It simply is experience undergone that leaves no significant residue. I can scratch my head, touch the table on which I am writing, read a sign before me, hear a sound, eat a meal, say hello to a friend, even have an extended conversation without having an experience that affects my life one way or the other. Such experiences are inconsequential.

There is a second kind of experience that Dewey calls miseducative. Miseducative experience arrests growth and/or develops dispositions toward a domain of human experience that limit or diminish the probability of growth in that area. More generally, experiences that result in phobias or anxieties, that prohibit the enjoyment or participation in wholesome human activities, that limit perception, that promote prejudice, or that diminish rationality—all of these experiences, because they limit growth, are miseducational in character.

Educational experience, the third kind of experience Dewey identifies, fosters the growth of human intelligence, nurtures curiosity, and yields satisfactions in the doing of those things worth doing. Educational experience is what we hope students will have in school, but schooling per se does not guarantee it. Educational experience is the major desired outcome of schooling, but clearly it can occur whenever human beings have intercourse with the world.

What is problematic and contestable, and therefore interesting, is the fact that although people might agree that education is a growth-producing process, there is more than one opinion about what constitutes growth. In previous work (Eisner, 1985b) I have described major value orientations in education in order to show how different views of what is important in schools are reflected in the kinds of curricula that are provided. I referred to these orientations as *academic rationalism, social adaptation–social reconstruction, personal relevance, development of cognitive processes,* and *curriculum as technology.* I shall not reiterate here the values embedded in these orientations to school programs. I mention them merely to illustrate the fact that although people might agree that education is concerned with fostering growth, what people regard as growth differs.

For that form of qualitative inquiry called educational criticism, the evaluation of what is seen is vital. Unlike the so-called detached observer who, somehow, is capable of simply describing, educational critics have the task of appraising as well. The reason for performing this function is clear. To describe students' work, or the processes of classroom life, without being able to determine if this work or these processes are miseducational, noneducational, or educational, is to describe a set of conditions without knowing if those conditions contribute to a state of educational health or illness. If you went to a physician who knew how to describe, even interpret, your physical state of being without being able to judge whether you were healthy or ill, you probably would seek another physician—particularly if you weren't feeling well.

Now the task of determining the educational value of school practice and student experience is far more complicated than judging the state of someone's physical health. First, what constitutes health is much less contentious than what constitutes education. Second, the means through which a person's state of health can be determined are, in general, far more precise and reliable than are the tools available to evaluate the educational "health" of schools. The task of educational critics is more subtle, more complex, and always related to context. This complexity means that the criticism we use to appraise what is occurring may differ from student to student. Nevertheless, the fact that it is complex, subtle, and context-specific does not mean we can avoid making judgments about the educational value of what we have seen. If we do not know what we have, there is no way of knowing what direction we ought to take. If we can't tell if we are moving ahead or backward, we are without both a rudder and a compass. In short, we are paralyzed.

The moral of this story is that there can be no evaluation without value judgments. There can be no claim about the state of education without a conception of what is educationally virtuous. "Value-free evaluation," like value-free education, is an oxymoron.

There is an interesting and complex tension in evaluation in a realm concerned with the development of personal idiosyncrasy. Sir Herbert Read, one of England's major philosopher-critics, has argued (Read, 1944) that the summum bonum of education is to assist individuals—children, adolescents, adults—to become what they have the potential to be. Since these potentialities are uniquely configured, at its best the educational experience the school engenders will lead to increased individuation. Within increased individuation, the appropriateness of comparing students becomes increasingly problematic. Comparisons are more acceptable when the material or performance is commensurate; the application of a common metric, the stopwatch for example, is best when all the runners are on the same track, start at the same place, and have the same destination. But as the "track" begins to differ and as the destinations vary from student to student, meaningful comparisons become less appropriate and more difficult. It is, of course, possible to measure the weight and the mass of bananas, tangerines, and oranges. We can even array them according to size, but such a description, although precise and useful for some purposes, does not tell us much about their distinctive features. To know if we have a good tangerine, we must know the tangerine we have and what good tangerines are like.

For children the evaluation problem is even more complex. We can try to know who we have, but we are less certain what the "end state" for a particular child is. We are, and we must be, guided by an image of virtue for *this child*, and as I have already indicated, that image is always as contestable as it is fallible.

To say that the recognition of incommensurability among children, teachers, and schools is one of the salient features of an approach to educational evaluation that is not reductionistic or simplistic in character is not to say that there are no criteria for appraising what we have seen. There may not be standards for measurement, but there are criteria for judgment.

The difference between applying a standard and employing a criterion is discussed with great insight by John Dewey in his chapter "Criticism and Perception" in *Art as Experience* (1934). He writes:

> There are three characteristics of a standard. It is a particular physical thing existing under specified physical conditions; it is not a value. The yard is a yard-stick, and the meter is a bar deposited in Paris. In the second place, standards are measures of definite things, of lengths, weights, capacities. The things measured are not values, although it is of great social value to be able to measure them, since the properties of things in the way of size, volume, weight, are important for commercial exchange. Finally, as standards of measure, standards define things with respect to quantity. To be able to measure quantities is a great aid to further judgments, but it is not itself a mode of judgment. The standard, being an external and public thing, is applied physically. The yard-stick is physically laid down upon the things measured to determine their length. . . .
>
> If there are no standards for works of art and hence none for criticism (in the sense in which there are standards of measurement), there are nevertheless criteria in judgment, so that criticism does not fall in the field of mere impressionism. The discussion of form in relation to matter, of the meaning of medium in art, of the nature of the expressive object, has been an attempt on the part of the writer to discover some of these criteria. But such criteria are not rules or prescriptions. They are the result of an endeavor to find out what a work of art is as an experience; the kind of experience which constitutes it. (pp. 307, 309)

It will not come as a surprise to experienced readers that historically the major function of educational measurement has been to apply standards to student performance in order to differentiate the positions of individual students on a distribution. One major objective of norm-referenced tests is to facilitate the comparison of students. Even in criterion-referenced testing, the aim is comparison, though not by comparing student to student, but rather student to criterion. What these two approaches to testing have in common is that both are comparative and that they are comparative with respect to a fixed or common criterion.

We can distinguish between criterion-referenced evaluation and norm-referenced evaluation as differences between comparing a student to a criterion and comparing a student to a group. We can distinguish further between these and *personally referenced evaluation*. Here also a comparison is made, but the comparison is to the student's past and present performance, not to others or to a fixed criterion. To make such comparisons requires the ability to appraise the qualities of the student's work and to have some sense of the direction in which it is going. The use of portfolios of student work can be helpful here, a practice long employed in the field of art education that is now catching hold in other areas of schooling. Again, the aim is not to mold a child to a fixed image or to turn out a product that meets a set of specifications: the model is not an industrial one. It is rather to gain a sense for the organic or biological direction of the student's work and to make appraisals on the basis of what the work is trying to become.

I realize that in speaking this way about children and their work I risk suggesting a form of biological determinism. I do not believe that what a student is able to do or be is biologically determined. I do believe that children have genetically determined proclivities or aptitudes and that one important function of schooling is to assist in their realization.[2]

In writing about evaluation this way, as in trying to appreciate the idiosyncratic features of children and adolescents, I know full well that I complicate an otherwise seemingly straightforward enterprise. The standard logic of evaluation calls for framing objectives in behavioral terms. These then provide the specifications against which educational effectiveness can be determined. Then instructional tasks for students are designed and sequenced according to their level of difficulty. They are taught to the students, and a test is employed whose items measure the extent to which objectives are achieved. The objectives are almost always common for a class of students, prespecified; little interaction between students and tasks is anticipated, and the same standards are applied to all students subject to the same objectives. It is a classic means-ends model of human purposive behavior. It is a tidy model with much appeal.

This model works reasonably well[3] in industrial settings where interaction effects can be minimized or anticipated with precision. It is possible in such settings to establish a set of procedures that can become predictable routines, which time after time yield a predictable desired outcome.

Neither children nor adolescents are quite so accommodating. They have their own ideas, motives, needs, and feelings about what they want to do and be. When a group of twenty-five or thirty get together, our ability to predict and control outcomes or processes becomes even more questionable. But even if a way could be found to control outcomes, it would be useful for only a small segment of what educational practice is intended to achieve. Productive unpredictability—creative thinking—is not characterized by conformity to a predetermined standard. Furthermore, the idea that schools should turn out identical products is antithetical to the image of education represented in this book. That such an aim would make the life of the evaluator easier is beside the point. I see no virtue in having a technology of evaluation define our educational aspirations, regardless of how "practical" such a technology might be.

Thematics

One of the differences between works of art and works of criticism is that works of art tell their larger, more generalized stories as an integral part of their total form. The author of a play does not provide an explanation of the moral of the story at the end: the reader either gets it or misses the point of the play. In criticism the point of the critic's story is often made explicit in the critical analysis.

In educational criticism a story is told, perhaps about a class and its teacher. The class is vividly described so that readers can visualize the scene, the meanings of the actions within the classroom are explained, and the educational value of the events described and interpreted is discussed. It would seem that a critic does all that can be done when description, interpretation, and evaluation have been completed. But there is more.

Every classroom, school, teacher, student, book, or building displays not only itself, but features it has in common with other classrooms, schools, teachers, books, and buildings. That is, every particular is also a sample of a larger class. In this sense, what has been learned about a particular can have relevance for the class to which it belongs. The theme, embedded in the particular situation, extends beyond the situation itself.

That theme is applied to other situations through a process known as *naturalistic generalization* (Stake, 1975), as contrasted with *formal generalization* (Donmoyer, 1980). In statistical studies, where formal generalization prevails, samples must be drawn randomly from a population so that the findings that emerge from the study of the sample can be generalized to the population from which it was selected. In studies of cases, such sampling procedures will not work. The sample is seldom random. Further, the process of inference operates by providing a guide to perception, rather than formally forecasting the features of other states of affairs. Experienced teachers, Donmoyer reminds us, learn from nonrandom experience. What one learns about one school can raise one's consciousness to features that might be found in other schools; the study does not claim that other schools will share identical or even similar features but rather that these are features one might look for in other schools.

The process of naturalistic generalization is a ubiquitous aspect of our normal generalizing tendencies. No one leads life by randomly selecting events in order to establish formal generalizations. We live and learn. We try to make sense out of the situations in and through which we live and to use what we learn to guide us in the future.

The use of particulars to provide guidelines for the future is a central function of both folktales and proverbs. In the case of the folktale, the story is to be appreciated not only for its interesting narrative or its humorous qualities, but also because there is an important lesson to be learned from it. The point of learning a lesson is that it is intended to influence our understanding or behavior; it has some instrumental utility. The same is true of the proverb. More compact than the story, it too encapsulates an idea that has instrumental utility. "Fools rush in where angels fear to tread" is a statement about neither fools nor angels, but caution and prudence. Aesop's tale about the tortoise and the hare is about neither tortoises nor hares, but perseverance. My point here is not simply to describe the utilities of folk wisdom, but to illustrate the fact that the process of generalizing is a pervasive feature of life and that it takes many forms.

The formulation of themes *within* an educational criticism means identifying the recurring messages that pervade the situation about which the critic writes. Themes are the dominant features of the situation or person, those qualities of place, person, or object that define or describe identity. In a sense, a theme is like a pervasive quality. Pervasive qualities tend to permeate and unify situations and objects. Although a painting usually has only one pervasive quality, classrooms and schools may have many. A qualitative study of a classroom, teacher, or school can yield multiple themes. These themes are distillations of what has been encountered. In a sense, they provide a summary of the essential features. They also provide clues or cues to the perceptions of other situations like the situation from which the themes were extracted. An example of a theme is found in Powell, Farrar, and Cohen's (1985) description of "treaties," those forms of mutual accommodation between high school students and their teachers that make their lives easier. They write:

> In her class on *The Catcher in the Rye* Mrs. Austin made it clear that the treaty that was offered substituted relaxation for engagement. When she asked a student what Salinger had intended in a passage read aloud, the student objected that the assignment had only been to tell why she liked the passage; Mrs. Austin immediately backed off and did not ask another probing question the entire period. During the quiz game the quality of the questions was never at issue. Since they dealt only with details rather than with plot or meaning, the answers were always brief and always right or wrong. The questions did not lend themselves to discussion or debate, and there was none.
>
> Mrs. Austin emphasized her desire to work in an enjoyable,

trouble-free environment and was proud that neither she nor the school was afflicted with many disruptive students: "We have an attitude here that works. Students have learned to be respectful." Part of the reason for the school's and her own success, she said, was that people had learned to leave each other alone. There was no "authoritarian" atmosphere: "We don't have big brother looking over your shoulder all the time." Not only were teachers free from administrative pressures, but "students don't have pressures from teachers." Everybody gained from that treaty, she believed. "It works out just fine." (p. 75)

Powell, Farrar, and Cohen saw relationships occurring within high schools that they believe are important. They tell us why they are important and give them a name, *treaties*, which allows us to hold onto the qualities they have perceived. The fresh awareness of these qualities, now given a special presence through a name, not only enables us to get the essence of their observations in schools, but to look for similar qualities in other schools. Their theme provides us with a guide, not a guarantee.

It is important to note that Powell, Farrar, and Cohen did not form the concept of treaties before their empirical look at high schools; they were not engaged in hypothesis testing. The high schools they looked at were not randomly selected, but those whose principals agreed to allow them to visit. The concept of "treaty" emerged after, not before, investigation. It was, so to speak, inductively developed and then named. Although Powell, Farrar, and Cohen brought to the schools they studied a highly differentiated perceptual set, treaties were not a part of it. Now they can be a part of ours. I shall have more to say about such matters in chapter 8, when I try to answer the question, "Do qualitative case studies have lessons to teach?"

The four dimensions I have described—description, interpretation, evaluation, and thematics—constitute the structure of educational criticism. But what about its validity? That will be the subject of the next chapter.

Notes

1. It might be argued that one of the major functions of criticism is to provide the content through which readers of different critics can compare and contrast competing interpretations of the same work and thus deepen their understanding of its multiple layers. This view of one of the important functions of criticism is as applicable to the criticism of culture and society as to the criticism of works of art.

2. For a comprehensive discussion of cognitive proclivities that are both culturally and genetically influenced with respect to intelligences, see H. Gardner (1985), *Frames of Mind: The Theory of Multiple Intelligences*.

3. I should emphasize that my qualification of "this model works *reasonably* well" is made to underscore the fact that assembly lines do work. They are not, however, without their problems. Workers on such lines typically find them boring, and absentee rates are high, particularly on Fridays and Mondays. Enlightened corporations are trying to invent better ways to design production activities so that worker satisfaction can be increased. For some, particularly neo-Marxists, such solutions are particularly pernicious since they do not alter the fundamental conditions of work in a capitalistic society. Hence, they seduce workers away from the real problems of their work life and thus delay the prospects of significant change.

Chapter VI

Validity in Educational Criticism

It's true, even if it didn't happen.

Ken Kesey

Facts are the enemy of truth.

Miguel de Cervantes

How Do You Know that You Know?

One of the persistent sources of difficulty for those using qualitative methods of research and evaluation pertains to questions about the validity of their work. There are some who believe that what is personal, literary, and at times even poetic cannot be a valid source of knowledge. Denis Phillips (1987), someone who is more than a little skeptical about artistically oriented qualitative research and evaluation, writes:

> like genuine poets, qualitative researchers are supposed to have keen powers of observation, heightened self-awareness and realization of how their own personalities can shape their work, and a sensitive command of the language in which they are going to report their observations. There is, however, one important respect in which poets and qualitative researchers differ—the works produced by poets may be intended to be enjoyable, insightful, and stimulating, but usually it is not necessary that they be accepted as true. "Half a league, half a league, half a league onward," and the rest, is a poetic rendering of the charge of the Light Brigade, but only the innocent (or the Hollywood scriptwriter) would take it to be a factual description of what actually happened on that fateful day in the Crimea. Indeed, in many cases, the notion of "truth" does not seem applicable to poetry at all; consider the lines of John Keats: "Thou still unravish'd bride of quietness, Thou foster-child of Silence and slow Time." These words are magical—they are evocative and communicate a great deal; to ask whether they are true or not is to make a serious "category mistake."
>
> On the other hand, qualitative researchers generally do intend for their findings to be taken as veridical. To say that a description of a classroom, or of life in an urban gang, or of village life in some exotic culture, is evocative but is not meant to be true or false is merely another category mistake (it is to identify qualitative research as being

poetry, or something similar). Moreover, it is a mistake that is fatal for qualitative research; if a qualitative description or analysis is not true or false (i.e., if these terms are not applicable to it), then the issue of whether that description or analysis is to be believed or acted upon cannot arise—it is not sensible to say that one believes the lines by Keats, just as it is not sensible to say that one believes Mozart's clarinet concerto and is prepared to base policy or social intervention on it! (pp. 9–10)

Phillips comments that poets and, I suppose by implication, novelists, create works that "may be intended to be enjoyable, insightful and stimulating, but usually it is not necessary that they be accepted as true." What does Phillips mean by "true"? He apparently means literally true. Works of poetry and literature are not true in the literal sense, but they can be true in a metaphorical sense. To restrict truth, as Phillips suggests, to literal truth alone, is to restrict knowledge to those forms of discourse that can be literally true. The reason this must be so for Phillips is because knowledge for him depends upon claims capable of literal falsification. He believes that if a claim cannot be falsified in the literal sense, it cannot be falsified at all.

His view leaves us with a very restricted view of knowledge, even for the kind of knowledge that science provides. Scientific knowledge is seldom true in the literal sense that Phillips implies. Especially in the social sciences where metaphor, analogical reasoning, and hypothetical constructs abound, literal truths are scarce. When we use literature, for example, to enlarge understanding, *literal* truth becomes an irrelevant criterion for appraising its utility. A piece of fiction can be true and still be fiction. Fiction, in the metaphorical sense of truth, is "true to life"; it helps us to perceive, experience, and understand what we have previously neglected. Art as well as science performs an epistemic function, and, I would argue, science itself is more of an art than Phillips seems to understand. Literal truth? What social science provides it? As Goodman (1978) indicates, truth can be regarded as a subset of rightness, and as Toulmin (1982) reminds us, doxai are about as good as we can get. The recognition of the plurality of ways to know the world is an invitation to open not a Pandora's box, but one's mind.

Given Phillips's view, when Clifford Geertz (1973) writes "that man is caught in webs of significance that he himself has spun," or that "the aim of ethnography is to increase the precision with which we vex each other," he is writing poetry that has little or nothing to teach us either about humankind or about anthropology. When Robert Nisbet (1976) writes about sociology as an art form and describes the great sociologists in terms of portraitists and landscapists, according to Phillips's view, Nisbet's poetic metaphors have little or nothing to tell us about either sociology or society. When Freud writes about the ego and the mechanisms of defense, according to Phillips, such talk, bordering on allusion and metaphor as it does, has little or nothing to do with understanding the way in which people function. Geertz, Nisbet, and Freud are, it seems, "merely" making poetic allusions that need not be taken seriously.

Now if Phillips does believe that these major figures in the social sciences should be taken seriously, he is apparently ready to open the door to the contributions of the poetic imagination to the problem of understanding how the social world ticks. If he does not, and if we were to restrict our view of knowledge to his, we would need to purge the social sciences of most of what they have to offer.

Before describing the techniques or means through which educational criticism is rendered credible, I wish to comment upon validity when it comes to matters as complex and subtle as the description, interpretation, and evaluation of teaching and life in classrooms.

First, we are not seeking a purchase on reality "as it really is." As I have argued in chapter 3, *that* aspiration is, in principle, impossible to attain. We will always have to be content with a mind-mediated version of what we take to be the case. Second, because we can secure no unmediated grasp of things as they "really are," we cannot ever be certain of having found Truth. We are always "stuck" with judgments and interpretations. Criticism is inherently an act of judgment.[1] Third, the fact that we make judgments does not mean we can have no basis for judging the soundness of the judgments we make. We must consider the evidentiary bases of our judgments; whatever they are, they will always be fallible. It is reasonable to expect that we have good grounds for the judgments we make, but not that our judgments are certain.

Even in law, a process in which the ultimate penalty can be applied, we do not require certainty; we require only that there be no *reasonable* doubt about the validity of the verdict. In clinical diagnosis, whether physical or psychological, we do not expect certainty, but the best evidence we can secure given the circumstances. In statistically driven research we estimate probabilities, not certainties. Furthermore, the probabilities that hold for a group may or may not apply to an individual; even here probabilities are compromised or made less probable than the inferential statistics we apply to samples or populations.

In clinical settings and in legal situations such as courts of law, inference is made on other grounds. We do not randomly sample. We try to put together a case that is credible. We don't say that "anything goes" in courts, nor does "anything go" in qualitative studies. The issue turns on what counts as evidence. And here different people have different criteria. Those who claim that the only "real" way to know something is through experiment must, of necessity, restrict their conception of knowledge to those things for which there is experimental evidence. Experimental evidence is nice to have when we can get it, but we can't always get it. If we needed experimental evidence to justify what we do in schools, we would have to close our schools tomorrow—maybe sooner. Furthermore, the kind of controls needed for the true experiment simply is not the kind available to those who work with children in schools. What then can we trust? More pointedly, what are the ways in which educational criticism can meet reasonable standards of credibility? Three sources of evidence are used in educational criticism: *structural corroboration, consensual validation,* and *referential adequacy* (Eisner, 1985b). I will consider each in turn.

Structural Corroboration

Structural corroboration, like the process of triangulation, is a means through which multiple types of data are related to each other to support or contradict the interpretation and evaluation of a state of affairs. These data come from direct observation of classrooms, from interviews with students and teachers (including a teacher's colleagues), from the analysis of materials used (tests, textbooks, projects assigned, workbooks, record sheets), and from quantitative information related to the interpretation or evaluation. We seek a confluence of evidence that breeds credibility, that allows us to feel confident about our observations, interpretations, and conclusions.

In seeking structural corroboration we look for recurrent behaviors or actions, those theme-like features of a situation that inspire confidence that the events interpreted and appraised are not aberrant or exceptional, but rather characteristic of the situation. They are what Alfred Schutz and Thomas Luckman (1973) call "typifications."

Putting the pieces together to form a compelling whole, one that is believable, has become a hallmark of detective work. One can readily recall Sherlock Holmes, or the work of canny Hercule Poirot, who was able through bits and pieces of evidence to determine who killed Mr. Ratchett on the Orient Express. In our own relationships with people we listen for evidence to support the credibility of the teller's tale or to have confidence in our image of the individual. The more skeptical we become, the more evidence it takes to persuade us to set aside our skepticism. The use of multiple types of data is one way to foster credibility.[2]

In all studies evidence can be used selectively. In qualitative approaches to research the scope is wide for people to see what they choose to see, or to interpret what they see according to their own theoretical lights. In conventional research methodology, procedural objectivity, when it is present, provides much less scope for personal interpretation or for description: a measured performance or a counted incident is less subject to the influence of personal orientation. In *that* sense, the qualitative study is less reliable. Qualitative research methodology in general, and educational criticism in particular, provides greater space for the researcher's personal inclinations, and therefore greater potential for heterogeneity. But one must not forget that a description is shaped not only by virtue of what an individual researcher or evaluator brings to a scene, but also by virtue of what a method or approach leaves out. Both omission and commission affect what we convey. Uniformity among observers in description, interpretation, and evaluation may simply reflect shared method. Procedural objectivity is intended to ensure such uniformity.

To point this out is not to sanction or justify the intentional neglect of evidence contrary to one's vested interests or educational values. On the contrary, because qualitative methods are vulnerable to such effects, *it is especially important not only to use multiple types of data, but also to consider disconfirming evidence and contradictory interpretations or appraisals* when one presents one's own conclusions. In saying this I do not mean that educational critics are obliged to provide readers with every possible interpretation and appraisal of a situation they write about; such a procedure would not only be cumbersome and graceless, it would not have much utility. I do mean that it is both prudent and important to consider those alternative interpretations and appraisals that one considers reasonably credible. There is no measure for determining such credibility; it too is a matter of judgment. The issue is one of fairness, of considering reasonable alternative interpretations. It does not mean relinquishing one's own view.

Structural corroboration in educational criticism, as in law, requires the mustering of evidence. The weight of evidence becomes persuasive. It is compelling. In a sense, matters of weight and coherence appeal to aesthetic criteria. They are qualities felt as a result of what is revealed. The *tight* argument, the *coherent* case, the *strength* of evidence are terms that suggest rightness of fit: echoes of Goodman (1978).

At the same time it should be recognized that most situations about which an educational criticism is written will not be crystal clear or unambiguous; most of life is riddled with dilemmas, trade-offs, ambiguities. There are always virtues to be found in the most troublesome classrooms and vices in the most virtuous ones. I mention this because it is unrealistic to assume that where a situation is punctuated with virtues and vices, with features that are focused and diffused, with clarity and ambiguity, it is possible to write an educational criticism that itself is without uncertainty. Precision can be concocted, but that doesn't make it useful.

Finally, in writing educational criticism the critic can allude to the multiple data sources in order to provide warrant for interpretations and appraisals. The form through which such warrant is provided is left to the critic. Like criticism in the arts and humanities, the manner in which criticism is written should bear the signature of the writer. Indeed, Geertz regards the author's voice as one source of the work's authority (1988). The last thing I want is a standardized format for a form of disclosure premised upon the unique sensibilities of the writer.

Consensual Validation

Consensual validation is, at base, agreement among competent others that the description, interpretation, evaluation, and thematics of an educational situation are right. Such agreement may exist on all or any of the permutations possible: One might secure validation on description, but not on interpretation or the rest. One might differ with someone on description, but agree on interpretation, and so forth. Consensual validation can occur in multiple ways. First, evidence secured through structural corroboration may enlist it. Given the evidence presented, consensus is engendered. Second, consensual validation may occur by having more than one educational critic *independently* prepare an educational criticism of the same school or classroom. Although this procedure is rare in educational contexts, it did emerge in the educational criticisms, or portraits, as Lightfoot calls them, published in the fall 1981 issue of *Daedalus*. Philip Jackson (1981 a, b, c) and Sarah Lightfoot (1981 a, b, c) visited three high schools and independently prepared educational criticisms about each school. One can read these criticisms and determine the extent to which they overlap.

One should not expect isomorphism in such exercises. Clearly, critics bring their own background to the scene and have their own particular way of describing and interpreting events. Writing styles also differ. But in the case of Lightfoot and Jackson, the observations substantially overlap. There are differences, to be sure, but the areas of agreement, in my view, far outweigh them.

In art and literature, literally hundreds of criticisms are written about the same works (Hoy, 1963). In dealing with a painting or a novel, one is dealing with something that is essentially stable; what changes are the contexts and the critics. Hence one might expect somewhat more stability among critics dealing with stable phenomena than in those dealing with phenomena that change—classrooms and schools, for example.

Yet even on stable objects, critics have different views. Shall we consider as valid only those portions of a work where there is unanimity or consensus? Should we try to extract a mean, median, or mode? Hardly. Instead we consider what each critic has had to say and assess the critic's reasons. We mainly use the criticism as a check against our own experience with a particular painting or novel. I will have more to say about this process in a moment, but for now the point is that consensual validation in the arts and humanities is not secured by seeking consensus among critics, but by considering the reasons critics give, the descriptions they provide, the cogency of their arguments, the incisiveness of their observations, the coherence of the case, and, undoubtedly, the elegance of the language. Rhetoric has a place in criticism as it does in science (Gusfield, 1981).

In the procedures I have just described, we may find critics with very different views of the same situation or the same work. What are we to do with such differences? In standard research methodology, we might dismiss the critics as incompetent and find new ones who can independently agree, or we might look to our own criteria and methods, for these might be at fault. Our methods might not be clear or, if clear, they might be incomplete, or our instructions to our critics (or judges) might be ambiguous. The point is, we would not trust differences of view; such a circumstance indicates statistical unreliability. We would try to achieve reliability among judges. As a last resort, perhaps, we might decide to limit what the critics were to attend to. By simplification we might achieve a higher level of intercritic agreement, even if in the process we compromised validity.

In criticism, differences between judges are no necessary index of unreliability. Different critics might be attending to different dimensions of the same work. They might be bringing different perspectives to the work. They might be sensitive to different aspects of the work. Internal coherence and structural corroboration within a piece of criticism are far more important than the degree to which there is consensus among judges. There are, perhaps, more than five thousand criticisms of Shakespeare's play *Hamlet* (Hoy, 1963). No one knowledgeable in literature would dream of trying to calculate a mean among critics as an adequate test of a critic's work. Consensual validation in criticism is typically a consensus won from readers who are persuaded by what the critic has had to say, not by consensus among several critics. Social criticisms written by critics with different political persuasions are not likely to overlap much. Indeed, if we know critics, we read their works with their view or orientation in mind. We do not expect a Jacques Barzun and an Ivan Illich to agree on what is right and what is wrong with schooling, but that does not mean there is not much to learn from each of them. How does such learning occur? This question brings us to the third and most important criterion for assessing educational criticism.

Referential Adequacy

The major function of educational criticism, like all criticism, is the expansion of perception and the enlargement of understanding. Critics speak so others can see and comprehend; criticism is an educational venture. If criticism does not illuminate its subject matter, if it does not bring about more complex and sensitive human perception and understanding, it fails in its primary aim. It is this aim that underlies *referential adequacy.* Criticism is referentially adequate to the extent to which a reader is able to locate in its subject matter the qualities the critic addresses and the meanings he or she ascribes to them. In this sense criticism is utterly empirical;[3] its referential adequacy is tested not in abstractions removed from qualities, but in the perception and interpretation of the qualities themselves. Thus the educational critic who describes classrooms, teachers, forms of student engagement, the atmosphere and ethos of schools, the pervasive features of the neighborhood in which the school resides, the political or social dispositions of the community, or the features both obvious and subtle of the textbooks students read deals primarily with the empirical world. This world is not only made vivid, it is interpreted and appraised. An educational critic's work is referentially adequate when readers are able to see what they would have missed without the critic's observations.

Educational Criticism and Its Audience

For whom is educational criticism written? And what ideals should guide its form and use? Let us consider the last question first.

The primary ideal for educational criticism is that it should contribute to the enhancement of the educational process and through it to the educational enhancement of students. In this sense educational criticism is an educational medium. It is not a detached, value-neutral descriptive vehicle concerned only with something called disinterested knowledge, but rather is concerned with understanding for educational improvement. The aim of the enterprise, like education itself, is normative, not simply descriptive. Thus the toughest test of educational criticism (and it is the same test I would apply to any form of *educational* research) is, does it contribute to the improvement of education?

Improvement may occur at several levels, each related to the audiences for educational criticism. One of these is teachers. Another is school administrators. A third is those who make educational policy.

Teaching is a professionally isolated enterprise. Teachers typically work alone. That is, they seldom coteach or have the benefits of sustained observation and feedback. Once they enter the school door their discretionary time is limited. Their day is spent with children or adolescents, and even when they have "free periods," assuming they teach in a departmentalized school, they are often in the company of students who come to visit or who seek extra help.

The result of a packed schedule and the paucity of time and space for reflection leaves teachers in a position of trying to find out, on their own, how they are doing. This is not an easy task. Most teachers are too close to themselves to secure a decent perspective. They try, on the way to or from school, to figure out how the day went and how they did. But they are never sure—never sure what they are missing, what they do not notice, and what they cannot see. All too often teachers suffer from *secondary ignorance*, that state of being in which we do not know that we do not know. (*Primary ignorance* is the state in which we know that we do not know and can do something about it.) Secondary ignorance is very difficult to deal with in any walk of life.

Given professional isolation and the difficulty it creates for improving performance, the potential importance of educational criticism becomes clear. To do good work educational critics must also be educational connoisseurs; they must be skilled in the art of appreciating, say, teaching. The potential benefits of having people who can appreciate teaching in a position to provide a supportive but critical analysis of what they have seen is not inconsequential. This kind of feedback is rare in educational institutions at all levels: neither universities nor elementary and secondary schools make much of an investment in the study and improvement of teaching *as it unfolds in classrooms*. Some in-service training programs are provided in some school districts, but they focus largely upon techniques or "steps" to good teaching, not on what real teachers do in their own classrooms. A teacher's specific difficulties or particular strengths are not likely to be addressed in such workshops. The occasional visits to classrooms by principals are often for purposes of monitoring and certification rather than for assisting teachers in their teaching. The observation schedules that are sometimes used by visiting evaluation teams are often reductionistic and either miss what is important in a particular classroom or so decontextualize the information they record that it is of little use to those to whom it is provided.[4]

Americans have designed schools that from a structural perspective make it difficult for teachers to improve at what they do, except by dint of their own reflectivity. Schools make little place for reflectivity. The result, in my view, is an institution that fosters little professional growth in teaching after the first three or four years. Once teachers internalize the routines and learn the content they are to teach, once they develop a good nose for smoke and learn to anticipate fires, their ability to cope is assured and with it the need to grow as teachers diminishes. To be sure, there are individual teachers who set their own professional agendas and who continue to grow throughout their careers, but they work in institutions that do little to make such growth possible or even to reward it. About half of all teachers leave the profession during the first five years of teaching. Ironically, once they have learned the ropes, half seek work elsewhere (Heyns, 1988).

The critical observation of performance is not taken seriously in schools—save in one location, athletics. It is on the playing field that coaches study their players' performance. Video tapes are made and careful analysis undertaken. The plays are dissected to help players understand their own moves and how to improve them. Where is the classroom counterpart to such scrupulous attention? Who scrutinizes the teacher's performance? Where is the feedback? Who does the coaching? Do we operate on the assumption that once someone gets a teaching credential the task of learning to teach has been completed? The answers to these questions are obvious. Yet the kind of observation and feedback I have suggested is seldom provided even though we do not accept the idea that the complex business of learning to teach is coterminous with a college degree or teaching credential. Educational criticism within schools should not be limited to a so-called visiting critic; it should be a part of the teacher's job. This will require redefining roles within schools and providing the time for teachers to assist each other.[5]

The improvement of teaching will require more than the provision of useful educational criticism of teaching; it will also require attention to the structural and evaluative dimensions of schooling I described in chapter 4. But the creation of opportunities through which teachers can secure useful criticism is not a bad place to begin. In any case, good educational critics would take into account the ways in which the important dimensions of schooling influence the growth opportunities for teachers. In short, they would consider the setting and the conditions within which teachers work. Helping teachers themselves appreciate the ways in which that setting affects their work is no small accomplishment.

What I have described above is an audience for educational criticism that consists of the two and a half million teachers employed in more than one hundred thousand schools in America. Their needs are especially acute since schools do not provide much opportunity to teachers to learn about their own teaching.

The isolation that teachers experience finds its counterpart among school administrators, particularly school principals. They, even more than teachers, perhaps, feel a sense of isolation. Teachers at least have other teachers in the same schools with whom to relate. There is only one principal. Yet principals, like teachers, could benefit from educational criticism focused upon their own stewardship. How they relate to teachers and to students in their schools, the muted but significant cues they provide to others, the tone they establish, and the values they tacitly endorse in their actions are relevant to the improvement of schools. I will not attempt here to specify the organizational arrangements that might be employed to provide such feedback; different schools and school districts will need to make arrangements suitable to their own situations. The point here is that feedback that is both critical and supportive is not restricted to those who teach; it also applies to those who are to provide leadership to schools.

In the previous sentence I used the phrase "critical and supportive." This phrase is crucial. Without a critical assessment there is no growth, without support there is no acceptance. Recall that the first ideal of educational criticism is that it conduces to growth. It is important to provide criticism in a form that leads to constructive, not destructive, results. This means that educational criticism must be written to fit its audience. More pointedly, it needs to be written so that it is likely to have constructive results. From a practical perspective this means that judgments should be made about the form and content of an educational criticism as it relates to a particular classroom, teacher, or school administrator. It is not necessary and might even be hurtful to "unload" everything that one notices that is problematic about a particular classroom or teacher. Exhaustiveness is not always salutary. How much to say, what to say, and how to say it require a consideration of its effects on the audience to whom one speaks or writes.

This "management of news" might be regarded by some as troublesome. Yet I would remind those who are concerned about candor that we do not tell all even to our best friends. And when articles submitted to scholarly journals are reviewed for consideration for publication, reviewers are often given a form that distinguishes between comments that are to be made to the editor and those to the author. These considerations reflect an awareness of the relationship of the message to the reader. Here, too, the criticism should be helpful. That criterion outweighs the abstract virtue of completeness when it is anticipated that completeness will, on balance, be harmful.

The admonition to attend to the anticipated consequences of an educational criticism is not to be conceived as a prescription for a "good news only" approach to feedback. It is a recommendation to reflect upon the consequences of a message in light of the leading principle guiding the use of educational criticism. This principle is especially important in an approach that is likely to be personal. When qualities are converted to data and when data are abstracted and numbers used to represent them, observations about practices are much more likely to be diffused and nonspecific. Often in educational criticism *particular* teachers, students, classrooms, and school administrators are made vivid. Under these circumstances, one has a special responsibility to those involved. In these matters there are also special ethical considerations, which I will consider in chapter 10. For the moment I pass on to the third major audience for educational criticism: policy makers.

Policies are guidelines intended to enhance organizational effectiveness by setting limits, providing direction and incentives, and listing proscriptions for individual behavior. Those who make policy define requirements, impose sanctions, provide rewards, determine eligibility, and define a host of other conditions designed to establish direction and maintain organizational stability. But policies, like intentions, do not always lead to the desired ends, and their formulation is not always based upon an adequate understanding of the problems they are intended to address. In educational matters the proliferation of policies based upon limited and sometimes erroneous conceptions is particularly egregious. Consider the following.

Since the early 1980s (and earlier), there has been widespread concern about the quality of public schools. The major indices of declining quality have been SAT scores, standardized test scores, and statements by employers that high school graduates do not have the basic skills needed to do their jobs. In addition, the armed forces have been obliged to create special schools to increase literacy. Even colleges and universities have found it necessary to increase the number of "bonehead" English courses they offer to incoming students. *A Nation at Risk* (USA Research, 1984), the most influential report on education that has been published in the fourth quarter of the twentieth century, regards U.S. schools as such a disaster that they are, in the opinion of its authors, a greater threat to national security than an invasion by a foreign army.

To ameliorate these problems, policies have been recommended and laws enacted to strengthen schools. These include increasing the number of weeks students attend school, extending the school day, and requiring tougher courses. It seems clear to virtually no one that requiring children to spend more time in a place that is deleterious to begin with might be quite the wrong prescription. I'm not suggesting that schools *are* deleterious to the young, only that if those who make policy believe them to be so, it makes no sense to require that more time be spent there. If students can't read, it seems reasonable to try to find out why, rather than to prescribe more of the same, or to "raise standards." The best way to find out why is to try to learn what goes on in schools. Educational connoisseurship and educational criticism can be very useful means for informing others about the state of schools.

Similar problems exist in other areas. As I already indicated, we now lose about half of all new teachers some five years after they begin teaching (Heyns, 1988). Why? And why is it that among those who leave, the most academically able leave first? The causes might be many, but it just might be the case that many teachers feel that nobody cares about what they do (Eisner, 1985), that they have to struggle to obtain minimum supplies, and that they have little incentive or opportunity to develop their own programs in school districts that are increasingly prescribing standardized curricula. How can policy makers deal effectively with educational problems without a decent understanding of what school is like for those who teach there? What should the general public know about the teachers' work and how should it be supported? The point here is simply that remedies to school problems that are developed as a reaction to symptoms are not likely to be responsive to causes. To understand problems it is necessary to pay attention to their sources, not only to their symptoms.

This process requires a presence in schools and an ability to see (not merely to look at) how they work.

The problems we encounter might be generated by our limited and essentially misguided conception of appropriate educational intentions, they might be a function of the way we have structured our institutions, they might be due to the content we teach or the way in which it is taught, or they might result from the inappropriate ways we evaluate our students, teachers, and schools. Perhaps all of these factors affect our school programs. Effective educational policy is more likely when we do more than look at test scores and shout, "The sky is falling, the sky is falling!" Educational criticism has something to offer.

Perhaps the most closely related counterpart to what I describe is found in the field of political science, particularly as it shapes public and foreign policy. A substantial segment of political science is interpretive. Students of domestic and foreign policy attempt to understand the context within which problems are posed, and from that context they formulate policy options for the legislative and executive branches of government. Alternative options are considered with respect to their probable consequences and the inevitable trade-offs that different potential courses of action may exact. The task is to provide a useful interpretive picture of a complex and dynamic state of affairs. As on a soccer field or basketball court, the policy maker needs to keep a close eye on the state of play in order to make the right moves. Trying to boost a team's score by raising standards or urging players to try harder is unlikely to prove effective. We need a careful analysis of the options and an understanding of the way the game is being played.

In the field of education we have roughly comparable analogues to public policy analysis in Goodlad's *A Place Called School* (1984), Sizer's *Horace's Compromise* (1984), Powell et al.'s *The Shopping Mall High School* (1985), and Boyer's *High School* (1983). All are examples of qualitative studies that are relevant to policy. Each attempts to penetrate the surface of schooling, to go beyond symptoms to their sources. Alas, their diagnoses suggest that a good deal more is necessary than longer school days and more school weeks per year. The changes in schooling they propose, ironically, are the most difficult to legislate. Yet in the long run it is better to appreciate the complexity of a complex problem than to be seduced by simplistic remedies that cannot work. Educational connoisseurship and criticism are intended to foster such appreciation. The next chapter will present a closer look at how this can happen.

Notes

1. One of the most illuminating sources concerning the functions of criticism is John Dewey's *Art as Experience*, especially chap. 14, "Criticism and Perception."

Dewey's entire book is an encomium to experience, a concept that is central to his philosophy. What criticism is about, writes Dewey, is the deepening and expansion of experience. In this sense, the critic is an educator and criticism an educational medium.

2. I believe that in matters of interpretation, credibility hinges upon a "feel" of coherence or what Goodman calls "rightness." There is, it seems to me, an undeniably aesthetic criterion that we employ in judging the believability of arguments or the relationship between what individuals say and how they behave. When this relationship is incongruent, there is a lack of fit. This lack of fit or lack of coherence is itself an aesthetic feature and gives us pause. The elegance, harmony, and beauty of a theoretical explanation, even in the hardest of the natural sciences, is an important consideration in its attractiveness. For a discussion of such matters, see T. Kuhn (1962), *The Structure of Scientific Revolutions*, and his *The Essential Tension* (1977).

3. The empirical features of educational criticism and criticism in general cannot be overstated. There is a tendency to regard empirical studies as those using quantitative procedures. While studies employing quantification do tend to be empirical, empiricism refers to experience, and experience is always of something fundamentally qualitative. The referential adequacy of an educational criticism is determined by locating the qualities to which the critic refers and appraising critical judgment by the way in which it helps us see and understand the subject matter it addresses. Rather than emphasizing abstraction far removed from the qualitative world, criticism is assessed by its intimacy with the qualities it describes, interprets, and appraises.

4. It is ironic that in the effort to improve teaching, teachers are subject to evaluation criteria that mince, dice, and slice their teaching into bits and pieces, thereby obscuring the necessary organic character of excellent teaching. In the name of objectivity and precision, observation schedules have been designed on the assumptions that elements in teaching can be identified and measured as discrete units and that through the summation of scores on such discrete units, a valid assessment of teaching performance can be made. This is analogous to appraising the quality of music by the incidence of F flats within a musical composition.

5. The improvement of teaching, in my view, will require a redefinition of the nature of a teacher's role in the school. What I believe is needed is a school that makes it possible for teachers to assume a variety of roles in the context of being a teacher so that from time to time they can free themselves from the constraints of their own classroom and assist other teachers and be assisted by them. At present there are basically two roles for a professional in a school: teacher or principal. I believe roles are needed that include mentoring responsibilities for new teachers by veteran teachers, opportunities for teachers to engage in curriculum development, opportunities for teachers to develop better assessment methods, and many opportunities for teachers to carry out research with their colleagues and with researchers from universities. In short, the school itself must be a center for professional growth for teachers as well as for students. This will require a reconceptualization of what it means to be a teacher.

Chapter VII

A Closer Look at Educational Criticism

Still, the fact that all linguistic expression is and remains "metaphorical" expression is proof that the capacity for objective representation can never become completely dominant in the domain of language. Metaphor constitutes an indispensable factor in language in its organic wholeness. Without metaphor language would lose its lifeblood and stiffen into a conventional system of signs.

Ernst Cassirer

The Criticism of Criticism

Although the roots of criticism are located in the observations and judgments of daily life, criticism reaches its most sophisticated form in literature and the arts. It will serve us well to take a brief look at the work of two American art critics, Harold Rosenberg and Leo Steinberg, and to go from their work to an examination of the semiotics of Roland Barthes and to Erving Goffman's classic study, *Asylums*.

The reason for examining these works is to display a family relationship: Educational criticism is part of a tradition that has long flourished in the arts and humanities, in philosophy, and later in the social sciences. Aristotle was a keen observer of the human condition, whose deep appreciation for the practical vicissitudes of life can be seen in his *Ethics*. Kant wrote anthropologically, and Marx, of course, gave the modern world the most influential critique of socioeconomic systems it has known. Writers like Alexis de Tocqueville, Hannah Arendt, Erich Fromm, Michel Foucault, and Bruno Bettelheim, as well as the writers whose work we will briefly encounter here, have also contributed significantly to our perception and understanding of the social world. Educational criticism is a part of this tradition—a tradition that has not had an important place in the methodology of educational research until rather recently.[1]

In the realm of art, critics follow artists. That is, critics do not provide the specifications artists are to fulfill; their relationship to artists is not one of architect to builder. Rather, critics are commentators, interpreters, evaluators, and, at their best, educators. In the realm of art, critics often focus on the context in which a work was produced to enable the reader to situate it in a field of ideas that makes its perception more acute. There are many different ways to achieve this. We will not examine all of them because in one sense there are as many versions of criticism as there are writers. But we can get a good sense of the critic's work by considering the following commentaries. The first, by Rosenberg, is on the retrospective exhibition of the work of the important American painter Ben Shahn. The second, by Steinberg, is on a painting by Picasso. Rosenberg writes:

> What links Shahn's art to the paintings of more literal contemporaries such as William Gropper, Jack Levine, Philip Evergood, and the Soyers is not shared manner, or even a common subject, but a pervasive moralizing and its perhaps inevitable accompaniment, an ineradicable drabness. These are embodied in Shahn's pinched drawing of faces and torsos, in his omnipresent walls as background, and in his watery and indecisive color. Even at his most spontaneous, exuberance seems outlawed by his conception of the nature of our times. It is interesting that when, in his later years, he turns to glorifying Old Testament texts, he resorts to interlacings of gold leaf, as if pigment were an inadequate vehicle for his enthusiasm.
>
> Among artists and intellectuals of the thirties, the moralizing impulse goes far deeper than particular political allegiances; it accounts for the sense of innocence and self-righteousness (for example, in Lillian Hellman's *Scoundrel Time*) which survives proof that they had been acting in the service of a hateful tyranny. Their moral universe was a closed sphere, complete in itself, and nothing done outside it could affect its rectitude. In the art of the thirties, a nude or an interior often seemed to make a moral point of the same order as a painting appealing for better health care (Shahn's *The Clinic*) or deploring the victims of Nazism (*Concentration Camp*). In Shahn's *Spring*, the couple lying in the grass are right to be there, as it is right for Shahn as a Jewish artist to make symbolic patterns out of the Hebrew alphabet (*Pleiades, Tenth Commandment*), even if he isn't religious and doesn't know Hebrew. (Rosenberg, 1985, p. 92)

What comes through in Rosenberg's essay is both a sense of erudition and a sense of style. He is reviewing not a single painting or even a set of paintings, but the work of a leading American artist—a retrospective at that. Rosenberg has comments to make about Shahn's work, serious reservations about its significance. These comments are made in a context that Rosenberg builds. He compares Shahn's work to the work of other painters—Gropper, Levine, Evergood, and the Soyers. He relates the impulse of their work to Shahn's, and he sets all of their work in a social frame, which includes Lillian Hellman's *Scoundrel Time* (1976), a story about McCarthyism and the Hollywood notables who failed to display the courage needed to defy it. What Rosenberg does in his writing is twofold. First, he displays his credentials; he knows both the art scene and the intellectual scene in America, past and present. Second, he comments on the quality of Shahn's work, not on individual paintings, but upon the corpus of the work, and he has penetrating things to say about it. In the end his comments are devastating: "What was needed," he writes of Shahn, "was not a wider range of topics—that could only result in further dilution—but a new approach to art."

This kind of criticism is at once both general and penetrating. Rosenberg's writing carries authority. His conclusions are, to be sure, contentious. Some readers will reject them as downright wrongheaded; many consider Ben Shahn to be a great American painter. Yet, even in dispute, Rosenberg gives readers something to chew on. That itself, insofar as it opens up a deeper consideration of the work, is not a trivial critical accomplishment.

Leo Steinberg, an important contemporary art historian, takes a very different approach to art criticism. Consider his comments regarding a common theme in Picasso's painting, *Sleepwatchers:*

> A Picasso watercolor of the Blue Period presents the artist at twenty-three. He is doing none of the things self-portrayed artists usually do. He is not searching his mirror reflection, nor staring defiance, nor eyeing a model. He appears neither at work nor at ease but deeply engaged in inaction: watching a girl sleep.
>
> The girl lies in a pool of light, one raised arm cradling her head. She lies within arm's reach, yet almost glides away, and her wallpapered corner dissolves in the warm glow of noonday sleep. It is the painter's figure that conveys an oppressive awareness of circumstance. Dusky blues ink even his cup and hair. His cold shadow contrasts with her brightness; his sitting up with her lying down; his solid frame with the tremulous trace of her skin. Their opposition is total. And as her radiance suggests the pure bliss of the body, his perplexed consciousness becomes a condition of exile.
>
> These early pictures are curtain raisers. They introduce the subject of the watched sleeper which was to become one of the haunted themes that recur continually in Picasso's work and give it constance. The artist must have known from the beginning that the subject was old. Scenes of sleeping nymphs observed by alerted males—scenes concerned with looking and longing—are part of the grand tradition of art, in antiquity and again since the Renaissance. But the young Picasso appropriates the universal theme as though he had found it within closed doors in his own private depths. So that the watch-sleep confrontation enters his work almost like a confession. And this may be why his further explorations of the subject were long postponed; the Cubist enterprise then being launched had no use for its sentiment. But before putting the subject away, Picasso stripped it of its private emotional connotations: in a powerful painting of 1908 the wake-slumber theme is depersonalized. (Steinberg, 1972, pp. 93–95)

From Steinberg we get an elegance of language and a depth of insight into individual works. He picks up subtle but important qualities in the works he writes about:

> And though the woman's recumbent pose set off against an upright male posture seems somehow familiar and fitting, there is no satisfactory meeting of opposites here, only mutual exclusion: He standing in darkness, in modern dress, exhausted, irresolute; while the girl's naked sleep leaves her simple and whole. (1972, p. 93)

Steinberg achieves a poetic grace that seems to go to the heart of the works he attends to. His comments are focused less on context than Rosenberg's, although context is not absent, and more on the rendering of the work through language, not simply to create a parallel art form, but to open up qualities of the work for the viewer, to give the work a setting from which its qualities can be reconsidered.

The features about which both Rosenberg and Steinberg speak are not the monopoly of paintings. They appear in the ways teachers teach and schools function, and how children treat each other. Criticism is in no way limited to the fine arts. Even the most prosaic aspects of our culture are candidates for criticism. Consider the comments of Roland Barthes as he writes about toys in his own French culture.

> French toys: one could not find a better illustration of the fact that the adult Frenchman sees the child as another self. All the toys one commonly sees are essentially a microcosm of the adult world; they are all reduced copies of human objects, as if in the eyes of the public the child was, all told, nothing but a smaller man, a homunculus to whom must be supplied objects of his own size.
>
> Invented forms are very rare: a few sets of blocks, which appeal to the spirit of do-it-yourself, are the only ones which offer dynamic forms. As for the others, French toys always mean something, and this something is always entirely socialized, constituted by the myths or the techniques of modern adult life: the Army, Broadcasting, the Post Office, Medicine (miniature instrument-cases, operating theatres for dolls), School, Hair-Styling (driers for permanent-waving), the Air Force (Parachutists), Transport (trains, Citroens, Vedettes, Vespas, petrol-stations), Science (Martian toys).
>
> The fact that French toys literally prefigure the world of adult functions obviously cannot but prepare the child to accept them all, by constituting for him, even before he can think about it, the alibi of a Nature which has at all times created soldiers, postmen and Vespas. Toys here reveal the list of all the things the adult does not find unusual: war, bureaucracy, ugliness, Martians, etc. It is not so much, in fact, the imitation which is the sign of an abdication, as its literalness: French toys are like a Jivaro head, in which one recognizes, shrunken to the size of an apple, the wrinkles and hair of an adult. There exist, for instance, dolls which urinate; they have an oesophagus, one gives

them a bottle, they wet their nappies; soon, no doubt, milk will turn to water in their stomachs. This is meant to prepare the little girl for the causality of house-keeping, to "condition" her to her future role as mother. However, faced with this world of faithful and complicated objects, the child can only identify himself as owner, as user, never as creator; he does not invent the world, he uses it: there are, prepared for him, actions without adventure, without wonder, without joy. He is turned into a little stay-at-home householder who does not even have to invent the mainsprings of adult causality; they are supplied to him ready-made: he has only to help himself, he is never allowed to discover anything from start to finish. The merest set of blocks, provided it is not too refined, implies a very different learning of the world: then, the child does not in any way create meaningful objects, it matters little to him whether they have an adult name; the actions he performs are not those of a user but those of a demiurge. He creates forms which walk, which roll, he creates life, not property: objects now act by themselves, they are no longer an inert and complicated material in the palm of his hand. But such toys are rather rare: French toys are usually based on imitation, they are meant to produce children who are users, not creators.

The bourgeois status of toys can be recognized not only in their forms, which are all functional, but also in their substances. Current toys are made of a graceless material, the product of chemistry, not of nature. Many are now molded from complicated mixtures; the plastic material of which they are made has an appearance at once gross and hygienic, it destroys all the pleasure, the sweetness, the humanity of touch. A sign which fills one with consternation is the gradual disappearance of wood, in spite of its being an ideal material because of its firmness and its softness, and the natural warmth of its touch. Wood removes, from all the forms which it supports, the wounding quality of angles which are too sharp, the chemical coldness of metal. When the child handles it and knocks it, it neither vibrates nor grates, it has a sound at once muffled and sharp. It is a familiar and poetic substance, which does not sever the child from close contact with the tree, the table, the floor. Wood does not wound or break down; it does not shatter, it wears out, it can last a long time, live with the child, alter little by little the relations between the object and the hand. If it dies, it is in dwindling, not in swelling out like those mechanical toys which disappear behind the hernia of a broken spring. Wood makes essential objects, objects for all time. Yet there hardly remain any of these wooden toys from the Vosges, these fretwork farms with their animals, which were only possible, it is true, in the days of the craftsman. Henceforth, toys are chemical in substance and color; their very material introduces one to a coenaesthesis of use, not pleasure. These toys die in fact very quickly, and once dead, they have no posthumous life for the child. (Barthes, 1972, pp. 53–55)

There are several messages to be received from Barthes's work, as well as from Rosenberg's and Steinberg's. One of these is that even the seemingly trivial can take on substantial significance, if seen as significant and if the appropriate context for its significance can be provided. Barthes attends to the importance of wood in children's toys, something that is likely to be overlooked as a source of significant meaning. Rosenberg comments that Shahn "resorts" to gold leaf, as if pigment were an inadequate vehicle for his art. Steinberg comments on the psychological impact of the placement of two figures in a painting: "Again a male watcher, this time a hunger-bitten wraith of a man: He stares at a girl sleeping in a low bed—at his feet, but at a distance which his inordinate height makes seem inaccessible." Each critic gives point to what otherwise might not be seen, or if seen, regarded as unimportant.[2]

The ability to write such criticism—and Rosenberg, Steinberg, and Barthes are masters of their craft—requires the ability to notice and to appreciate the symbolic import of social objects and activity. The initial achievement requires an awareness of qualitative features and their significance—for Rosenberg, the use of gold leaf, for Steinberg, the treatment of space and scale, for Barthes, the absence of wood. In the field of education, we can ask: What are our classrooms made of? What is the character of the tasks we ask students to engage in? Do they, too, deny children the opportunity to create their own solutions or to define their own problems, as Barthes claims is the case for French children and their toys?

My aim here is not to make a point about the features of American schools but rather to show that the kinds of qualities that critics take into account in art and in social life are not unlike those that can be addressed in the study of schools. One major challenge to the research community is to prepare scholars who have the penetrating insight and sensitivity displayed by the critics whose work we have examined.

Before turning our attention to examples of educational criticism, consider the work of an important social scientist, Erving Goffman, whose work *Asylums* (1961) powerfully reveals the impact of total institutions on individual identity. One brief section of Goffman's book illustrates his ability to help us understand what it means to be in a mental hospital.

> The inmate, then, finds certain roles are lost to him by virtue of the barrier that separates him from the outside world. The process of entrance typically brings other kinds of loss and mortification as well. We very generally find staff employing what are called admission procedures, such as taking a life history, photographing, weighing, fingerprinting, assigning numbers, searching, listing personal possessions for storage, undressing, bathing, disinfecting, haircutting, issuing institutional clothing, instructing as to rules, and assigning to quarters. Admission procedures might better be called "trimming" or "programming" because in thus being squared away the new arrival

allows himself to be shaped and coded into an object that can be fed into the administrative machinery of the establishment, to be worked on smoothly by routine operations. Many of these procedures depend upon attributes such as weight or fingerprints that the individual possesses merely because he is a member of the largest and most abstract of social categories, that of human being. Action taken on the basis of such attributes necessarily ignores most of his previous bases of self-identification. (1961, p. 16)

The foregoing passage, like the ones that preceded it, exemplifies both insight and a way of describing it. Art critics bring to bear upon works of art a deep understanding of the conditions of their creation and the traditions in which they participate. For social scientists and French semiologists, it is a matter of perceiving the social import of those seemingly trivial features of social reality that are, for most, so easy to neglect. But how do such approaches to the world relate to education? It will be useful to look briefly at the work of Theodore Sizer.

Horace's Compromise (Sizer, 1984) is a book that examines the American high school through the perspective of the composite personage Horace Smith, a veteran high school social studies teacher. Here, Sizer sets the stage for his study:

Here is an English teacher, Horace Smith. He's fifty-three, a twenty-eight-year veteran of high school classrooms, what one calls an old pro. He's proud, respected, and committed to his practice. He'd do nothing else. Teaching is too much fun, too rewarding, to yield to another line of work.

Horace has been at Franklin High in a suburb of a big city for nineteen years. He served for eight years as English department chairman, but turned the job over to a colleague, because he felt that even the minimal administrative chores of that post interfered with the teaching he loved best.

He arises at 5:45 A.M., careful not to awaken either his wife or grown daughter. He likes to be at school by 7:00, and the drive there from his home takes forty minutes. He wishes he owned a home near the school, but he can't afford it. Only a few of his colleagues live in the school's town, and they are the wives of executives whose salaries can handle the mortgages. His wife's job at the liquor store that she, he, and her brother own doesn't start until 10:00 A.M., and their daughter, a new associate in a law firm in the city, likes to sleep until the last possible minute and skip breakfast. He washes and dresses on tiptoe.

Horace prepares the coffee, makes some toast, and leaves the house at 6:20. He's not the first at school. The custodians and other, usually older, teachers are already there, "puttering around," one of the teachers says.

The teachers' room is large, really two rooms. The inner portion, windowless, is arranged in a honeycomb of carrels, one for each older teacher. Younger or newer teachers share carrels. Each has a built-in desk and a chair. Most have file cabinets. The walls on three sides, five feet high, are festooned with posters, photographs, lists, little sayings, notes from colleagues on issues long past. Horace: Call home. Horace: The following students in the chorus are excused from your Period 7 class—Adelson, Cartwright, Donato. . . .

Horace goes to his carrel, puts down his briefcase, picks up his mug, and walks to the coffee pot at the corner of the outer portion of the teachers' room, a space well lit by wide windows and fitted with a clutter of tables, vinyl-covered sofas, and chairs. The space is a familiar, comfortable jumble, fragrant with the smell of cigarettes smoked hours before. Horace lights up a fresh one, almost involuntarily, as a way perhaps to counteract yesterday's dead vapors. After pouring himself some coffee, he chats with some colleagues, mostly other English teachers.

The warning bell rings at 7:20. Horace smothers his cigarette, takes his still partly filled cup back to his carrel and adds it to the shuffle on his desk, collects some books and papers, and, with his briefcase, carries them down the hall to his classroom. Students are already clattering in, friendly, noisy, most of them ignoring him completely— not thoughtlessly, but without thinking. Horace often thinks of the importance of this semantic difference. Many adults are thoughtless about us teachers. Most students, however, just don't know we're here at all, people to think about. Innocents, he concludes.

7:30, and its bell. There are seventeen students here; there should be twenty-two. Bill Adams is ill; Horace has been told that by the office. Joyce Lezcowitz is at her grandmother's funeral; Horace hasn't been officially told that, but he knows it to be true. He marks Joyce "Ex Ab"—excused absence—on his attendance list. Looking up from the list, he sees two more students arrive, hustling to seats. You're late. Sorry. . .Sorry. . .The bus. . .Horace ignores the apologies and excuses and checks the two off on his list. One name is yet unaccounted for. Where is Jimmy Tibbetts? Silence. Tibbetts gets an "Abs" after his name. (Sizer, 1984, pp. 9–11)

Sizer enables the reader to identify with Horace Smith the man and to get some sense of his family, his home, his work. The writing is vivid; readers have no difficulty visualizing the scenes in which Horace Smith plays a central role. One sees in these scenes images of the past. For those who have attended American high schools, the 7:30 bell, the absent students, the excuses of those who are late, the ubiquitous movement, the minor difficulties of schedule, the teen-age humor are no strangers. The picture that Sizer paints is congruent with our own experience; it displays authenticity.

Such pictures are an important part of what is required to understand the situations we care about. They provide an imaginable context through which our often more abstracted conclusions can take on meaning. Sizer gives both Horace Smith and the school in which he teaches a human face.

The face that Sizer paints in *Horace's Compromise* allows us to ask some fresh questions about the meaning of school life for high school teachers. New questions lead to new theory. Generating theory depends upon acutely perceiving those qualities that collectively constitute the life of schools. This is enhanced by being able to see and interpret what one has seen. Without the former, there is no interpretation. Without interpretation, no theory development is possible. Theory, therefore, grows in the light of perception. Perception gives rise to consciousness, and interpretation confers meaning upon it.

Educational Criticism Presented, Compared, and Examined

So far, we have read excerpts written in a critical mode by two art critics, a semiologist, a social scientist, and an educator. Now we will consider an example of educational criticism. I wrote the piece under unusual circumstances.

In the fall of 1985, Secretary of Education William Bennett went to the Banneker High School near Washington, D.C., to teach a lesson on James Madison's *Federalist Papers*. The event, televised nationally, was meant to show a Washington bureaucrat getting in touch with the reality of schools and, in a sense, demonstrating how substantive teaching could be provided to America's youth. Bennett's forty-five-minute lesson was videotaped, and the American Educational Research Association (AERA) invited four scholars who study teaching to analyze the performance in their own modes and to present the results at a session of the annual meeting of the AERA. I was one of the four. At the convention, several hundred people saw brief excerpts from the videotape and heard each of the four analyses presented by its author. What follows here is my contribution and, by way of contrast, a paper by another panelist, Roger Shuy.

Each of these analyses reflects a particular approach to the study of teaching. Shuy is a linguist, and his paper reflects his focus and his methods. My paper is a special sample of an educational criticism. I say "special" because educational criticism is not ordinarily written about a forty-five-minute videotape. The observations are normally "live" and often require one to spend several weeks in a classroom or school. Furthermore, we had no opportunity to learn about the context first-hand, to interview the students or their teacher, or to examine written materials and other data. Because of the circumstances, this sample of educational criticism, like Roger Shuy's, is atypical. Furthermore, because these papers were prepared for presentation at an AERA convention, their length was limited to what each presenter could say in twenty minutes or less. Typically, an educational criticism is several times the length of what I reprint here. Yet, because this piece is short and because I have a unique opportunity to contrast it with another analysis of the same event, I believe it will serve my purposes well. They will be followed by another educational criticism written by James Kuntz, S.J., which I will analyze for form and content.

After reading Shuy's article and my own, readers will find it useful to compare and contrast them. Shuy brings to bear upon the analysis of discourse a variety of concepts and methods that make it possible for him to reveal the linguistic moves and discourse structures that operate in Bennett's classroom. In a sense, Shuy is searching for the skeleton of the dialogue in order to understand the way in which the discourse game is played. My own analysis attempts to portray Bennett as a person and as a teacher. It addresses the significance of the ideas that he and his students examined, and it tries to provide a feel for and an image of the setting and what Bennett emphasizes when he teaches. My own analysis omits much of what Shuy includes, and vice versa. The lesson to be learned here is that what teaching is like and how it is regarded depend in no small measure on the form of analysis that is brought to bear upon it.

A Secretary in the Classroom
Elliot W. Eisner

In this corner, at 175 pounds, we have William, The Cat, Bennett! Reporters surround the ring. Microphones create a small mountain on the desk before him—all the networks, it seems, are hooked in. Lights are everywhere, creating a level of heat that brings beads of perspiration to our champion. The clicks of the photographers' shutters surrounding the ring create a constant din reminding all who view the scene that this is no mere civics lesson. It is the Secretary of Education himself—our educational leader—preparing for his first high school bout with Banneker High's best and brightest.

That the Secretary of Education, once a professor of philosophy, should take to the classroom at the start of a new school year to teach a multiracial class of high school students the lessons to be learned from James Madison's *Federalist Papers* is not a common event. No Secretary of Education in my recollection has ever made such a journey, and on live national television. Yet here we have a slightly paunchy, forty-five-ish former academic exposing himself live to the vicissitudes of American secondary education. How will he do? Can this man teach adolescents? What will his manner be? And what about all of those lights, the mountain of rising mikes on the desk before him, the throng of the press who line the classroom's walls, the wires hooked up to his belt and tie? Few teachers, I think, would relish such an assignment.

From the start, one gets a sense of purpose and intensity. Adjusting the electronic equipment to which he has been attached, Bennett makes his opening foray by acknowledging sarcastically, "This is a typical day at Banneker," and then telling the class, "If you want to, turn around and say hi." "Hi, Mom!" he says, and the twenty-five or so students do likewise amidst giggles acknowledging his wit and displaying their understanding that for them, too, this is no typical day at Banneker.

"All right, let's get to work. I'm putting my name on the board so you can write me if I make mistakes."

Sarcastic? Hard to tell. Neither Bennett nor the students laugh. Perhaps he is serious. With preliminaries over, our champion takes off his suit coat, hangs it on the chair adjacent to the desk, rolls up his sleeves, and begins to pace back and forth in front of the room. "Why read *Federalist* 10?—Why bother? Why not watch the Georgia-Alabama game?" His voice, his slight crouch, his hand gestures—but most of all the intensity of his gaze—leave no doubt that this is a serious encounter. "Let's get to work"—his opening phrase is apt. Today's lesson will be no "once over lightly," no open-ended superficial discussion of anything on anyone's mind, but a serious examination of ideas, which he seems to care about deeply.

The task Bennett has set for these students is to read and understand James Madison's *Federalist Papers*, specifically Paper 10. The students attend an academic high school from which, according to Bennett, all graduates go on to college. Again, not only is the day special, so are the students. The fact that at least half are black serves well to illustrate to the millions who will be watching Bennett and the class on television that blacks too can deal with concepts as abstract as the tension between liberty and majority rule.

The aim of Bennett's lesson is twofold—at least from the vantage point of a television viewer. First is his interest in helping his students understand the philosophic assumptions upon which our government rests. He wishes them to understand that all assumptions about government are built upon a conception of human nature. Madison's view of human nature shapes the way in which he believes our government should be formed.

Second, Bennett is interested in developing the students' analytic and critical abilities. His teaching oozes with tactics typically employed in the teaching of the humanities. Thus, what animates his activity as a teacher is an interest in sharing nontrivial ideas about the nature of a just government and the joy of helping the young slowly discover what he has already learned. This material, for Bennett, is no stranger. It is obvious that he has taught it before, and often. How do we know? He repeats passages verbatim from Madison's *Federalist* 10. The book he uses he proudly tells the class is "properly dog-eared." And dog-eared it is, almost falling apart in his hands. In some ways its condition is reminiscent of the overly loved teddy bear that has grown into middle age. Madison and Bennett are old friends. "What is a faction?" he asks, "and why is it a problem in a society like ours? Why does liberty cause the problem of faction?" Liberty, faction, self-interest. These are nontrivial ideas that bear not only upon Madison's time, but on our own.

"Liberty provides the opportunity to hold different opinions," one student responds. "If you get liberty and give it to people, people will have different views about liberty."

Clearly a problem is posed—or beginning to be posed. "How do we solve the problem of faction?" Bennett asks. "Remove liberty," he responds, and then follows quickly and quietly with a question, "Why not remove liberty?"

This problem of faction has at least two alternative solutions. The first is to remove liberty. But do that and the ball game is over. That cure, to quote Madison, is worse than the disease. Second, give everybody the same opinion. But that will not do either. How then does one keep a self interested majority from exploiting the interests of a minority while maintaining the liberty that all wish to have?

The pattern of the repartee on such heady issues is predictable. Bennett asks an open-ended question, one that requires recollection of the material read and an interpretive understanding of it. Students respond with an answer designed to satisfy the question. Bennett then responds by asking for elaboration or clarification. At times he rejects the explanation—hardly ever directly, usually by a quizzical look, a humorous comment, or another question. Students then elaborate their response. Finally, Bennett expounds upon the student's elaboration and gives it a context that none of the students is able to provide.

Bennett's responses, in general, are seven to ten times longer than his students' responses. His verbal salvos last from 60 to 120 seconds. Students typically speak for 10 to 20 seconds.

The articulateness of some of the students is particularly impressive. They provide a rationally connected verbal chain that even when marginally missing Madison's points is nonetheless laudable.

Bennett uses two pedagogical moves that are often acknowledged but seldom employed. He summarizes the major ideas the class has discussed at several intervals during the forty-five-minute lesson. He puts the issues in almost syllogistic form.

"Give people liberty, and you get differences of opinion."

"Get differences of opinion, and you get violence."

"How do we control the violence?"

"How do you, in a free society, prevent the majority from tyrannizing the minority?"

His intensity is fierce; he paces, paces, paces. Sometimes he clenches his fist. His eyes dart from side to side. Nothing apathetic here. He is on camera, and he knows it. But one senses it is more than this. Bennett seems to *care* about what he is teaching. The ideas he is teaching are part of himself. His voice, his comportment, his earnestness—yes, it is his earnestness that comes through the most. This, for him, is no mere game, even if it did originate as a public relations gambit. He knows the material too well for that. His pedagogical moves are too intense for that. For Bennett this is important stuff, and he is intent on helping his students understand just how important it is.

I said that there were two pedagogical moves that Bennett uses with his students; summarizing the main ideas is only one of them. The other is teaching for transfer.

Factions, he says, is an old-fashioned word. What terms do we use today? "Special-interest groups," one of his students says. "Exactly," he responds.

"I get so frustrated when I hear people talk about special-interest groups as though they were a new thing. Madison had to deal with them in his own time. Pick up a newspaper—you read a newspaper each day, don't you?" he knowingly and sarcastically asks the class, gibing them in the process to do so. "Pick up any newspaper and you'll find special interests pleading their case." He demonstrates his point with the local paper he brought with him to class.

He illustrates the self-interested nature of human beings by describing a situation in which a crowd of 150 people is trying to buy 25 Bruce Springsteen concert tickets. He tries to put the complex abstract notions of *Federalist* 10 in a form his seventeen- and eighteen-year-old students can relate to. He tries to help them see the intimate connection between the concerns and remedies produced by those "young men, barely eighteen years older than you are, at most," and the issues, dilemmas, aspirations of today.

He goes even further. Bennett not only tries to establish firm linkages of past and present, he relates the problem of self-interest and violence to his own college days, when one of his buddies from Boston was almost mugged by a group of New York college students because he gloated over the victory of the Celtics over New York. Bennett reveals a small part of himself in the process.

Perhaps because such a large percentage of his students are black, Bennett relates Madison's views to the Civil War and Lincoln's desire to save the Union. "Was the Union saved?" he asks. He talks about Lincoln's priorities and the tension between "two goods," the liberty of slaves and the maintenance of the Union. At least five times during the course of his lesson such connections are made; this lesson, he appears convinced, is not to be a dry historical relic having no bearing upon today's world or the real interests of the students he is teaching.

"The heart of the heart of the heart of *Federalist* 10 is located in Madison's observation that the latent causes of faction are thus sown in the nature of man."

Human nature, therefore, breeds potential conflict and violence. Government is a means through which self-interest can be reconciled with the public good. Bennett's latent lesson, it seems to me, not only is about Madison's views of constitutional rights, it is about the virtues of our view of people and government. There are, to be sure, other governments with other views, but our government's views, though sometimes flawed in practice, are the most virtuous. This message is not conveyed explicitly. It's not even what one might call a "soft sell." But it is there nevertheless. Bennett has a mission *and* message. He shares what he thinks is of profound importance to his students. He relishes the fight, he cultivates, he probes, and he challenges the students with whom he works. The crowd assembled has seen a tough boxer in the ring displaying his skills. Bennett is no lightweight. And judging by the applause he receives at the end of the fifteenth round, he seems to have won by a unanimous decision.

Are there some lessons to be learned from such an incursion into the colonial period? I think there are. One is that full command of the ideas one is teaching can free one to take on all comers—responses to questions and statements by students can be treated with style if one knows one's intellectual turf. Bennett, in this material at least, surely does. What does such competence mean to those of us interested in the improvement of teaching? To what extent is it likely that a teacher will have pedagogical grace if the teacher does not have a firm grasp on the content to be taught? Psychologists often study teaching as if it were a contentless process. Can teaching be effectively studied that way? Can one teach for transfer if one does not see the connections through which such transfer is made?

Another lesson or theme that we might extract from the tape focuses on the pedagogical virtues of emotional intensity. Bennett models intellectual interests, not mere academic ones. There is not a word about grades, points, or deadlines that must be met. No student is asked a question in a perfunctory way. The questions Bennett asks are asked intensely, and have point. They are designed to lead the student through the main ideas of the material. Are there perils to such an approach? Of course. One can accuse Bennett of conducting a lecture that is disguised as a discussion. After all, he knew just where he wanted the class to end up when he began. There were no questions by students directed to other students. He could be accused of using a "ping-pong" approach to teaching. Yet I find such objections objectionable. In any performance one can find flaws—God never made anything without a crack in it. Bennett directs his students' attention to very important issues. He cares about what he is teaching. He raises questions that move them forward through the major points of *Federalist* 10. He summarizes at intervals the distance they have traveled. He expresses enthusiasm and pleasure at the competence of their responses. He helps them see the connections of a piece written in 1787 to the problems of the Civil War, and to our own society today. He uses wit to stimulate when it is needed, and he keeps the door open for competing views. There is much to learn from him. After having studied teaching and learning in high schools for the past two and a half years, I can tell you with confidence, there is much to learn here. (Eisner, 1986)

Secretary Bennett's Teaching:
An Argument for Responsive Teaching
Roger W. Shuy
Georgetown University

As a discourse analyst concerned about education issues, I approached this videotape as I would any other data which are offered as a discrete unit. The event of a classroom has been well documented (for example, Mehan, 1979; Sinclair & Coulthard, 1975, Stubbs, 1976). The classroom teaching event, like the sales encounter event, the doctor-patient medical history event or the police interrogation event, has by now a rather well-defined structure. Like most human communicative events, it has an opening segment, a main body segment, and a closing or concluding segment. This structure corresponds, in fact, to the simple three stages of most human conversation: Hello–Topic Interactions–Goodbye. Greeting and closing segments have been studied by specialists in ritual or formulaic language (for example, Irvine, 1974). Such studies have been very useful, especially for cross-cultural understandings. Within a culture and on the topic of classroom interaction, however, our main concerns are with the main body of the structure, the topic initiations, and responses in particular.

A useful way to view teaching is to consider it a type of dialogue. Under the best of circumstances, a person will dialogue with one other person. Most of our effective communication and learning outside of schools, in fact, is carried out in dialogue. Other forms of teaching are carried out through monologue, sermons, and lectures, for example, where the communication is entirely one way, from speaker to silent learner. An implicit theory in education is that the older the student, the more monologue is used. Somewhere between actual dialogue and one-way monologue is what passes for communication in most secondary education. Researchers in classroom interaction have documented that for the past eighty years at least, the dominant type of classroom talk is referred to as the recitation pattern (Hoetker & Ahlbrand, 1969). More recently this pattern has been documented in American schools and is referred to as the Question-Response-Evaluation Model by Mehan (1979). As Schneider et al. (1985) point out, "Recitation may test students' existing knowledge but it does not teach" (p. 113). The emphasis of recitation teaching is on what they call "lower level facts and ideas, literal detail and the already known" (p. 113).

In contrast with the recitation model, Gallimore and Tharp (1983) describe something called responsive teaching, in which the teacher assists the students to reach the upper end of what Vygotsky (1978) refers to as the zone of proximal development, that is, the potential level of comprehension that they may someday achieve. Using contingency questioning (rather than evaluation questioning), the teacher makes adjustments to support student thinking and expression of ideas, stretching them beyond where they are to the next higher level of functioning. Such a practice comes closer to dialogue than does recitation teaching.

These structures of classroom talk can be viewed as a kind of continuum between the one-way lecture at one end of the continuum and everyday dialogue at the other, as shown in Table 1.

Those who advocate the responsive teaching model, most notably utilized in the Kamehameha Early Education Project in Hawaii (Gallimore & Tharp, 1983), believe that it comes closer to the type of language used most effectively for learning in virtually all life contexts other than in schools. Their position is supported from research in other communication events, such as doctor-patient interaction, where medical histories have been demonstrated to elicit more accurate and complete information from patients when physicians conduct their interviews as dialogue rather than in the strict question-answer recitation model (Shuy, 1979). Even automobile salesmen understand the need to get their customers involved in expressing their own preferences and resources before moving into any standard sales pitch routines.

We may ask how it is that education has developed a practice in which recitation teaching dominates in a world in which virtually all learning before school, and a great deal of learning after school, is

Table 1
Varieties of Structure in Classroom Talk

Communication Structure:	Monologue	Recitation Teaching	Responsive Teaching	Dialogue
Examples:	Sermon Lecture	Most U.S. classrooms Doctor/patient interviews Courtroom testimony		Adult-adult talk Adult-child talk Child-child talk
Communication mode:	One-way	One-way	Two-way	Two-way

achieved very efficiently through dialogic interaction. The answers, not surprisingly, have little to do with learning or teaching as such, but instead grow out of economic interests. Teachers faced with thirty or more students in one classroom find it difficult to dialogue in an effective way with one student in any developmentally productive way. The same teachers are faced with still another handicap from the traditional value of quietness. Should students be encouraged to dialogue with each other, the noise level of classrooms becomes unacceptable to by-now-well-developed prejudice against classroom talk. "No talking," in fact, is an oft-repeated admonition of most teachers.

Another traditional value that interferes with developmentally productive dialogue in the classroom is the democratic principle of turn taking: one student should not dominate and each student should get a turn. However democratic this is, it does not lead to assisting students to develop potential levels of comprehension individually. At best, such development in the thirty-student classroom is vicarious and inferred.

This framework of potential communication structures available to Mr. Bennett as he taught his class at Banneker High school in Washington, D.C., is a necessary beginning point in a discourse analysis of his classroom interaction. The first step is to determine the overall structure of the teaching event. In his case, it is the traditional recitation teaching model. Evidence that it is this model makes use of the following tools of discourse analysis:

Setting

Question sequencing analysis

Topic analysis

Response analysis

Evaluation analysis

Setting

Perhaps it is not fair to Secretary Bennett to consider the video classroom event analyzed here as a teaching event. The presence of the television media, the fact that the Secretary of Education should be considered the best at the field he heads up, and the public relations intent of this event might be enough, in themselves, to disqualify this even as a teaching event and to label it, instead, a public relations event.

But since the media regard it as a teaching event, since Mr. Bennett refers to himself as their teacher, and since the setting is a real-life classroom in which education is alleged to be taking place, it will be analyzed as though its purpose were no different from that of any other teaching event. We will assume here that the event captured on tape here in this classroom is representative of what Mr. Bennett would do if he were the regular, year-long teacher. Indeed, by his willingness to be videotaped he is giving silent assent to such an assumption. He is saying, in effect, "I am a teacher. I am good enough to be videotaped. In fact, my teaching here today might serve as a model to other teachers."

There is much that is good and effective in Bennett's style of teaching. He teaches with friendliness and humor. He evaluates positively on most occasions and encourages the students to go a bit farther in their answers. He provides frequent summaries (six times) or road maps of where they have reached so far, and he attempts, with some success, to relate *Federalist* 10 to current life in America. He is in complete control and it is clear from his occasional managerial remarks that he has a definite course plotted and will brook no deviation. He makes frequent comments about the need to involve other students in the discussion and he insists on a hand-raising, turn-taking procedure.

It is clear, in fact, that he is quite successful in managing to get the students to do what he wants them to do with his topics. The serious question to ask is whether or not the students were extended to go beyond their current levels of understanding to a level higher than they had reached before the class began.

Question Sequencing Analysis

As an ethnographer, the first question I ask of this event is, "What is going on here?" The answer may seem simple but it has many complex discourse features. Mr. Bennett is leading a class of high school students through a lesson in Madison's *Federalist* Paper No. 10. Presumably, the students were assigned it as homework and were to come to class prepared to discuss it. It is also clear that Mr. Bennett considers the assignment appropriately challenging for a class of very intelligent students. For this reason, we can expect his teaching of this class to focus on higher-order questions concerning cause and effect or inferencing of the text to current life situations, rather than on mere factual recall of the details of the text itself.

Schneider et al. (1985) vividly describe the questioning strategies used for a similar class of high-achieving students in California but also contrast their questioning approach in that class with another, low-achieving class in the same school on the same day and on the same topic, the relationship of the U.S. Constitution to a lawsuit involving the flag salute. To the high-achieving class, the teacher's questioning pattern moved from open-ended to "wh-" questions, in an effort to provide the type of guided assistance that will enable the student to move from mere factual recall to generalizations about causes and effect, or inferences about relationships of the topic to current situations, personal or not.

To the low-achieving class, the teacher began with the same broad question strategy, an open-ended question, but did not achieve the same quick generalizations and inferences that he achieved in the high-achieving class. The questioning pattern here, then, looks like this:

Teacher question		Student response
Open-ended	→	Nil
↓		
"Wh-"	→	Nil or partial
↓		
"Yes/no	→	Successful
↓		
"Wh-"	→	Successful

The end results in the two classes were somewhat the same, the major difference being in the questioning patterns utilized by the teacher to get there. Both classes had the same zone of proximal development, but one achieved it with minimal assistance, and the other achieved it only by the agency of the teacher's carefully chosen and well-timed questions.

Of crucial interest to us as we analyze Mr. Bennett's teaching is an issue highlighted by Schneider et al. (1985), namely, the teacher did not really know what to do once the high-achieving class quickly achieved the appropriate generalizations and inferences. That is, what was *their* next level of development? Where next should they be taken through effective teaching? Put in terms of "recitation teaching" vs. "responsive teaching," it is clear that in responsive teaching, that which came closer to dialogue and which leads the student to higher levels of development in a self-generated fashion, it is much easier to achieve the desired generalizations and inferences but much harder to go beyond this level,

Table 2
Types of Questions Asked According to Source of Answer

Source of Answer	Type of Question	
Student-generated answer	Open-ended	0
	"Wh-" "why"	14
Teacher-generated answer	Factual "wh-"	49
	"Yes/no"	29
	Tag	7
Total		99

largely because teachers do not really know where to go or what the next zone of proximal development really is.

Mr. Bennett's questioning strategies in the Banneker School lesson are instructive in this regard. Excluding rhetorical questions, Mr. Bennett asks a total of ninety-nine questions, broken down as shown in Table 2.

In an earlier study of teacher questions in the classroom it was shown that teachers who asked more than twice as many "wh-" questions as "yes/no" questions were considerably more effective than those teachers who relied on "yes/no" and tag questions primarily (Shuy, in press). In this study of 114 elementary school children in six classrooms, few if any "why" questions were asked in the twelve lessons examined. No open-ended questions were discovered.

Mr. Bennett, teaching a high school class, could be expected to ask more "why" and other "wh-" questions. He did so, as two-thirds of his questions were the higher-order types. Furthermore, his question-asking sequence was appropriate for first permitting the students to self-generate (from his "wh-" questions), then probing and specifying their answers with factual "wh-" questions (such as "where," "what," and "when"). If Mr. Bennett still did not elicit the specificity he desired, he asked a "yes/no" question and then immediately moved back up the question scale to "wh-" again. Within the recitation model of teaching, Bennett's question-asking strategy is an excellent model for other classroom teachers to follow. It can be diagrammed as follows:

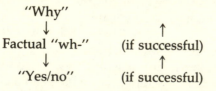

```
    "Why"
      ↓              ↑
Factual "wh-"    (if successful)
      ↓              ↑
  "Yes/no"       (if successful)
```

That is, Bennett began with higher-order questions which should lead the student to generalize, infer appropriate relationships, or develop his or her own theories of cause and effect. If the student failed to do this, Bennett supported the student by asking a recall question (usually with "what," "where" or "who") which could then serve as the basis for the generalization, inference, or cause and effect. If this still did not yield the desired response, Bennett then moved to a "yes/no" question, not as an end in itself and not as a test of the student's knowledge or recall, but rather as a pump-priming basis for the journey back up the question ladder to the ultimate "why" question again. Then, better reinforced with the specific knowledge necessary to think through the "why" question, the student was supported, rather directly, by an effective question-asking sequence.

It should be noted that the reason for there being no genuine open-ended questions in this lesson may well be the pressure of time caused by the on-camera performance. Bennett timed his lesson rather well and, for the sake of the public inspection that he knew would follow, he could not afford to be too broad in his focus. Instead of open-ended, "tell-me-all-you-know" types of questions, Bennett relied on fourteen well placed "why" questions as his higher-order agenda.

A different structure of this lesson can be observed if one focuses on the placement of these "why" questions. A full transcript of this lesson covers twenty-seven typewritten pages. If the entire lesson is divided into thirds, nine pages each, it can be seen that seven "why" questions occurred in the first third, only one in the second third, and six in the final third of the lesson. Correlating with this division of "why" questions is the distribution of responses by male against female students, as shown in Table 3.

That is, during the periods of male performance in question answering, Bennett asked the most "why" questions. Or, put another way, males responded during peak periods of Bennett's "why" questions much more than did females. This male-female difference will be explored further.

Table 3
Distribution of Male and Female Students' Responses to All Questions Compared with Distribution of "Why" Questions at Different Stages of the Lesson

Pages of Transcript	No. Responses By Males (N = 10 Respondents)	No. Responses By Females (N = 12 Respondents)	No. of "Why" Questions
1–9	22	9	7
10–18	2	30	1
19–27	27	0	6
Total	51	39	14

Twenty-two students responded to Bennett's questions: ten males and twelve females. The males uttered 634 words over 51 turns of talk for an average of 12.4 words per turn. The females uttered 419 words over 39 turns for an average of 10.7 words per turn. Bennett interrupted the males in 19 percent of their responses and the females in 27 percent of their answers to his questions. Males averaged 5.1 turns of talk apiece while females averaged only 3.35 turns apiece. These facts point to the need for further study of female student interaction in high school classrooms.

The data represented here might suggest the following about females during this lesson in relation to males:

1. Less willingness to participate at the beginning of the class.
2. Less willingness to participate at the end of the class.
3. Most willingness to participate in the middle of the class.
4. Less willingness to respond to "why" questions involving generalizations, inferences, or cause and effect.
5. More apt to be interrupted.
6. Fewer words per turn.
7. Fewer turns of talk.
8. More willingness to respond to "yes/no" questions or "wh-" questions involving "where" or "what" facts rather than "why" or "how" facts.
9. More willingness to ask questions during the period designated as Bennett's time to ask questions.
10. Less willingness to ask questions during the period designated as student question period.
11. Fewer generalizations, responses of cause and effect, or inferential relationships.

In terms of his question sequencing, Bennett followed the traditional recitation model of teaching rather than the responsive model. That is, Bennett controlled the questioning and, as we shall see next, the topics introduced. It must be pointed out, however, that Bennett utilized the recitation model of teaching about as well as it could be done. The question sequencing analysis carried out here also suggests an avenue of research on student responses based on gender. It is difficult to determine whether Bennett's turn-taking assignments or the students' own natural selection of questions to be answered is the cause of the sharp differences noted here in response to higher-order questions. Such findings, however, point to further analyses of teacher-student classroom interaction.

Topic Analysis

We now turn our attention to whether or not it is possible to assist students to reach the upper end of their zones of proximal development within the recitation teaching model. Schneider et al. (1985) found this a very frustrating task. They found that their more advanced class achieved the appropriate generalizations, relationships, and inferences rather quickly and left little else to accomplish within the recitation model. They further suggest that a responsive teaching model might be more appropriate.

One way to determine what a responsive teaching model might lead to is in the topics introduced by both teacher and student. The topics that people introduce in conversation are clues to their agendas or concerns. They tell us what they are really interested in. Topic analysis simply marks all the topics introduced and recycled throughout the event. Recycled topics, in fact, suggest an even stronger agenda than singly introduced topics. In this lesson, Bennett introduced eight topics and recycled one of them for a total of nine topics. The students introduced three, all of which were questions. One question was introduced during Bennett's topic sequence. The other two questions were introduced during the designated question period. Bennett's topics were as follows:

Topic	Text Page	
1	1	Why read *Federalist* 10?
2	3	Why is it relevant now?
3	4	How do we solve the problem of factions?
4	7	Human nature is evil.
5	10	The government protects our rights.
6	11	(recycling topic 4) Human nature is evil.
7	15	How can we control our passions?
8	20	Representative government is the answer.
9	23	Even representative government has problems.

From the questions asked by the students, we can adduce their three topics as follows:

Topic	Text Page	
1	15 F9	Suppose the majority really believes race is an important issue?
2	25 M2	Does paper money constitute a serious problem and pervade the whole Union?
3	26 M10	Why was *Federalist* 10 addressed to the people of New York only?

A speaker's topics give a very strong indication of that person's agenda in a conversation. In a classroom, however, the rules of speaking are stacked against discovering what the real agendas of the students are. They have no real voice unless the structure of the event permits them to have one. To Bennett's credit, he permitted the students to raise their own topics in the brief question period at the end of the class. But even this question period was highly ritualized, as it is in most classes. The topics of the main discussion have been declared very important by the power figure, the teacher. It is clear from the context and from the way Bennett opened the floor for student topics that such topics were expected to be directly relevant to his own.

In sharp contrast to the designated question period, however, was the lone question introduced by F9 during Bennett's designated topic segment of the class. It concerned the fear that many blacks have, namely, that although race is a serious matter, not trivial or frivolous, the majority "may push it as a relatively important distinction" and turn race into a serious and heinous problem for the black minority. Bennett should not be accused of racism in his response to F9, for he pointed out that race is a serious issue, but it is clear that F9's concern or agenda was in the area of race relations and constitutional matters. It is likely, in an all-black classroom in Washington, D.C., that this was also the concern of other students.

Bennett's topics, on the other hand, show evidence of being on more than American history. The topic that he recycles, in this case the evils of human nature, took up almost one-fourth of the class time. The essential problem, Bennett stated over and over again, lies in the evil nature of all humanity.

Once again, we must emphasize that Bennett's teaching was located in the style of recitation teaching. He was quite successful in managing to get the students to do what he wanted them to do with his own topics. Like the advanced class of Schneider et al. (1985), Bennett's students moved very quickly into generalizations, cause and effect, and relational thinking on his topics. But responsive teaching is closer to dialogue, to normal conversation. In responsive teaching, like dialogue, students will introduce their own topics in such a way that the teacher can guide them in generalizing, determining cause and effect, and inferring to their own topics, concerns, and agendas. But this cannot be done without first allowing the students to put forth their own topics. When this is permitted to happen, teachers join in by responding and teaching through their responses to the self-generated and important issues of the students.

Even in the recitation teaching analyzed here, there are evidences of student topics upon which responsive teaching might be based, giving a small hint of how much there might have been had Bennett chosen to teach in a consistently responsive mode.

Response Analysis

Response analysis is still another discourse analysis routine that is applicable to this lesson. In this lesson, students responded to Bennett's questions and Bennett evaluated and responded to the students' answers.

There were twenty-seven responses of the students to Bennett's fourteen higher-level "why" questions. Twenty-one were made by males and only six by females. These responses were of the type:

X because of Y
X so that Y
X therefore Y

The three equal segments of the class noted earlier display the distribution of responses to "why" questions shown in Table 4.

Of the twenty-two students who responded to all ninety-nine of Bennett's questions, only eight were involved in responding to these higher-level questions, four males and four females, as shown in Table 5.

What is noteworthy is that two males accounted for over half of these responses. The research issue here, of course, concerns what actual percent of students carry the higher-level question load for the whole class. Also of interest is to compare the perceptions about such load carrying by the teacher and/or the viewers of this tape. Do teachers really *see* such imbalance when they hear a good answer, or do they assume that other students are also capable of making the same response?

Response analysis of this classroom, then, suggests areas of needed research on male-female differentiation of questions responded to, but it

Table 4
Distribution of Male and Female Students' Responses to "Why" Questions at Different Stages of the Lesson

Pages of Transcript	No. of Male Student Responses to "Why" Questions	No. of Female Student Responses to "Why" Questions	No. of "Why" Questions
1–9	11	1	7
10–18	2	5	1
19–27	8	0	6
Total	21	6	14

Table 5
Distribution of Responses to "Why" Questions Across Individual Students (n = 8 Students)

Student code no.	M1	M2	M7	F1	M3	F7	F9	F10	Total
No. of responses to "why" questions	10	5	4	3	2	1	1	1	27

Note: M signifies males; F signifies females.

also shows that the students in this class were providing generalizations, causal relationships, and inferences from the outset of the lesson and throughout. The teacher who perceives such effective responding can take such clues as an indication that the recitation model of teaching is not capable of moving them to the upper limits of their development. Continued recitation teaching, under these circumstances, can lead only to repetitive recitation, reflecting little about what is possible and repeating, over and over, what is obvious. The theory seems to be that if a little is good, a lot is better. Such a theory would make little sense in most other areas of life, such as cooking, in which a little salt may be good but a lot may prove disastrous.

Evaluation Analysis

Also interesting are the evaluative responses of Bennett to the students' answers to his questions. He was polite at all times and treated their answers with dignity, even when they were not quite what he wanted. He gave essentially four types of evaluative responses to their answers: negative, challenge, neutral, and positive.

All Bennett's negative evaluations were mitigated, or softened. Examples include, "It's more than that, isn't it?" "Well, I wouldn't think. . .," or "It's simpler than that now, isn't it?" His neutral evaluations neither praised nor condemned. They usually took the form of "Okay" or "All right," spoken with flat intonation. Bennett's challenges usually repeated the words of the student in a question intonation such as "Democrats and Republicans are factions?" indicating that part of the answer was right but not all of it, or he asked the student to say the answer in another way. Bennett's positive evaluations usually took the form of "Right" or "Very nice." To one student, who provided a particularly acceptable inferential answer, Bennett said: "Right. Terrific. Exactly. Can't improve on it. Can't improve on it. That's it. That's right."

Once again, however, a breakdown of Bennett's evaluations by type and by the student's gender is most instructive. Bennett did not

Table 6
Distribution of Secretary Bennett's Evaluations Across Types of Evaluation and Across Student Gender

Student Gender	Types of Evaluation (%)			
	Positive	Neutral	Challenge	Negative
Male	45	0	30	25
Female	50	30	0	20

evaluate over half of the student answers. Table 6 displays the evaluations he did make as percentages.

What are of interest here, of course, are Bennett's neutral and challenge evaluations. He offered challenges only to male students and he offered neutral evaluations only to females. Again, the data from this single classroom are limited, but they suggest interesting further analyses of classroom evaluations. Do teachers challenge males more than females? Do male teachers challenge males, while female teachers challenge females? From the discourse analysis perspective, do challenges come closer to responsive teaching in that they encourage discourse and seem more like dialogue? Should teachers challenge more and use fewer positive, negative, or neutral evaluations?

What a Response Model Might Look Like

We noted earlier that Gallimore and Tharp (1983) and Schneider et al. (1985) posed their own frustration about how to *extend* students who move quickly toward the generalizations, inferential relationships, or cause and effect understandings desired by the teacher. These researchers suggest that the answer to this frustration is in moving from the recitation model of teaching to the response model. We also noted earlier that the response model is closer to conversational dialogue, a two-way communication mode with both parties initiating topics, changing the direction of the lesson, and relating it to their own lives.

The lesson analyzed here is a very good recitation model, but it is also no more than a recitation model. This model would have worked better, perhaps, with a less intelligent, less motivated, less prepared group of students. It is clear from the very beginning of this class, however, that students were not only providing the desired factual answers, but they also were displaying clear evidence of their ability to see causal relationships, infer appropriately, and generalize from the past to the present. Such responses can be easily seen in their use of words like "because," "if X then Y" constructions, and "X so that Y" sentences. The major reason that students did this so frequently and so well is that Bennett asked the "why" questions that made such answers possible.

Had Bennett attempted a response model teaching event, he would have done more with student questions such as the one about race relations noted earlier. There would have been student questions, comments, or opinions throughout the lesson, not just at the end during the designated question period. There would have been less rigidity about turn-taking rules. There would have been a conscious effort to get the students' agendas or topics on the floor for discussion.

Response teaching might not work in all classes but from what Gallimore and Tharp (1983), Schneider et al. (1985), and the Banneker classroom analysis indicate, it might have been more appropriate here, for this rather sophisticated class.

A deeper and perhaps more serious theoretical question remains unanswered, however. It is assumed that higher-order questions are somehow better than mere fact-recitation, memory-oriented ones. Although this seems self-evident and true, what research base do we have to support it? How do we know that students extend themselves to their next level of proximal development when higher-order questions are used? We probably will not know the answer to this question until we study, ethnographically and linguistically, classes in which such responsive teaching actually takes place. At the moment, there seem to be very few of these available.

References

Gallimore, R., & Tharp, R. G. (1983). *The regulatory effect of teacher questions: a microanalysis of reading comprehension lessons* (Report No. 109). Honolulu: Centre for the Development of Early Education, The Kamehameha Schools.

Hoetker, J., & Ahlbrand, W. (1969). The persistence of recitation. *American Educational Research Journal, 6,* 145–167.

Irvine, J. (1974). Strategies of status manipulation in the Wolof greeting. In R. Bauman & J. Sherzer (Eds.), *Explorations in the ethnography of speaking* (pp. 167–191). Cambridge: Cambridge University Press.

Mehan, H. (1979). *Learning lessons.* Cambridge: Cambridge University Press.

Schneider, P., Hyland, J., and Gallimore, R. (1985). The zone of proximal development in eighth grade social studies. *Quarterly Newsletter of the Laboratory of Comparative Human Cognition, 7,* 113–119.

Shuy, R. (1979). Language policy in medicine. *Language in Public Life.* Washington, D.C.: Georgetown University Press.

Shuy, R. (in press). Question asking strategies in the classroom. In J. Green, J. Harker, & C. Wallat (Eds.), *Multiple Analysis of Classroom Discourse Processes.* Norwood, NJ: Ablex.

Sinclair, J., & Coulthard, R. (1975). *Towards an analysis of discourse*. New York: Oxford University Press.

Stubbs, M. (1976). *Language, schools and classrooms*. London: Methuen.

Vygotsky, L. S. (1978). *Mind in society*. Cambridge, MA: Harvard University Press.

(Shuy, 1986)

The foregoing essays focused upon the work of a single teacher teaching a single lesson to a group of students he had not seen before. These essays—one an educational criticism and the other a linguistic analysis—were prepared from a forty-five-minute videotape. As I have indicated, the circumstances for which they were prepared are atypical. The essays were included in this chapter to provide a sense of what different approaches to classroom analysis might reveal, but the conditions under which they were written and the setting for which they were prepared—delivery at an AERA annual meeting—do not represent the conditions under which educational criticisms are typically prepared. What follows does.

What you are about to read is the work of James Kuntz, S.J. The work formed part of a doctoral dissertation at Stanford University (Kuntz, 1986) done under my supervision and included in part here, with his permission. Kuntz's aim was to describe, interpret, and appraise the ways in which values pertaining to social justice, a value central to Jesuit education, are transmitted. He examined two classrooms, one each in two Jesuit high schools in the Bay area of California, for about three months. I have excerpted 23 pages of text from his 483-page dissertation, followed by my analysis of his educational criticism. Each paragraph of his text is numbered, and I refer to the paragraphs by number in my comments. Not every paragraph will be commented upon.

Outerworld/Schoolworld
St. James: Tradition and History
James Kuntz

1. Several years after the founding of Berchmans Hall [one of the two high schools Kuntz studied], Jesuit fathers begin a small educational mission in Mount Hermon. Though set "in a hole surrounded by sand hills," in the words of an early Jesuit at St. James, the secondary school survives during its early years as a small part of a larger Jesuit institution formed to serve many constituencies. Mount Hermon prospers during the nineteenth century, and within its urban surroundings, St. James grows accordingly.

2. With its clear separation from the other Jesuit institutions, St. James begins a new phase in its history. Neither the Depression nor the Second World War seriously threatens its existence, and the local Catholic community contributes generously to the maintenance of the school, and the construction of a new physical plant for its campus.

3. In other ways, the development of St. James mirrors that of Berchmans. The Jesuits and their lay colleagues realize that the immigrants and other Catholics of Mount Hermon desire the security and sense of community which a parochial school education provides. In the 1960s and 1970s, the expectations of these Catholics change, or more precisely, expand to include not just the development of faith and acceptable academic skills, but also the highest quality of college preparation. The educators at St. James confront the same ambivalent goals as those at Berchmans: Would the desired and desirable goal of academic excellence preclude the transmission of religious values, especially those which concern the demands of social justice in Christian teaching?

St. James

4. The houses are all the same. Some wear different colors; in others, the shape of a picture window or the position of a garage distinguishes a home from its neighbor. The overwhelming impression, however, is that of sameness: developers saw plots of land and designed structures which maximized profit at the expense of diversity. Row upon row, city street after city street, St. James' neighborhood retains its character by the force of its homogeneity.

5. At first glance, St. James High School, encircled by uniformity, presents a contrasting face. Its buildings look down upon its neighbors, and its shape suggests purposes far different from the surrounding suburban dwellings. Classrooms, playing fields, student parking areas—all signal "school" to the passing motorists who drive past the campus on the nearby highway.

6. Morning arrival and afternoon dismissal times reinforce these first impressions. Hordes of students suddenly appear around the school. Some of the older boys drive to St. James in their own cars; a larger number arrives by bus or other means of public transportation, and a few even walk to school. The students generally come from a middle-class background and 85 percent are baptized Catholics. On rare occasions during the school year, the students wear coat and tie but otherwise school uniforms and strict dress codes are, as at Berchmans, a thing of the past.

7. During most of the school day, the students remain in classrooms or in designated areas, and the school begins to resemble in greater detail

those houses that surround it. Outside visitors call infrequently and the school structures describe an island paralleling the square blocks which encompass them, but separate, apart, and self-enclosed. For like the homes that surround it, St. James is a private dwelling, whose facade signifies not just educational or ecclesiastical tradition, but separation and insularity.

8. St. James has in common with its neighbors a desire to blend the most helpful of the new into a well-defined past that shapes all future vision. Talk of conservatism, patriotism, loyalty and tradition echoes in the halls of St. James without ironic reverberations. Students move from class to class through the corridors like soldiers falling in: chaotic intensity directed toward a regimented goal. Though quite lovely in appearance and design, the recently built school houses quite traditional classrooms: square spaces with the customary teachers' and students' desks, surrounded by blackboards and narrow windows.

9. The thirty-four students who attended Jim Reardon's Theology III course each day after lunch possessed a sense of that separation. They rated St. James above the local public and other Catholic schools not just on academic matters, but in relation to its tradition for Catholic Mount Hermon. Classroom 209 did not differ substantially from any of the other classrooms at St. James, nor even from classrooms in previous St. James buildings, and the student body, with some significant exceptions, remained white, middle-class Catholics, from the traditional European nationalities that had supplied students to St. James for decades. Whatever embodied tradition—which at St. James included literary and dramatic presentations, past and present athletic triumphs, academic success and alumni accomplishments in political, religious and economic circles—assumed great importance for the school community.

10. Though clothed in contemporary finery, tradition remained a formidable influence at St. James in the minds of the students as well as faculty and staff. Within that environment, Jim Reardon confronted a considerable challenge in teaching *Theology III/Moral Decision-making*. Not only did students almost invariably possess a background shaped by traditional Church teachings, they might expect those teachings to be introduced in familiar ways. Concerned not just with social justice and traditional Church teachings, but also with appropriate methods for approaching moral questions, Jim Reardon faced two tasks: teaching the material of his course, and also reaching his students' hearts and minds.

Classroom 209

11. Classroom 209 looked down upon a courtyard but very few students looked out its windows. The students' desks formed a U-shaped ar-

rangement around three of the four walls of the square room, and one or two rows of desks prevented easy access to the windows. One entered the classroom at the front of the room facing the windows: the teacher's desk lay straight ahead, between the two legs of the U; the blackboard panels hung suspended from the wall to the right, as did a permanent film screen, and the students sat to the left, in their assigned places. During quizzes and tests, the teacher had the students rearrange the desks in rows to prevent cheating, though with mixed success. The teacher signaled that times of evaluation called for stricter measures; the students cheated anyway.

12. Four large, square light fixtures furnished the classroom with light on the days when sunshine did not flood the classroom. Toward the back of the room, a large overhead projector sat on a cart next to a large bookcase filled with a variety of textbooks and other volumes. The pale walls and green carpet softened the otherwise regimented organization and structured feel of the room.

13. A poster placed on the bulletin board just to the left of the door read "If You Want Peace, Work for Justice," though no student, nor the teacher, ever referred to it during the months of my observation. The rest of the classroom wall space occasionally carried newspaper clippings or articles of note, but very little in the way of decoration. The carpeting and the natural light which made its way into the room through the narrow windows saved the room from a cheerless fate.

14. In discussing which class I should observe, Jim Reardon expressed the opinion that the period right after lunch would be his most difficult, and as it turned out, that was the class I chose. Indeed, Jim did encounter occasional problems with the students, and the rather smallish classroom and its midday warmth contributed to Jim's difficulties, as one student frankly stated:

> It was a hot classroom. After lunch—sleep time.
> (Todd Longo, interview, April 22nd)

Lunchtime athletic contests contributed to this midday slump as well: students frequently came to class hot and sweaty, with clothes in disarray. As a result, their attention wandered and they had to struggle to stay awake.

15. Class interruptions figured in my observations at St. James as they had at Berchmans, but at St. James, they took on a more intrusive and intentional cast. The administration used the public address system with some regularity during the fifth period, at least every other day, and most frequently for disciplinary reasons. On February 3rd, for instance, Jim Reardon was conducting a discussion on a comparison of the Nazi

concentration camps and American conduct during the My Lai massacre in Vietnam. Just as he was carefully detailing the comparisons and contrasts between those two horrors, the voice of the school disciplinarian came over the loudspeaker:

> It would please me very much if teachers would give detention to those in the hallway.
>
> (Administrator, class, February 3rd)

The teacher immediately stopped his lesson and went out into the hallway where he managed to catch one or two students who had been loitering in the corridors. The students in the corridor, who had also heard the announcement, had taken to their heels so only a couple of students served their detention period with the school disciplinarian after school, but even though Jim Reardon attempted to link up the lesson with the interruption— "Excuse me, I was just following orders"— the momentum of the lesson had been lost in the service of a very minor disciplinary obligation. But at St. James, few disciplinary matters were minor and one of the traditions school authorities strove to uphold was that of order, even at the expense of teacher comfort, or as in this case, educational instruction.

16. But students provided the most striking suspension of a teaching lesson that I observed during my time at Berchmans and St. James; what is more, the school supported the students in this interruption. On January 18th, Jim Reardon had begun the lesson with a discussion of journal entries, and how the students should produce them. With no previous warning and without even knocking, two St. James basketball players wearing their letter sweaters walked into class and announced that they had tickets for sale for that week's home basketball game. Arrested in mid-sentence, the teacher reacted not with anger but with mild acquiescence.

17. As the marketing job began, he stood back and watched with interest. Nor did the students take this interruption amiss; neither did they seize the opportunity to waste a great deal of time. The Mount Hermon newspaper had that day designated one of our visitors as a "bona fide high school All-American"; some students gently teased him about his publicity, which he uncomfortably acknowledged, as his teammate sold tickets to four or five of the students. Once the students had completed their transactions, the two basketball players thanked Mr. Reardon and left the room to move on to other classes. The teacher resumed the class at the point where he had been interrupted and the class returned to its consideration of the journals.

18. When I questioned Jim Reardon about this occurrence, he began his answer by stating that he attempted to encourage St. James students,

especially seniors, to chart an independent course for themselves in their dealings with teachers and in choosing classes. He confessed that he was surprised that he had stopped teaching in this instance, because he had previously denied a student permission to sell tickets when that young man had attempted to come into the class during the prayer with which Mr. Reardon customarily began his lesson. That this refusal angered the student suggests that, in the area of athletics at least, the administration and faculty granted the students a fair amount of independence; that Jim Reardon allowed a suspension of a class lesson but not a prayer indicates that he considered athletics a constitutive part of the educational experience at St. James, though not its top priority, and he did in fact wear the school colors on the days home basketball games were scheduled:

> I do support kids in activities, not necessarily athletics only. The 8 A.M. to 2 P.M. kids are wasting their time and money here.
> (Jim Reardon, interview, January 26th)

Jim's views struck a responsive chord in students who looked for more than academics at St. James. Students agreed quite strongly with Jim that school involved more than academics. Todd Longo reasoned that a student needed the time to reflect upon the many changes he was experiencing and that school offered the opportunity in a way that his home could not:

> Some classes are boring for many reasons but to get a sense of yourself is hard and there is time for it at school more than home. You can be in a disagreeable mood at school and some resent the authority here. But you're changing and you should enjoy your time here.
> (Todd Longo, interview, April 22nd)

19. Interruptions such as PA announcements concerning disciplinary enforcement and students selling basketball tickets, along with the unfavorable scheduling of this class of thirty-four students directly after lunch, added complicating factors to the challenge Jim Reardon faced in the Moral Decision-Making course. . . .Moral decision courses in Catholic religious curricula included within their syllabi not just the conclusions or content resulting from proper moral decisions but the moral reasoning that contributed to those decisions. External factors like those mentioned above complicated this process because the students generally came from traditional Catholic backgrounds. Subliminal messages concerning the importance of discipline and athletics even in respect to academics could only reinforce the students' resistance to new ways of thinking, as well as to conclusions or moral stances in opposition to the emphases in moral questions which their previous education had stressed. Jim Reardon's teaching style took on even greater significance

in the face of these conditions because he had to overcome administrative practices, student resistance and narrowly traditional moral teachings as he outlined the difficult path of moral decision-making.

Teacherworld

Teaching Style

20. James Reardon exemplified the type of student St. James' teachers and administrators wanted to develop. An alumnus of the school, he had earned a Master of Divinity degree from one of the country's most prestigious universities, and then returned to his alma mater to share the benefits of his education with its students. About thirty years of age, he was married, and his wife was expecting their third child. Dedicated to his profession, he derived great satisfaction from his teaching though he realized that a high school faculty position would never reward him with substantial sums of money. But the pleasure of teaching and the conviction of its importance outweighed the financial sacrifices he was making.

21. Part of the satisfaction Reardon enjoyed included a view of Christian community which he believed that St. James illustrated, at least when it functioned at its best. He referred to the eighteenth century American Congregational theologian Jonathan Edwards and his vision of the heart as the center for religious experience and knowledge, and believed that the best education offered at St. James included not just the academic or religious but athletics and other activities as well. He thought that all these factors contributed to Christian community and so he attempted to support students in their various after-school activities, as well as during lunch hour intramural contests, and other similar events. His presence added weight to his beliefs about how the St. James community should function:

> The kids say that the contents are not critical but "the teacher knows
> my name and knows I was in the play. He says hi to me outside of
> school time or away from school." Faculty awareness and support is
> important.
>
> (Jim Reardon, interview, January 26th)

22. Jim contrasted the potential for community which he observed at St. James with that of another Catholic high school where he had worked several years before. I had questioned him about the role of athletics and activities at St. James based on the basketball tickets incident during class on January 18th:

> [The incident] reflects the Athletic Department style here but not the
> whole school's. At my previous school, the brothers, the coaches and

the lay faculty all placed the top priority on athletics. St. James has a much better flow. But among students, if you're not jocks, you won't get recognition.

(Jim Reardon, interview, January 26th)

Though the teacher believed that Christian community could flourish at St. James, he understood that other values might obstruct its growth, and at St. James, concern for athletics in the institution and among the students could provide formidable competition.

23. Jim Reardon also saw the background and formation of the students as possible impediments for learning about moral decision-making. He considered the makeup of the student body quite similar to what it was when he attended St. James: white, West European, Catholic boys. The two changes he had observed, that more students now came from outside the city boundaries of Mount Hermon, and that fewer blue collar parents sent their sons to St. James, only increased the resistance he had experienced in his three years at the school.

24. The teacher strongly believed in the importance of students' knowing their own values and of acknowledging the significance of integrity in the process of making moral decisions. By encouraging the students then to utilize this process in looking at the world around them, Reardon believed that students could learn to make good moral decisions, given the proper schooling in moral principles. But some of the student values most strongly held acted as a deterrent to moral growth. Many students at St. James abused alcohol and displayed very macho attitudes toward women, according to the teacher, while showing very little sympathy toward those whose attitudes differed from their own, and the biggest putdown with which one student could label another was "fag."

25. Reardon also detected a conservative leaning among the students concerning the question of racism. His attempts to discuss racism invariably met with the student response that reverse discrimination invited equal condemnation, something Reardon denied. He questioned whether any white students had faced discrimination, and thought that racism lurked beneath the surface in the resentment expressed against students who dressed distinctively, or against ethnic clubs for black, Hispanic or Oriental students.

26. Reardon considered teaching an art, not a science, and believed that he could best serve his students with an eclectic repertoire of teaching techniques mixed with enthusiasm for his students and his field. But his methods for grading and evaluation placed very structured demands upon the students, while allowing them some creative leeway in the choice of topic and approach. These demands included fifteen journal entries each quarter, eight typed homework/project options, five quizzes

and active participation in classroom discussions. The teacher deducted points from a student's grade for a late assignment and expected the students to submit assignments that were neat, and grammatically correct.

27. The teacher's desire for accountability extended to almost daily evaluations of students. On February 9th, for instance, the teacher completed one section of his material and then asked the students to take out their books and note-taking apparatus while he placed a note in his mark book opposite the names of those who did not have them. He sternly encouraged those students to prepare for class with more zeal; the students looked somewhat brow beaten at the end of this lecture.

28. On February 16th, the teacher collected a homework assignment by systematically moving from desk to desk, notebook in hand. To those students who did not have the assignment, the teacher simply said:

> You'd better get it in before you go home today.
> (Jim Reardon, class, February 16th)

29. The combination of academic demands, the importance the teacher placed on his subject, the challenge of the material and some of the attitudes students held produced some resentment, which occasionally led to breaches in discipline. Though by no means their customary response, improper student behavior occurred with enough frequency to indicate that some students some of the time chose this manner to reject what the teacher was teaching, and that the catalyst for their rejection was the teacher's style.

30. Interestingly enough, Jim Reardon believed that discipline problems in the school tended to be few in number, because teachers could afford to be lenient in the context of the strong disciplinary stance the institution maintained. In fact, he stated:

> In the evaluations I hand out at the end of the year, few students feel that my discipline policies are arbitrary. More think they are too loose.
> (Jim Reardon, interview, April 22nd)

But the teacher corrected the students for a number of shortcomings or disciplinary infractions during the time I observed his class, while some student reactions to his demands, though muted, represented a rebellious attitude on the part of at least a couple of students. While some of the infractions illustrated general student playfulness, others hinted at teacher frustration and student resistance.

31. Two incidents illustrate the playful type of infraction which the teacher, if he even noticed, was inclined to ignore, and which presented no direct challenge to his authority. On January 13th, as the teacher con-

cluded his remarks about ideal human behavior as the norm by which moral actions should be judged, a student in the corridor, waiting for the sixth period class, did an imitation of a person smoking a joint of marijuana. Wrapped up in his analysis, the teacher did not observe this amusing counterpoint to his lecture, though several sitting near me just barely held back their laughter.

32. On March 1st, two students outside class were keeping a third student from regaining his lacrosse stick. Finally, one of the boys tossed the stick through the door at the front of the class, while the teacher was moving about the classroom, challenging the students about their generally poor grades. The boy who owned the stick unobtrusively sidled in, picked up his lacrosse stick and returned to his friends in the corridor, to the silent relief of us all. The product of student energy more than anything else, such instances of misbehavior bore little resemblance to incidents that characterized a strained relationship between teacher and student.

33. That type of incident might develop from teacher frustration or from student opposition, but in either case, signaled at least a partial breakdown in the relationship between them. At times, the teacher reacted to disciplinary violations. On January 27th, two students were disturbing each other during the prayer at the beginning of class, and two other students walked into class several minutes late. Obviously annoyed, the teacher wrote out detention slips for the two latecomers and then ordered the two boys who had disturbed the prayer to see him after class.

34. On other occasions, the teacher reacted to academic shortcomings, the failure of students to study for quizzes, read assigned material, hand in journal reports or take an active part in discussions. By February 24th, the teacher decided to send a student to mandatory study hall, held in a classroom at the end of the school day, for not having read a chapter after the teacher had urged him to do so the preceding week. And in the space of five minutes on March 4th, Mr. Reardon noticed one person who was not listening to the lecture and told the boy to see him after class, stared at one student who came in with a slip and then just backed into his seat when he saw the look on the teacher's face, and summoned a student into the corridor to give him detention for misbehavior.

35. Jim Reardon expressed his disappointment with the students involved in these incidents both individually, and to the class as a whole. A third type of encounter took on more personal overtones. When the teacher corrected a student at the time of an incident, occasionally the young man reacted angrily. When the teacher's patience had been exhausted, he also grew angry, and sharp words ensued. On February

3rd, for example, the teacher gave a detention slip to a student for being late, and the student snatched the slip from the teacher's hand. Mr. Reardon then told the student that he had just earned another detention for attitude, which only stoked the young man's defiance. He returned to his seat and sat with his arms folded for the duration of the class.

36. Students usually reacted mildly in these confrontations, but on a rare occasion, a student might not restrain himself. On February 18th, a student returned to class wearing a sweatshirt after the teacher had sent him to the office for sporting a T-shirt advertising a type of beer. The school dress code prohibited both types of shirt. As the student returned to class for the second time, the teacher went to the door of the classroom to confer with another teacher. Behind his back, the student made an obscene gesture in full view of the class, and though the teacher turned around when the class laughed, he did not observe what had taken place.

37. During the class on March 4th, Jim Reardon and a student engaged in a heated debate concerning the issue of whether homosexual teachers should be allowed to teach. After several sharp and increasingly pointed remarks had been exchanged concerning the student's failure to use moral principles in his argumentation, the student began to make a point by saying "I think" but was interrupted by Jim, who said: "I think not." After a short silence, the teacher recognized another student's question, and the first student muttered under his breath: "That's because you're a jerk, Jim."

38. While such heated exchanges represented a small portion of the interactions between teacher and students, a more pleasant tone characterized the greater number of exchanges. At the beginning of class on February 22nd, the teacher related several anecdotes from his own days as a student at St. James. Just as he began the lesson for the day, the school's disciplinarian employed the PA to summon a student to his office. One of the class members asked Jim if the disciplinarian had been strict in his day, and Jim replied that he had been exceedingly demanding. In fact, the students in the school understood some of the coded phrases utilized by this man. In particular, when the words ". . .and bring your books" came at the end of the announcement, they signaled that the disciplinarian had decided to expel the student. The class grew silent as they considered the harsh conditions that previous generations of students had faced, and Jim and the class shared the common bond of attendance at St. James in a very real fashion. Class went very well that day.

39. Jim did not emphasize his role as a teacher, or the authority he had over the students. In fact, he frequently employed humor in his class, with himself as the object of the jest. On February 24th, Jim summarized

an argument incorrectly because he had failed to listen carefully to the point the student was making about cheating. When the student glee-fully pointed this out, the teacher slapped his own wrist for not listen-ing clearly, an accusation he continually made against the students. And when he asked the students if he should cop their grades from other teachers, the class laughed enthusiastically, with some students suggest-ing that he consult with them as to which teacher's grades he should appropriate.

40. The teacher's demanding and challenging style combined with the students' attitudes on some moral questions to create a provocative, charged, and on rare occasions, hostile atmosphere in Classroom 209. Students did not blame Mr. Reardon for his frustration during the times they proved inadequate in class, but they did express surprise at his oc-casional disappointment with them concerning material he considered important:

> Today we talked about the 10 Commandments. Our class whipped them out fairly fast but it did take a little digging. . . .We could see he was fairly upset at the fact that the other classes had trouble with the big ten. I almost feel that he gets disappointed with our behav-ior.
>
> (Larry Tautolo, journal, March 1st)

The teacher's challenge met at varying times with acceptance, con-fusion and occasionally anger on the part of the students, but even those students who disliked the course, or even Jim Reardon personally, conceded that he was a fine teacher:

> I don't like class with Mr. Reardon and I don't like him. . . .But he is a great teacher.
>
> (Todd Bratton, interview, March 17th)

41. Mr. Reardon's teaching style elicited a variety of responses from the students and his three years of teaching at St. James had provided him with some pedagogical techniques to take advantage of those responses. By capitalizing on the students' competitiveness, and his own emphasis on accountability and the taking of responsibility for one's own actions, Jim Reardon managed to guide the students toward some understanding of the principles of moral decision-making, and their own responsibility in using those principles in the conduct of their lives.

Pedagogical Techniques

42. Though Mr. Reardon on several occasions brought his class together with another teacher's, either to view a film or to discuss one, he spent the overwhelming majority of his class time teaching thirty-four juniors

in Room 209. Though occasionally the students formed small groups to discuss a question and then reported back to the large group, the usual class followed a familiar pattern. Mr. Reardon began with a period of silence, in which he asked students to pray for their own intentions. This moment of silence usually evoked several public petitions from students dealing with such concerns as family problems or illness, national emergencies or issues like the mass layoffs of workers in a particular industry, and even some broader concerns such as peace in the world or an end to world hunger.

43. After taking attendance, the teacher began instruction with a statement about the topic for that day, and a reference to the homework assignment, text or class material pertinent to the discussion of that issue. After asking if students had questions, Mr. Reardon generally presented a brief summary of the state of the question, along with background material not available in the student text, *Deciding* by Michele McCarty. But his short introduction generally yielded to the style of instruction most characteristic of Mr. Reardon's class: a strong emphasis on the Socratic method, the teacher questioning the class and individual class members with a probing intensity that served several functions.

44. First, the Socratic method involved many students in the discussion and underlined Mr. Reardon's claim that each student bore the responsibility for class preparation and, in a wider sense, for all his actions. This individual questioning occasionally led to conflicts such as those mentioned previously.

45. Second, Jim Reardon did not allow the class to be too teacher-centered, but encouraged the students to respond with their opinions after he had ascertained that they had grasped the assigned material. While Mr. Reardon did express an interest in student opinion. . .some students believed that he was biased, in large part because his understanding of moral principles enabled him to "win" debates with students by the force of his argumentation. Finally, the use of the Socratic method promoted student attention, and generally prevented students from causing disciplinary problems.

46. The teacher also emphasized less traditional means of engaging the students, occasionally with marked success. On February 10th, Mr. Reardon was explaining the power of peer pressure and used a contest to exhibit that power to the students. He began by giving instructions to the students:

> *Teacher:*   Put your pens down. This is an endurance test—you
> will compete by rows. As a group, follow these

> directions: First, no noise from the row; second, sit
> straight, feet on the floor, one arm parallel to the floor,
> and one arm perpendicular. To make this worth your
> while, for your homework assignment—full credit to
> the winning team. The longest any of my other classes
> went was thirteen minutes.

Student: What's the point of the game?

Teacher: We'll talk about that later.

> (Class, February 10th)

47. The students grew eerily quiet. Not only did each one want to win
in order to avoid a homework assignment, no one wanted to fail in front
of the others in his row. When the teacher ruled that one member of a
group had broken position, he eliminated that group from the competition, and if any member of an eliminated group talked, the group received one day of detention for each person in the row, per person. No
one wanted six days of detention; no one spoke.

48. The silence bound the groups together but individualized each student. Some boys gazed stonily at the back of the boy in front of them,
while others let their eyes wander around the room. Here and there, a
student shut his eyes as if to go into a trance. As the contest continued,
the silence came to be almost palpable, as did the sore joints and stiff
necks so obviously, if quietly, endured.

49. After two minutes, Group 2 was eliminated, followed by Group 6 at
five minutes, Group 5 at seven minutes and Group 3 at eight minutes.
Groups 1 and 4 continued their noiseless contest until one boy in Group
1 uttered a groan, and broke position: Group 4 had won the battle of
wills after ten minutes and forty seconds.

50. After a round of applause all the more striking because of the silence that preceded it, Jim Reardon asked the group for reactions. The
students focused on the challenge of holding the position, even after the
pain set in, and they spoke about keeping their minds off their own dis-
comfort. When the teacher asked them the purpose of the exercise, several students shouted: "Concentration!" But Mr. Reardon replied that he
wanted to pose two questions to the students:

> First, did the group have influence? Second, did a tangible payoff
> have anything to do with it?
>
> (Jim Reardon, class, February 10th)

After graphically demonstrating the power of peer pressure, and
harnessing the competitiveness of his students, the teacher distributed a
handout concerning Christian morality: "To Be Human Is to Be Moral,
to Be Moral Is to Be Human." The linking of the group exercise with the

content of the handout hinted at a lesson for the students: that whether they made moral choices depended on how they associated with a group, and upon what constituted a tangible payoff for them as human beings.

51. The commonplaces of the curriculum did not strongly support this message, nor did they work against it; rather, they provided a backdrop of a traditional sort. The content of the course followed normal academic lines, and the approach, though more Socratic than most, was generally traditional. The classroom with its square shape, blackboards and desks resembled countless classrooms in other schools. Though the teacher did challenge the students to make this course their own, and attempted forcefully to involve the students in decision-making processes, both teachers and students realized that Jim Reardon had determined the content and the style of the class, and the students made that point with irony:

> *Teacher:* It's your course.
>
> *Student:* Great, it's our course. Now what?
> (Class, January 13th)

In most of the commonplaces, Jim did not practice innovation. . . .

52. But in a very real sense, Jim Reardon utilized the constant practice of accountability as a pedagogical technique, in a way similar to his use of Socratic questioning. The continual stream of demands for journals, studying for quizzes and tests, active participation in class and so on, reflected the teacher's commitment to his subject, and his desire for students to view moral decision-making as their normal way of living, and not as a bothersome appendix.

53. On March 2nd, for example, Mr. Reardon asked the students to write down their explanation of phrases taken from the Beatitudes in Matthew 5:3–12 on a handout he had given them. While the students bent to their task, jotting down their sentences next to phrases like "the poor in spirit," and "persecuted for the sake of right," the teacher moved about the class placing notes in his mark book. When a student asked a question, the teacher's voice took on an almost threatening quality and he impressed upon the students the need for quality and efficiency as they answered the questions.

54. Toward the end of the time allotted for the exercise, Mr. Reardon systematically called the roll and asked each student whether or not he had read the assignment necessary for completing the exercise. When he had finished his survey of the students and the tension in the class concerning grades had reached its highest level, the teacher announced that the entire assignment had been an exercise in self-study, and would not

be graded. The class expressed feelings of relief, and the implicit ac-knowledgment that the pressure of accountability had motivated them to concentrate on the assigned task. The teacher had pressured the students to perform, but then had called the exercise a self-study, presumably for the students' benefit. What lesson actually was learned is not clear.

55. By means of his strong emphasis on accountability, Jim Reardon illustrated the key points of his course. The teacher's explanation of his grading policy included the phrases: "insightful comments," "openness and critical thought," "completeness," and "willingness to share insights, questions, interpretations and observations." By stressing the need for insights into moral questions, and the value of sharing those insights with a wider community, Jim Reardon summarized his approach to moral decision-making. His method included a thorough explanation of moral principles and what contributed to the making of a moral decision, as well as an expression of the importance of tradition and community in concepts such as Ideal Human Behavior, law, infallibility, and sin. He also made a point of equating what is truly human with what is truly moral, thus emphasizing that human beings at their best acted as moral beings. (Kuntz, 1986, pp. 216-239)

I wish to comment upon a number of features in the material you have just read. First, notice that in the introductory paragraph, Kuntz provides what might be regarded as an advance-organizer (Ausubel, 1978). He sets the school he will be studying in a historical context, a context that also relates one of the schools he observed to the other. He lets readers know about the kind of people who send their children to St. James, the values they embrace, and the changes that have occurred in their values over the years. He implies that changed community expectations have consequences for the school, if not in what it emphasizes, then in what its students value. These new expectations create a tension, which Kuntz identifies, and as readers identify the tension between spiritual and rational development and success in college, the readers' interest is tapped.

From the general historical picture in paragraphs 1, 2, and 3, Kuntz moves toward greater specificity by focusing on St. James, its neighborhood, and its physical and human features. Notice here that the repetition in "row upon row, city street after city street, St. James' neighborhood retains its character by the force of its homogeneity" reinforces the literal content of the paragraph: the sameness or repetitiveness of the houses that make up its neighborhood. In this brief phrase we see how form can effectively convey the ideas the writer intends readers to grasp.

In paragraph 5 the metaphor "signal school" captures the immediately apprehended difference between the school and the houses that surround it. "Signal" works; it connotes immediacy and a radical shift in awareness. In paragraph 6 the scene Kuntz describes narrows even further. He moves from a picture of the school in its setting to the activities of those who inhabit it. The funnel, so to speak, becomes more pointed and gradually readers are given a focus that eventually, in paragraph 9, leads to the classroom and the hero of the piece, Jim Reardon. En route, small details and facts—85 per cent of the students are baptized Catholics—inspire confidence that the writer has done his homework.

Throughout the early pages Kuntz employs metaphors to give power and depth—"school structures describe an island paralleling the square blocks that encompass them, but separate, apart, and self-enclosed." And "students move from class to class through the corridors like soldiers falling in: chaotic intensity directed toward a regimented goal." The writing is metaphorically descriptive. Kuntz's aim is to describe a scene, to enable the reader to see St. James and to understand a bit of the history of expectations of those who send their children through its portals. The major substantive theme through paragraph 8 is the faculty's need to reconcile or integrate the new without losing tradition, the old. How does a school that is historically committed to spiritual values also prepare students for the instrumentally oriented life they will lead when they leave St. James? Indeed, the integration of these values without sacrificing the former to the latter is not simply a need to be met in the future, but one that exists for students and teachers at present.

Kuntz not only provides a visual picture of place, but also helps the reader become aware of a potential conflict of values—one not limited by any means to Catholic schools. Finally, in paragraph 10, Kuntz brings us directly to the course Jim Reardon is teaching, and in paragraph 11 to Classroom 209, where the scene that constitutes this chapter will unfold.

Again, Kuntz's first description of the classroom enables the reader to picture its features: "The students' desks formed a U-shaped arrangement. . . .One entered the classroom at the front of the room facing the windows: the teacher's desk lay straight ahead. . . ."

One learns of the teacher's apparent distrust of the students during quizzes, manifest in his requirement that they rearrange their desks. Kuntz reveals attributes in his description of details and candidly discloses the futility of the teacher's effort to curb cheating in a course devoted to social justice.

In paragraphs 12 and 13 Kuntz provides more detail, filling in the picture of the setting and capping it off with the astute comment that the poster "if you want peace, work for justice" was never commented upon by either students or teacher during the time he was in class. Comments such as this impress because of the subtlety of perception they reveal; not only do they display an awareness of something that might have been easily missed, they also indicate that the neglect of such material means that even well-intentioned efforts to use visuals for educational purposes might erode into neglected decoration.

In paragraph 14 Kuntz points out that according to Jim Reardon, the period after lunch is his most difficult; this is the period Kuntz chose—but he does not say why. Readers are likely to be curious and not to have their curiosity satisfied.

The comments in paragraphs 14 and 15 continue to contribute to the sense of candor the writing displays; Kuntz is apparently quite willing to reveal problems frankly. The irony expressed in paragraph 15—the interruption of a discussion of a Nazi concentration camp by the school disciplinarian, speaking over the loudspeaker, requesting teachers to "give detention slips to those in the hallway" is especially poignant.

All of the text up to this point is intended to set the stage for the substantive pedagogical description to follow. One gets a taste or glimpse of the community, the school, and the general classroom atmosphere in which the action of the chapter will emerge.

In most social situations values are complex and often compete for saliency; that is, individuals are often torn between allegiance to one value and another at odds with it. In paragraph 18 we get a sense of such a situation. Jim Reardon values school spirit and knows that school athletics are important to it. He also values solid academic work, and prayer in the classroom is a top priority for his work as a teacher. Here we find the selling of basketball tickets by student athletes interrupting a class lesson—something he wishes to protect—for school spirit, something he prizes. We glimpse the extraneous factors with which teachers must cope as they try to teach. Combined with after-lunch lethargy, Jim Reardon's task, we have no trouble imagining, is not easy. Yet his job is not atypical.

Notice also how in paragraph 20 Kuntz slips in biographical information about Jim Reardon. It is part of the flow of narrative, not a mechanical resume given "up front"; it becomes an integrated part of the picture. Its logic is organic, rather than geometric.

Notice also that when Kuntz makes general conclusions about Jim Reardon's views, he often includes short direct quotations, as in paragraphs 21 and 22, to support them. This useful technique provides evidence to support the statements and increases their credibility.

In paragraph 25 a quotation or a concrete description of the conversation Kuntz describes would have strengthened his observation. There are, of course, formal considerations limiting the number of direct quotations one can include in a narrative without losing coherence and interrupting the flow of text. The writer wants to provide neither disconnected text nor a full transcript of all that has taken place. Hence there is always selection, structure, and editing in the production of narrative. This process occurs not only in the creation of text, but also in perception itself. The trick is to provide as much detail as is necessary for meeting evidentiary requirements. The trouble is that the level of specificity deemed necessary varies with the epistemological inclinations of readers. One needs to avoid using a level of specificity that is so reductionistic and mechanistic that it trivializes what it seeks to portray or one that is so light on evidence and logic that it breeds no credibility. Kuntz's material avoids both of those pitfalls. Just how well he does so would become even more vivid if the 450-plus pages not included here were read.

In Kuntz's work the text shifts from statements that interpret or describe Jim Reardon's beliefs and attention to detail to quotations that encapsulate and support those interpretations and descriptions. Examples of this shift in focus appear throughout the text and are especially vivid in paragraphs 31, 32, 33, and 34. In paragraph 35 we have no trouble "seeing" the scene of an angry exchange and a defiant student. We learn something about Jim Reardon through such images.

Kuntz also uses subheadings to give his text focus and to alert the reader to the chapter's orientation. All writers of educational criticism have to cope with organizing their text. How can one structure a narrative that makes it possible for readers to understand the scene? A chronological account might do, but it might not be best. The critic has experienced a myriad of events, his or her notes of these events are likely to be full, other sources of data have been secured; the task is to create a coherent narrative that illuminates the classroom or school or teacher. Kuntz has decided to focus on topics that he believes are important in *this* particular work and to organize these topics from the top down, that is, from the general to the particular. Although we do not get a sense of chronology, we do learn about the dimensions of the situation that Kuntz believes are important.[3]

One other point. Good educational criticism requires good writing. It is very difficult for an unskilled writer to reveal the qualities of classroom life in narrative. Kuntz writes well. The language flows, the paragraphs relate to each other. We have no difficulty understanding the text. Kuntz's writing is not offered as the most expressive, aesthetic, or artistic one might read in this genre, but it is felicitous, more than enough so to help the reader see and understand the situation about which he writes.

Notes

1. Although it is clear that interest in qualitative inquiry in education has grown considerably in the past two decades, most of this interest has emerged among researchers who analogize such inquiry to one of the social sciences, especially anthropology, or who attempt to reduce qualitative forms of inquiry to a soft form of positivism. There are relatively few scholars who have related their work

to the arts and humanities. Maxine Greene, Madeline Grumet, William Pinar, Robert Donmoyer, Tom Barone, and Gail McCutcheon are among those few. I anticipate that the move toward the arts and humanities as sources for methods for the study of educational practice will continue to grow as deeper understanding is developed concerning the relationship between methods and what can be learned from their use.

2. One way in which critics, like artists, call our attention to what we have not noticed is through "defamiliarization." By using a striking metaphor or creating a fresh connection for putting an object, process, or idea into a new context, critics cause us to sit up and take notice. Such decontextualization defamiliarizes us with the subject matter addressed, and hence we are more likely to see it freshly.

3. The analysis in which I have just engaged can be regarded as a meta-criticism of Kuntz's work. I have provided a kind of criticism of a criticism. In some ways this is like a meta-analysis of an experimental, correlational, or statistical report. Its aim is to explicate further what has been explained, to understand the strategies and tactics used by the writer, and to appraise their adequacies, particularly with respect to the conventional studies: the problem of assessing "conclusions," or themes as I have called them, is often more complex and more subtle. These themes typically pervade the language that the critic uses as the critic attempts to describe the features of a situation. The very act of selecting which features to attend to is both evaluative and interpretive. It is evaluative since one normally does not attempt to describe what one believes is trivial. It is interpretive since the significance of an event is related to the kind of meaning one secures from it.

Chapter VIII

The Meaning of Method in Qualitative Inquiry

The denial of complexity is the beginning of tyranny

Anonymous

The Primacy of Judgment

For readers who seek a procedure, a formula, or a set of rules for doing qualitative inquiry, this chapter will be a disappointment. I know of no "method" for the conduct of qualitative inquiry in general or for educational criticism in particular. There is no codified body of procedures that will tell someone how to produce a perceptive, insightful, or illuminating study of the educational world. Unfortunately—or fortunately—in qualitative matters cookbooks ensure nothing.

What I can provide in this chapter are some of the considerations that can be taken into account when studying some aspect of the educational world: how schools operate, how teachers teach, what students do in their free time in school, what kind of ideas are examined in classrooms, and what sort of values are promulgated by textbooks and other instructional materials. The considerations addressed in this chapter should be treated as an array of heuristics, not a set of algorithms. They are born of experience working in schools, but they provide no road to certain success.

The reason for the paucity of methodological prescriptions is related to the nature of qualitative inquiry itself. First, qualitative inquiry places a high premium on the idiosyncratic, on the exploitation of the researcher's unique strengths, rather than on standardization and uniformity. Hence, investigators who study schools or classrooms and who engage in that craft called field work will do things in ways that makes sense to them, given the problem in which they are interested, the aptitude they possess, and the context in which they work.

Second, all forms are influenced by style, and since style is personal, an inevitable personal dimension enters into qualitative work—a dimension that conventional research methodology typically tries to minimize. In qualitative inquiry, personal stylistic features are neither liabilities nor elements that are easily replicable. Qualitative inquirers confer their own signature on their work.

Third, qualitative research often takes weeks, months, or even years to conduct. It is simply not possible to predict the flow of events as they unfold, so researchers must adjust their course of action based upon emerging conditions that could not have been anticipated. As in a basketball game, spectators might have some reasonable expectations about what they are likely to see, but the particular events on the court are impossible to predict. How players respond depends upon the state of play itself; they might do one thing with twenty minutes left and quite another two minutes from the final buzzer. Thus, qualitative inquiry works best if researchers remain aware of the emerging configurations and make appropriate adjustments accordingly. A preformulated plan of procedure indifferent to emerging conditions is the surest path to disaster.[1]

Flexibility, adjustment, and iterativity are three hallmarks of qualitative "method." Even aims may change in the course of inquiry, depending upon what happens in the situation. Such an attitude toward method is diametrically opposed to the aspiration to bring everything under control so that effects can be unambiguously explained.

Fourth, my conception of method also implies that it is as unreasonable as it is unwise to expect qualitative research proposals to take on the kind of finality and specificity we often see in research proposals using quantitative methods. The idea that one knows beforehand what the significant variables are and can predict their magnitude in cells describing the anticipated effects of some treatment is simply inappropriate for qualitative research. This does not mean that there is no rhyme or reason to qualitative research, but rather that the course of its development is contingent upon the features of a future no one can fully anticipate. Qualitative inquiry requires a considerable faith that researchers will be sensitive to the significant and able to make the right moves in context. It means that the lines for the research will be less specific; more is left to opportunism and the adventitious. As in a good conversation, one listens to the other, and how, when, and what one says depends upon what the other has said.

Again, this introduction to method is not an apologia for sloppy planning or wishful thinking; it is a recognition that qualitative inquiry participates in a conceptual paradigm that does not aim to control variables in a laboratory-like setting in order to identify the contribution of each variable to the effects achieved. Its function is to highlight the complexity of such work and its dependency on the sensibilities and good judgment of the qualitative researcher. There are no routines to prescribe, no rules to direct one's steps, no algorithms to calculate. There are desires, flexible aims, and the need to remain in touch with what's important.

Access: Getting and Keeping It

The most obvious and significant locales for qualitative research in education are schools and classrooms. Access to schools and classrooms is not something that one can take for granted.

At one time in the history of American education it was comparatively easy for researchers from universities to locate schools and classrooms in which to collect data. The researchers' status was substantially higher than the teachers', and teachers usually offered little or no resistance to entry. The researchers' presence in schools or classrooms was usually brief, and their findings were often so abstract that the anonymity of teachers or students was pretty much assured. More often than not it was the experiment that was being tested, not the students or the school, and it was the experimenter who assumed responsibility for the experiment, not the teacher.

In qualitative research this is no longer true. Researchers do not typically hit and run; they stick around (Becker, 1986). The teacher and school are no longer faceless abstractions, they are often identifiable, even with pseudonyms—hence they are at risk. And finally, teachers are less willing than they once were to tolerate unilateral decision-making that affects them. Their willingness to cooperate with a researcher is often predicated upon quid pro quo; teachers justifiably expect some return for the access they provide.[2]

One would think that the provision of feedback on the basis of what a researcher has learned about a school or classroom would have been a standard and reasonable practice. It is provided less frequently than we might wish to believe, and for several reasons. First, researchers typically focus on journals read by other members of the research community rather than on the teachers and school administrators who made the study possible. Second, the form in which research reports are written is frequently incomprehensible to practitioners unfamiliar with technical jargon or statistics. Third, practitioners often expect little from researchers; teachers often regard the relevance of the researcher's work as marginal—a belief confirmed, it seems, by their days as students in teacher-training programs. For some practitioners the motive for allowing researchers access is not that they expect results that will help them modify their own practices, but that variety is interesting and association with a university is a sign of being forward-looking.

The net result of these expectations is that education has been, and is in large measure today, a bifurcated field. Researchers get brownie points for technical publications, and practitioners focus on the practical, paying little attention to research journals or research reports, aside from occasionally using their distilled and translated findings to legitimate what they already believe. Thus the issue regarding access is part of a still larger issue concerning the power relationship of researchers to practitioners. For the most part, teachers see researchers in their schools and classrooms as strangers in their midst rather than as colleagues with whom they can work. I am happy to say that this kind of relationship, which is still dominant in teacher-professor relationships, is beginning to change, largely as a result of the growing interest among university researchers in the nature of educational practice (Atkin, Kennedy, and Patrick, 1989) and in part because of the increased professional self-esteem and autonomy of teachers.

Access is a delicate matter. We need the consent of those we study in order to do our work. They ought to understand, as far as we can explain, the aims of the research and how the study is to proceed. They ought to know what they, as people who provide consent, may expect as an outcome of the work. By this I do not mean that an educational critic or any other qualitative researcher is in a position at the outset to tell a teacher precisely what will be learned. If the results were known in advance, the study would be unnecessary. But practitioners should know how feedback, if any, will be provided and to what uses the research will be put.

There is, of course, a special difficulty in meeting such commitments in qualitative research. Because the qualitative researcher is devoting substantial time to the study of a situation, and because human situations change, it is often difficult to know if the aims or intentions formulated in advance will remain relevant, interesting, or important later on. And because qualitative research typically develops a focus gradually, clarity of aim is not its hallmark at the initial stages of inquiry. Thus it is better for researchers to provide a general rather than a specific description of aims, if for no other reason than so they can shift gears when necessary. This practice does not imply deception; it implies some degree of appropriate flexibility and the understanding that in matters as unpredictable as schools and classrooms it is typically difficult to know in advance exactly what issues are most significant in any particular situation. Thus, gaining access is accompanied by tension. On the one hand, researchers want, as far as possible, to help those who provide access to understand the aims of the enterprise and the methods, time, and obligations that both parties incur. On the other hand, in qualitative studies, researchers take their cues from what emerges; it is not unusual for qualitative researchers to have only a general, even a vague, idea about the directions or course of action they will take until they experience the setting. In a way, the form and focus a qualitative study may gradually take are closer to the creation of a collage than to the construction of a building. A finished collage depends upon in-process decisions made because of the look of the configuration as it unfolds. In constructing a building one follows specifications. In a collage, the artist controls the qualities and is cued by them. In a school the qualities "unfurl" and the qualitative researcher sees and selects.

Regardless of unpredictability, gaining access by providing information to those working in the setting is critical. How researchers go about securing permission varies with the situation, but in a school district, permission from the superintendent—and even at times from the school board—may be necessary. Such permission increases the probability that permission will be provided in turn by the principal and by the teachers. In a large study of six high schools (Eisner, 1985c) that I conducted, I not only secured permission from the superintendents of six school districts and the principals of the schools, but in each case asked to meet with the entire high school faculty to describe the study and to ask for their cooperation. To secure faculty assent in a confidential way in one school, I sent each faculty member a postcard, addressed to me, to be returned anonymously with his or her vote. I did not want to invade their school with a bevy of graduate research assistants to observe their classrooms without their strong consent—which was, in fact, secured.

Must all qualitative researchers seek permission from the entire faculty before beginning their work? No, if the study does not require the participation of all of them. The general "rule" is that researchers should seek the consent of those whom they expect to provide information or to be observed. Even here, judgment is necessary. If contact is indirect or very brief—say, a simple conversation during a part of an hour—consent for the study as a whole may not be necessary from everyone. Individuals who elect not to provide assistance can make their wishes known when asked. In the case I described earlier, all of the teachers were candidates for observation, hence permission was sought from all, and although no teacher objected to being observed, had one done so I would have honored his or her request, regardless of "biasing the sample."

In another study in which I was co–principal investigator (Eisner and Walker, 1988), the school district was the recipient of foundation funds, and we had been asked by the foundation to conduct a qualitative evaluation of the program. In this case, we did not seek specific permission from each teacher, since it was a part of the school district's agreement with the foundation that access would be provided. Different situations call for different criteria and different procedures. Insensitivity to the feelings of those observed, however, regardless of invitations by foundations, courts disaster.

In seeking access to a school or classroom initially researchers may need to rely upon the principal for approval of the project or study as a whole, but obtaining permission from teachers is another matter. In general, researchers are their own best advocate for convincing teachers that the study is important. It is dangerous to try to secure permission by having a principal or someone else describe a study to teachers, for several reasons. First, the description may not be accurate. Second, the principal may not be enthusiastic. Third, the answers given to teachers' questions may not be the ones the researcher would want to give. And perhaps most important, one never knows what image of the researcher teachers or others hold. Is this researcher going to be supportive and sympathetic or hostile and suspicious? Is there a hidden agenda behind the research? Does the researcher "understand" students and teachers? The best person to allay such fears is the researcher. After the principal has given tentative approval, the researcher should talk directly with the teachers.

Two factors that often emerge during the course of work in a school are potential sources of difficulty. First, teachers may expect the researcher to become a kind of teacher's assistant in the classroom; students, especially young ones, may also develop such expectations. Second, teachers may make requests, often subtle, for evaluative feedback: "How am I doing?" or "What do you think of my teaching?"

It is often the wiser course of action not to accede to these requests. Assuming responsibility as a teacher's aide can distract the researcher from attending to what is important for the study; giving immediate feedback to the teacher is fine when the evaluation is positive, but can be disastrous for the study when it is negative. Furthermore, if qualitative researchers are interested in the way things are in *typical* circumstances, their presence in a classroom creates some degree of atypicality—which will only be exacerbated by their functioning as a coach to the teacher or as a source of approbation.

Keeping access is as delicate as getting it. One way to maintain access is not to forget that on the site, in all interactions, researchers are first and foremost students of the situation: virtually everything can be data. Agreement on the researchers' role during the course of the observation is also important. They should make it clear, for example, that the reason they can't be a teacher's aide is not that they want to avoid work, but that they could be seriously distracted from what they need to see.

In describing such understandings between the researcher and the teacher, I should make two other observations. First, there may be situations in which functioning as a teacher's aide is appropriate and useful. Nothing replaces judgment in deciding what is appropriate in particular situations. My recommendations are to be interpreted as general ones. Second, the way in which mutual understanding and agreements are reached between the researcher and the teacher is very important. Researchers can generate both anxiety and awkward formality by approaching practitioners with an attitude that reeks of a legal and binding contract: they need to be moderately clear, appropriately general, and personally supportive rather than stiff, formal, and highly specific. Interpersonal comfort and mutual trust are the critical elements.

Access is influenced by both the manner in which people are approached and the understandings and agreements that are reached with them. Increasingly, practitioners expect, as is their right, some benefit from those they allow in. In earlier days, association with a university research project was thought to be sufficient payment. This is seldom enough today. Agreements, I have indicated, need to be sufficiently general so as not to tie one to aims and procedures that fetter after one enters the field.

Yet, they should be clear enough to give those observed a decent understanding of what the researcher is interested in. I know this is something of a tightrope to walk, but I cannot provide greater specificity; the context must be taken into account.

Sometimes access is made conditional on review of the study's results by the individual or group studied. Because qualitative studies often focus on individual schools, the reputation of the school or particular teachers can be at stake. What rights, if any, do those studied have to review the material written in advance of its public dissemination? Here we enter difficult waters. I believe that copies of the research product should be shared with the relevant parties before they are made public. I believe their reaction should be solicited. I believe the researcher or evaluator should consider what they have to say. But in the final analysis, the decision to disseminate or publicize should rest with the researcher. The researcher should assume responsibility for what is said, even if those studied do not concur with matters of fact or interpretation.[3]

Once researchers agree to give others a veto power, their intellectual integrity is compromised—even if they are mistaken. Researchers have the right to be mistaken. A researcher can elect to provide practitioners with an opportunity to prepare a rejoinder to the report and to have it included, but giving someone else the right of approval or disapproval as a condition for dissemination is to undermine the competence of the writer whose name is on the work.

Finally, with respect to access, another dimension needs to be considered, not because it affects the researcher currently on the site, but because it will affect the opportunities others have to work on the site. I speak of what campers call "leaving the site clean." The affective state with which a researcher leaves a field site—the feeling of well-being and satisfaction the participants experience—can have a large influence on whether they will allow others to work there. Practically, one must attend to the matter of human relations, especially, but not only, during the closing periods of the research. Researchers must keep promises, provide feedback, clear up their own paperwork, tie up loose ends, express thanks, and take general care for the way they depart. Guests in our home who leave their sleeping quarters and the bathroom in a state of disarray are not likely to be welcomed back.[4]

Alas, it is easier to straighten up sleeping quarters and to leave the bathroom clean than it sometimes is to leave a school principal or a teacher happy. If, for example, the school principal provided permission for the study in the expectation that what the researcher had to say about the school would bring accolades from all who read it, if the principal's motive was political, and if the researcher's results lean in the opposite direction, the principal may very well be unhappy. It is unlikely that even a physically clean site would recompense for damage to the school's reputation and the principal's ego. One way to avoid such a feeling is for the researcher to say nothing but positive things about the school; in short, to omit everything that does not contribute to a positive school image. Acceding to such expectations would be engaging in a public relations campaign, not conducting a qualitative study.

These matters are tough. I mention them here because they come with the territory. Since I believe that *educational* researchers have a responsibility to appraise the educational merits of practice, a picture of only the positive side when there are other sides as well is an abrogation of that responsibility. Furthermore, the aspiration to be "neutral" is inherently flawed; there is no neutrality, even when one decides to be descriptive. One *chooses* what to describe. To conduct educational research, especially qualitative research, is to have to deal with these difficult moments. It is better to anticipate them at the outset than to be taken by surprise.

What to Look for: Prefigured and Emergent Foci

Once access has been secured, how do researchers decide what to look for in a classroom or school? What is worth paying attention to? There are no standard answers to such questions, although it is possible to identify—as I have done in chapter 5—dimensions of schooling that could be candidates for attention. Those dimensions are the *intentional*, the *structural*, the *curricular*, the *pedagogical*, and the *evaluative*.[5] It is also true that although one could enter a school or classroom with a specific observational target, what I call a *prefigured focus*, one can also allow the situation to speak for itself, that is, to allow for an *emergent focus*.

In a prefigured focus, for example, a researcher might decide to look for the ways in which competition or cooperation is fostered in the school or classroom. The researcher might be interested in the frequency, form, and quality of dialogue in a social studies class, or the way in which the structure of the school day influences the ways in which teachers plan their lessons. In each case a focus is selected and becomes the major object of the observer's attention. Everything that bears upon that objective is a candidate for interpretation.

Researchers can formulate a prefigured focus independently or in concert with teachers or school administrators who might want particular feedback on aspects of their teaching or school, about which there is some interest or concern. A teacher might, for example, want to know whether he talks too much, whether enough "space" is provided to students for comments, or whether students are treated fairly in his classroom. Such a focus can serve as the major object of attention or as a part of a prefigured agenda. Providing feedback on aspects of teaching or schools that are identified by teachers and administrators as important can contribute significantly to the quid pro quo I described earlier.

When there is a prefigured focus, the emergence of the unanticipated can command special attention. One of my students decided to observe a high school English teacher to determine the kind of critical approach she brought to the analysis of literature: Was her focus on the formal structure of the novel, on the kind of experience it generated in students, on its historical features or genre, or on its message and its relevance for the students' world? During the course of observation, it became clear that the teacher employed a great deal of irony in her teaching. She was not teaching irony in literature; the teacher herself used irony as a pedagogical device.

If we were to consult the *Handbook on Research on Teaching* (Wittrock, 1986) or the *Education Abstracts* (1988), we would find no entries under "irony in teaching." It simply was not a feature that my student could have predicted, yet it was a major feature of this teacher's performance. In this case, the focus shifted from the study of the novel to the use of irony in teaching. Openness to such qualities is often very revealing. Such openness leads to what Dewey has called *flexible purposing* (Dewey, 1938), as contrasted with fealty to a predefined set of objectives. Knowing when it is appropriate to shift gears and when to acknowledge the surprises of observation makes for both good science and good art.

Although one might understand why a term as seemingly remote as *irony* might not be listed in *Education Abstracts*, it is more difficult to understand why the term *artistry* is not listed in the seven-pound *Third Handbook of Research on Teaching*. Although the index of that monumental volume contains over eight hundred entries, art and artistry are nowhere to be found, *except* under the teaching of art, as contrasted with the art of teaching. Its omission signals further that artistry in teaching or the art of teaching has been removed somehow from research on teaching.

The Virtues and Vices of an Observation Schedule

An observation schedule specifies the variables or dimensions that the observer is to attend to. Once these variables or dimensions have been specified, rating scales are often designed to accompany them: outstanding, good, average, below average, and inadequate, or some version of the foregoing. The observer observes and then checks the appropriate box. If more than one observer does this, interrater reliability can be determined. For some purposes such a procedure can be useful. If what one wants to know is how many times something has occurred, a frequency count is just fine. Roger Shuy's study of William Bennett's teaching, which appears in chapter 6, is a good example of how frequency counts, along with interpretive commentary, can be intelligently used. But if one wants to describe or interpret the meaning, the relevance, or the appropriateness of something, using numbers and other highly reductionistic markers is likely to be less than helpful. Although a list of observable variables, features, or dimensions can be formulated and used to provide an abbreviated record momentarily, researchers should not be lulled into the false sense of security of believing that such a record is all that they need. First, the variables identified before they enter the scene may not be the ones that are the most educationally significant. Second, it is usually not the incidence of an event that gives it significance, but its quality and its relationship to the context in which it functions. Counting the incidence of isolated features may obscure rather than reveal what is important in the setting.[6] Third—and this has to do with recording rather than with focus—the idea that the qualities of a classroom or a school can be disclosed by "pointer readings" is questionable to say the least.

Keeping these caveats in mind one can choose to focus on the following dimensions or factors in classroom observation: the quality of the content being taught, the variety of forms of representation employed, the kinds of incentives employed, and the quality and form of student engagement. We will consider each in turn.

The Quality of the Content Being Taught

Surprisingly, the quality of the content being taught is frequently neglected in classroom observation. The reason, I think, is that those who observe teachers are often not specialists in the subject matter being taught and focus therefore on what the teacher and students do. Yet, as I have indicated earlier, the quality of what is taught is of crucial importance. It is no virtue teaching content that is trivial, regardless of how skilled the teaching is: what is not worth teaching is not worth teaching well.

In appraising the content, one can also look for the extent to which what is taught is made relevant to ideas in other content areas or to issues and situations outside of the school.

The line between content and process is not altogether clear. Indeed, the line is difficult to draw because how one teaches and what students do as a result are mediated by the activity through which the content is construed by students. If a biology teacher teaches so that students learn a set of significant ideas through a method that requires them to experiment, the meaning of the ideas learned is likely to be different from "the same" ideas learned as a part of an exercise studying textbook conclusions. The processes through which ideas are grasped and understood, which themselves are influenced by the conditions of teaching, give meaning to the content learned. Hence, *how* something is taught and *what* is taught are, from an experiential perspective, part of the same whole. One can attend to both the separable and the experiential, inseparable aspects of content.[7]

The Variety of Forms of Representation Employed

The world is presented to us as an array of qualities we learn to experience. Meaning is construed from those qualities by virtue of the experiences their features generate. These experiences provide the content for the forms of representation humans have learned to use to convey what they have experienced. These forms of representation can be visual, auditory, or kinesthetic, as well as discursive, poetic, figurative, and numeric. Their social counterparts are the visual arts, music, dance, science, poetry, literature, and mathematics in its various forms. Each type of representation emphasizes and makes accessible particular aspects of content. What we can convey through pictures or diagrams is often difficult or impossible to convey in words, and vice versa. What can be said through poetry cannot be said in prose (Langer, 1942; Goodman, 1976; Arnheim, 1986). Thus, the choice of forms of representation used by a teacher to help students understand, say, the Civil War, can have a major influence on what children have an opportunity to learn (Epstein, 1989). First, the kind of meaning students can secure is influenced by the forms of representation through which that meaning is constructed. Mathew Brady's Civil War photographs and the literary character of Lincoln's Gettysburg Address make unique kinds of meanings possible. Second, the modes of thinking children employ are influenced by the kinds of tasks in which they have an opportunity to engage. Each form of representation imposes its own cognitive requirements and requires its own skills (Eisner, 1982). The abilities needed to read or to create a musical score or an abstract painting are not the same. The ability to read a scientific account of the world is in important respects different from reading poetry or a historical novel. Third, the kinds of abilities and interests children have are relevant to their ability to cope constructively with content within a form of representation. Those who are interested or skilled in the use of visual forms of representation may be advantaged if material is presented to the class visually. Educational equity is more likely if the forms of representation are diverse rather than restricted. If the forms are restricted, those whose aptitudes and interests are relevant to the form emphasized will have an advantage over those whose aptitudes are neglected.[8]

In sum, it is important to attend to the array of forms of representation employed in a class because of the different kinds of meaning that each provides and the different kinds of thinking skills each develops, and because educational equity is likely to increase as the diversity of forms grows. Aside from Epstein's work (1989) and ongoing work by Singer

(1990) this area has received little empirical attention in the context of classrooms.

The Kinds of Incentives Employed in the Classroom

One major concern among those who teach is to maintain an appropriately high level of student motivation. One classical approach to matters of motivation is the use of the carrot and the stick. In the main, for primary school-age children, "carrot" incentive systems are prevalent. Praise by the teacher, brownie points, stars, and special privileges are all used to motivate and to maintain interest. Consider the following example:

Learning for the Sake of. . .

> Brenham, Texas middle school pupils who study hard will get more than good grades this month. They'll be taking home engraved watches and pens.
> A school incentive program bankrolled by businesses will reward eighth-graders who have maintained a 90-point average for $2\frac{1}{2}$ years with a $120 watch with a custom clock face.
> Under a similar program, the top sixth- and seventh-grade students in the Brenham School District will get engraved pens. And the student with the most dramatic increase in grade average also will receive a watch. (Palo Alto *Times Tribune*, February 9, 1988)

Some classroom teachers, in contrast, use a stick approach, employing something called aversive discipline (1980). The teacher writes the rules of classroom decorum on the blackboard and adjacent to them lists penalties for their infraction; this arrangement is something like a contract that students have no opportunity to negotiate. By making explicit the rules and consequences for breaking them, teachers standardize and rationalize expectations and penalties.

Yet standardization and rationalization of rules and consequences can interfere with learning about arbitration, negotiation, and the contextualization of actions. Furthermore, emphasis on rewards and penalties—"carrots" and "sticks"—can undermine deeper and sounder motives for action. A systematically employed extrinsic reward system may hook children on point acquisition as the major motive for study (Lepper & Greene, 1978). The threat of negative consequences can lead to the same result. The pedagogical trick is to arrange learning activities so that the incentives for learning are intrinsic to the activity. This is not the place to delve deeply into issues pertaining to incentives for learning and their consequences. Suffice it to say that the kind of incentives that are generally used are consequential and that attention to their form and effects is an important aspect of the study of schools.[9]

The Quality and Form of Student Engagement

One of the most common and disheartening findings about schools and classrooms is that they are boring places to be (Goodlad, 1984). While no one expects schools or classrooms to have the constant spirit of a Broadway musical, the idea that students should spend their childhood bored by school should at least give us pause. Must schools be that way? In fact, one of the most important and satisfying features of intellectual life is that it is exciting. When we talk with people who are intellectually engaged in what they do, there is an unmistakable sense of excitement in their voices, in their animation, and in the intensity with which they talk about their work; indeed, their excitement is often contagious. For such people satisfaction is intrinsic to their work.

I believe that the analysis and description of student engagement is an important dimension of the life of schooling. Students who are bored by what they study, unenthusiastic, and reluctant to act without reward are students we might well worry about. Hence, attention to the quality and form of student engagement is a nontrivial dimension of schooling and one that can justifiably command our attention.

One index of engagement is the students' voluntary activity. Do students come to school early? Would they rather work on classroom projects than go out to recess? Are they reluctant to leave at the end of the day? Do they choose to work on classroom projects during their free periods? Even so brief a list of questions suggests how formidable an array of criteria they would be for appraising the educational quality of classrooms and schools. We typically neglect such considerations and look at standardized achievement test scores as the main, if not sole, index of educational quality. Yet how students feel about what they are doing, as expressed in their actions, gestures, expressions, and comportment, is among the most robust and significant outcomes of schooling. If students are disengaged or do not like what they have studied, they are not likely to pursue it without compulsion.

The potential candidates for researchers' attention in schools and classrooms could constitute a veritable laundry list. Here, I will identify some of the aspects of school and classroom life that have been and could be important subjects for observation. Obviously, this list is illustrative, not comprehensive.

1. Wait time. How much time does the teacher provide for students to think about and elaborate their responses to a teacher-formulated question?
2. Academic engaged time. How much time during the school day is devoted to activities that are unambiguously academic (often more difficult to discern than one might suspect!)?

3. The character of the tasks, questions, and problems in which students are engaged.

4. The degree to which students are encouraged to define and structure their own problems in class.

5. The incidence of discussion, debate, and intelligent argument in class.

6. The prevalence, quality, and outcomes of small group activities.

7. The degree to which students participate in the formulation of solutions to problems of classroom disorder created by themselves and their peers.

8. The extent to which the teacher uses teaching routines that minimize the time needed to deal with nonintellectual and nonacademic matters.

9. The way teachers cope with excessive demands upon their time during the school day.

10. The relationships that are established between the various subjects students study and the way teachers facilitate such relationships.

One problem with such lists is that each item by itself is an isolated bit, independent of a framework or theoretical structure that would give it intellectual significance. What one elects to look for depends upon both the focus brought to the setting and the insistence of the setting upon the observer. Focus is deliberately formulated, while the setting insinuates itself into the observer's consciousness when the observer is open and the features of the setting are compelling. A *mere* list neither enjoys the benefit of purpose nor is necessarily relevant to the unique features of the setting observed.

Sources and Types of Data

Making sense of schools and classrooms is enhanced by paying attention to the variety of phenomena that emerge on their own and by setting up the conditions that elicit information that is unlikely to emerge directly. It also profits from looking for information in unexpected places. In general, the richest vein of information is struck through direct observation of school and classroom life. What people do and say, and how they do and say it, are prime candidates for attention. We live in a situation and try, by being self-conscious of our own experience and its relationship to the phenomenal world, to make sense of the complex social scene in which we live. These observations profit from a special kind of perception.

In ordinary circumstances, being situated in a state of affairs means essentially that the events will wash over us; we are often not particularly conscious of life as lived—ordinary experience is part of the ebb and flow of being. When we are functioning as connoisseurs, it is important to focus our attention on two targets: one of these is the events themselves, the other is what those events do to our experience. Obviously these two targets are not separable in the way I have suggested. I make the distinction because I wish to highlight the importance of being conscious of the experience we undergo and relating that experience to the qualities in the situation. This awareness provides the stuff out of which educational criticism is built. Thus, the kind of consciousness I am referring to is a kind of enlightened self-consciousness. Our ordinary experience is not characterized by such an acute level of awareness.

The Use of Interviews

Second in importance to direct observation is the use of the interview. We need to listen to what people have to say about their activities, their feelings, their lives. How does a teacher feel about the new evaluation system that the state has mandated and does she expect it to affect her teaching? If so, in what ways? If not, why not? How did another teacher choose the activities he asked the students to engage in? Where did the activities come from? What will he do with the results? What relevance do students construe from their work in class and what do they think is important in the material they are studying? What do teachers do with their free time after school? How much of it do they have? Do they have a second job? Do they need to have a second job in order to get by financially?

It is surprising how much people are willing to say to those whom they believe are really willing to listen. In the main, interviews need not—indeed, should not—be formal, questionnaire-oriented encounters. The aim is for the interviewer to put the person at ease, to have some sense of what he or she wants to know, but not to be either rigid or mechanical in method. It is wiser not to use a tape recorder for the first interview (and if it is necessary, one should always ask for permission to do so). Conducting a good interview is, in some ways, like participating in a good conversation: listening intently and asking questions that focus on concrete examples and feelings rather than on abstract speculations, which are less likely to provide genuinely meaningful information. Asking a teacher to describe briefly his or her philosophy of education is likely to elicit pious, canned proclamations that seem as though they had been snatched from a third-rate philosophy of education text. It is usually better to focus the interviewees' attention on the things they have done. It is often useful for researchers to ask teachers to explain something they said in class—the way they introduced a topic, responded to a student, or selected an issue for discussion.

Interviews can be conducted in the most unlikely and the most ordinary of places: in hallways, walking to the teachers' lounge, in cars, over lunch, on the parking lot, between classes—in fact, anywhere people are willing to talk about what they think or feel. In one qualitative study I conducted (Eisner, 1985c), each research assistant shadowed a high school student for a two-week period every day from 8:30 A.M. to 3:30 P.M. The twenty-one students who were shadowed provided both guidance and a passport to what was going on. Research assistants accompanied the students to classes and participated with them and their peers in social contexts outside of classes. They were able to secure an intimate glimpse of the school through the eyes of these high school students. While no formal interviews were conducted with most students, substantial interview information was secured. In addition, these students provided unusual access to the school—to the "sidelawners," to the jocks, to students of color, and to the mainstream.[10]

Documents and Artifacts

Another important source of information about schools and classrooms is the records and artifacts that frequently reveal what people will not or cannot say. Consider, for example, the kinds of tests that teachers construct or the sorts of homework that students are assigned. These artifacts, often available to researchers for the asking, provide a kind of operational definition of what teachers value. Tests presumably represent what the teacher believes is important. What kinds of content are students held responsible for? What kinds of questions are raised on the test? What kinds of answers are to be provided, and what responses are considered adequate? How much feedback is given to students? In what forms, if at all, are students asked to correct their responses? All of these questions point toward data that can reveal much about incentives and the values that are expressed in any particular classroom. It is one thing to proclaim that high-level cognitive skills are valued, and quite another to reinforce recall through tests that elicit and reward it. Indeed, two of the most significant indices of educational values are the kinds of content and processes that are elicited through the assessment instruments used, and the kinds of responses that are considered acceptable. Such features have much to say about what teachers and test makers value and what is conveyed as important to students.

Like tests, workbooks and homework assignments are rich sources of information about classrooms. What are students being asked to work on? How much time is required to complete homework assignments? And perhaps most important, how much and what kind of feedback is provided to students by teachers, and how long do students wait for it?

Artifacts such as these are frequently mute but telling testimony to the tasks teachers believe important or feel obliged to emphasize. They provide what Webb and colleagues have referred to as *unobtrusive measures* (1981), the indirect surrogates for values, expectations, and behaviors that might otherwise be difficult to see and assess.

Lest this identification of specific data sources become fragmented and atomic, I should emphasize that the context as a whole is a primary source of information; actions within it constitute a subtext that can reveal the meanings people share within that context. A quality observed or a datum secured becomes a meaningful source of information as it fits into or relates to a larger constellation of events or materials. In general, researchers look for large patterns, and when such patterns are hard to locate, individual occurrences are rendered meaningful by their place in smaller, more limited configurations.

The array of events and artifacts that can be used as a source of data is limited only by the researcher's sensitivity and insight: Announcements posted in rooms and hallways, posters that display forthcoming events, graffiti, locations on the school campus of various social groups, the voluntary seating arrangements in the lunch room or the assembly hall, and other such potentially telling indicators *become* data depending upon the questions put to them and the meaning the researcher construes from them.

School records, newspapers, and community statistics relevant to the issues a researcher wishes to address are also potentially relevant resources for generating a context in which meaning can be deepened. The use of multiple forms of data, as I indicated in chapter 5, tends to provide the material that contributes to credible interpretation. What is deemed relevant in such an effort depends upon the connections one is able to construct. Those, in turn, depend upon perceptivity and imagination.

Imagination might seem to be an oddity in a section describing relevant data sources. It is not. Information *becomes* data only if a researcher is able to make it meaningful. Without imagination, we are situated in the "booming, buzzing confusion" that William James described. It is imagination that gives the world nameable categories that package what might otherwise be unexperienced or chaotic: Goffman's "Flooding Out" (1961) and "Rules of Irrelevance" (1961); Weber's democratic, charismatic, and authoritarian forms of leadership (1968); Adorno's authoritarian personality (1950); and Freud's id, ego, and superego (1933) are examples of the work of the imagination in conferring order and providing meaning. These constructs give coherence to what would otherwise be little more than disconnected bits and pieces. When we try to formulate theoretical structures so that these and other constructs "fit," the imaginative tasks become even greater. Imagination—the creation of images—traverses the line from construing relationships among "simple" component qualities to the creation of grand models of mind and culture. Imagination is an absolutely essential resource in the conduct of any kind of research. When the data are messy, the processes studied unpredictable, and the contingencies complex, imagination enables us to make sense out of the situation. Without it research is likely to be pedestrian; with it, insightful and cogent. To the extent to which theory is made—a "fictio," as Geertz (1973) calls it—, theoretical interpretation is a fiction, something we make to satisfy our rationality and to help us get on with our lives. In the making, imagination is at work.

There is another point, one that I made earlier but wish to reiterate, about imagination and theory as it pertains to qualitative research. The kind of theory one uses to explain or interpret qualitative material can be derived from a variety of social sciences and philosophic disciplines. Political scientists, for example, attend to qualitative phenomena and try to describe and interpret those phenomena through concepts germane to political science, such as power, treaty, alignment, bloc, and so forth; psychologists interpret human behavior through psychological concepts, such as ego strength, reinforcement, aptitude, cognitive dissonance; anthropologists have developed concepts appropriate for their disciplinary aims, such as enculturation, mores, kin, nuclear family, emic and etic, and the like. The same can be said of educational theory in those all-too-few places in which educators have coined terms that are uniquely suited to educational phenomena: *turn-taking, conservation strategies* (Flinders, 1987), *goal-free evaluation* (Scriven, 1973), *expressive outcomes* (Eisner, 1969), and so forth.

Qualitative phenomena, therefore, can be interpreted using different frameworks located in different fields, typically with different aims. The importance of these theories or frameworks is not only that they provide a set of lenses through which to interpret what has been described, but also to the extent to which they are a part of the investigator's cognitive map, they steer the course of observation. We tend, as I have indicated earlier, to seek what we know how to find. What we know how to find is influenced by the tools we have learned to use. In this respect, theory is among the most useful tools we have, even when it is not up to the job of dealing with particularity.[11]

Coding, Organizing, and Codifying

At the outset I feel compelled to say that in qualitative inquiry *numbers are okay*. I want to say that again: Numbers are okay. My emphasis is due to the widespread belief that qualitative studies in general and educational criticism in particular cannot use numbers—that no counting is allowed.

Coding, Organizing, and Codifying

This is *not* the case, although a study that did *nothing* but count or measure qualities would not be a qualitative study. The way in which situations are represented is crucial, but to say that they need to be rendered vividly and interpretively is not to say that numbers can play no role in qualitative research. If the phenomena are best treated by numbers, the researcher should use numbers. If some things are best measured, they should be measured. If the researcher wants to know about the relationship between ethnicity or race and school failure, graphs will be useful—and graphs require numbers. When determining the percentage of drop-outs, researchers must use numbers. When such features predominate, however, the study will not be a qualitative study, but something else. That is no sin: it is simply not qualitative research.

The point of using qualitative means to render and interpret the educational world is that it enables researchers to say what cannot be said through numbers—or at least cannot be said as well. But it is not an argument against numbers. In fact, the use of numbers where appropriate in qualitative research often gives readers the sense that researchers were reflective about their methods and not doctrinaire. But if a researcher wants to describe or interpret the character and meaning of, say, kindergarten for students or teachers, observation and interview are likely to be the appropriate methods and qualitative description and interpretation the most appropriate vehicles.

I also wish to say explicitly that photographs, videotapes, and film can be very useful for displaying what a situation is like. We seldom see photos in research reports. The *American Educational Research Journal* has published only two photos in all of the articles appearing between its covers in the past twenty years (Levin, Shriberg, & Berg, 1983; Mastropieri, Scruggs, & Levin, 1987). The presence of photographs in other major journals in education such as the *Harvard Educational Review, The American Journal of Education,* or *Teachers College Record* is almost as rare. The norm is numbers and words. Recall the principle: Use what you need to use to say what you want to say. Photographs and films can say things that not only would require pages and pages of words to describe, but in the end could not be adequately described with words. To show what a classroom looks like, an excellent photo will do far more than the best of texts.

It is interesting to note that while visuals are very rarely used by research journals *if* those visuals are photographs, it's considered fine to use histograms, trend lines, scattergrams, and flow charts. Quantitative information visually displayed in graphs looks scientific and is acceptable. Yet by accepting histograms and the like the editors implicitly recognize that some information is best portrayed visually rather than through numbers or text. In fact, computer companies exploit the capacity of their computers and software to display data in living color, to create spreadsheets, pie charts, and graphics of every imaginable variety. Here too there is recognition that the provision of information can be enhanced and in many ways made possible through visual displays (Tufte, 1983).

Some anthropologists have recognized the importance of photographs and film in research. Early in their careers Margaret Mead and Gregory Bateson collaborated on making films (Bateson & Mead, 1952, 1954), and contemporary anthropologists such as Hockings have promulgated what is referred to as visual anthropology (1975).

Photographs, video, and film have enormous potential to help us see a scene and can provide the raw material for interpretation and analysis. Their general absence from educational research publications and from national conferences devoted to research and evaluation in education is slowly—very slowly—changing. The neglect of such potentially powerful resources is due to habit, custom, old norms, and limited views of the nature of knowledge. As these views expand, it will become increasingly acceptable to conduct a dissertation study or a qualitative postdissertation study in which the core of the work is a film or videotape, accompanied by an interpretive text. In some places (the Stanford University School of Education being one), this is already accepted, but only a few students actually do such work (McCutcheon, 1976; Jones, 1982). As we become increasingly aware of the way in which humans process, store, and retrieve information and as we increasingly appreciate the contributions of different forms of representation to the meanings we make, the use of photographs, video, and film will, I feel confident, be increasingly exploited in the future.

Earlier I indicated that note-taking and, at times, tape recordings are important tools in conducting qualitative research. I wish to reiterate their importance here. They are not simply important, they are crucial. They provide the reminders, the quotations, the details that make for credible description and convincing interpretation. What researchers record when they take notes depends initially upon their ability to perceive what is meaningful and significant: this too is the act of imagination at work. What is significant does not announce itself for all to hear. It does not carry an identification badge. The observer's task is both to see and to remember. Note-taking is a way of remembering. If we try to record everything, we are likely to see nothing, and in any case, we don't want a chronicle or a running account of "reality." *That* would swamp the reader and probably confuse the writer.

One way to decide about what to record is to decide before entry what to focus upon. In large measure, the prespecification of foci described earlier goes far to resolve that problem. With an emergent focus, however, significance is determined by selecting out of the interactions those that count, given the frame of reference, theory, conceptual system, or set of values the observer brings to the scene. The point here is that perceiving the significant is a cognitive achievement; indeed, it is what distinguishes the expert from the amateur. Experts know what to neglect (Berliner, 1988).

One common way to maintain a written record is to divide a page into halves vertically and to list on one side at the time of the occurrence what one believes important—this will provide something of a chronology—with interpretive comments alongside those occurrences.

Researchers can also include in such commentary how they feel about what they have seen, that is, what emotions the situation generates in them and why. Such comments can be used as sources for interpretation, although it is important to remember that in virtually all cases the story to be told is not about the researchers but about the situation they have experienced. This is a major difference between providing an autobiographical account and one that describes the features and significance of the situation studied, even though one's own biography is inevitably a part of any situation one describes.

Selecting a Focus and Building a Plot

Qualitative studies of classrooms, teachers, and schools are usually expressed in stories. That is, authors try to craft a picture of the situation, person, or community they have studied. Since not everything they have seen is usable, and since even a camera account of the scene in real time would be less than useful, the problem of finding a focus and selecting and organizing what they have to say is crucial. How is a researcher to take events occurring in real time and reduce them into what Lightfoot (1983) calls "a portrait" and what I call an educational criticism of what the observer—in my case, the educational connoisseur—has experienced? This is a task of storytelling, and in the telling of any story, theme, plot, and point are important considerations.

One format that is used for this purpose is the formulation of themes, those recurring messages construed from the events observed. The identification of themes requires researchers to distill the material they have put together. The notes and transcripts of interviews and index cards on which ideas and comments have been written can be used more or less inductively to generate thematic categories. One of my students conducted a study of a middle school classroom and used the following two themes to distill the major conclusions for her educational criticism:

Messages from the Children

Messages to the Children

In writing about the dynamics of encounters, Erving Goffman (1961) organized his material into the following themes:

Games, Play, and Gaming

Spontaneous Involvement

Ease and Tension

Incidents

Flooding Out

Structure and Process

Interaction Membrane

Conclusions

In writing about his experiences in studying a Christian fundamentalist school, Alan Peshkin (1988) employed the following themes:

The Setting, the Author, the Times

The Dictates of Doctrine

Called to Teach

Schooling for Spirituality

The Impact of Orthodoxy

Truth's Organizational Structure

The Structure of Control

Costs and Benefits

All of these categories represent efforts to distill the major themes that would provide a structure to the writing. Within this structure authors select material, which they then use to illuminate the themes they have formulated. To do this well authors must construct what is essential and use enough description to make the thematic content vivid. Themes also provide structures for the interpretation and appraisal of the events described.

In the process of portraying the situation it is important that the momentum of the writing not be lost. Many novice writers attempt to provide a detailed factual account of the events seriatim. This is done in the name of verisimilitude. Such an approach, however, often leads to a dull, lifeless chronicle. Tension must be maintained between accounts that do justice to a situation as seen and the literary quality necessary to maintain readers' attention and interest without violating a fair and credible picture of the situation. No narrative that seeks to portray life experience can be identical to the experience itself; editing, emphasizing, and neglecting through selection are all ineluctably at play. Hence we seek not a mirror but a tale, a revelation, or a portrayal of what we think is important to say about what we have come to know. This narrative should be supported by evidence, structurally corroborated and coherent, but it cannot be a disembodied listing of what somebody did or saw. It needs both a cast and a plot; it needs to have point. The thematic structures derived inductively from the material researchers have put together and from the observations they have made can provide the conceptual hubs around which the story can be told. The stories told around these thematic situations can then be used as material for a summary account of the story as a whole.

In working with the metaphor of a "story" I intend to emphasize the importance of the craft of conveying meaning through literary, expressive modes. It is difficult to overestimate the importance of the form of the language used and the persuasive structures employed by writers not only in the humanities, but in the social sciences as well. Facts are not simply discovered, they are selected or construed. If one agrees with Nelson Goodman (1978), facts are fabricated. Their rendering and placement in a text, even in one that has no literary pretensions, are consequential. Even in the most so-called objective accounts, rhetorical elements are at work. Rhetoric is the art of persuasion, and the facts alone are seldom enough to persuade. They must be couched in a story; that story has a structure; and that structure has tempo, coherence, and point. Stories without structure, tempo, coherence, and point simply are not read—and if read, they do not persuade. There is no telling it like it is, for in the telling there is making. The task is to do justice to the situation and yet to recognize that all stories, including those in the natural sciences, are fabrications—things made.

Thematic structures are one way to select a focus for a report. Another is to organize events over time. In this process events will inevitably be collapsed. The extent to which this occurs depends upon the level of detail the researcher wants to provide and how much data he or she has to work with. A four-month study of a school can be described in thirty pages—or in three hundred. How much reduction is too much? How much detail is enough? There is no single decontextualized answer possible. The choice depends upon the author's aims and the functions of the story. In a chronological account we sense the flow of events. That may or may not be important, depending upon what the author wants to say. To give readers a sense of someone's day, the author will need to communicate the flow of that day. Ted Sizer, in the introductory chapter of *Horace's Compromise* (1984), does a masterful job in portraying Horace Smith's day, from the time he rises to his work after school helping out in his brother-in-law's store. For this image to be developed, time is important, and Sizer provides that sense of time. In a brief thirty pages we come to know the central character of Sizer's book. Horace becomes a person, and through him we learn something of what it means to be a high school teacher.

Another way to organize material is to select a single day or episode that is sufficiently representational and rich to function as a vehicle for interpretation, appraisal, and thematics. John Fielders (1983) used this approach in his study of a big city school superintendent. He shadowed the superintendent for three months, made detailed notes, collected various materials, but selected one day in the superintendent's life—from 8:45 A.M. to 11:00 P.M.—as a way to describe how he functioned with subordinates, used information to maintain power and control, negotiated competing demands on his time, delegated responsibility, and so forth. The day—a single day in the life of an executive—became a structure for a very vivid and illuminating story.

It is important to point out that Fielder could not have written a book-length study of one day in the life of a superintendent of schools if he had not spent three months shadowing him. It was by virtue of his understanding of the context and the particularities of this specific person that the events occurring during any particular period took on more than superficial meaning. The meaning that Fielder was able to create was derived from his sensitivity to the situation and to the man himself, and these, in turn, were enhanced by what the writer was able to learn during his three months of observation.

How Long Is Long Enough?

One of the most frequently asked questions about educational criticism is, "How much time do I need to spend in a school or classroom?" Again, I wish I could provide a fixed, certain figure or an algorithm for calculating optimal observation periods. I cannot. Alan Peshkin spent eighteen months living in the home of an evangelical Christian while he was studying an evangelical school (1986). Sarah Lawrence Lightfoot (1981a, b), Philip Jackson (1981a, b, c), and Tom Barone (1983) spent three to five days in the schools about which they wrote. How much time is enough? If one is not perceptually acute, forever is not long enough. If one can read a scene rapidly, less than forever is fine. The question is not so much the length of time as the quality of the evidence the researcher has to support descriptions, interpretations, and appraisals. The more experience one has, on average, the shorter the observation time necessary. Experts can read a situation much more quickly than novices.

In saying this I am not arguing the case for commando raids or what Rist (1980) has called "blitzkrieg ethnography." Time to understand the situation is important, but how much time that takes depends upon the perceptivity and experience of the observer and the degree of subtlety in the situation. *In general*, for beginning researchers, two weeks in a classroom and four weeks in a school, full time or nearly so, is not unreasonable. When one remembers that those who evaluate teachers often spend less than an hour in a classroom, two weeks full time does not seem too little. Again, the major issue is not time per se, but the quality of the evidence needed to support observations.

The Use of Appendices

To conclude this chapter, I will comment on the use of an appendix in a qualitative research study. It is a marvelous invention, if for no other reason than because it provides a place in which typescripts, field notes, questionnaires, response sheets, and various other materials used in the study can be displayed. Although some of such material might be appropriately integrated into the body of the study, much of it would distract and break up the continuity that a good qualitative study should possess. The appendix comes to the rescue. Readers may want to know what the questionnaire included, or what the teacher said when interviewed, or they might want to see examples of homework assignments and teacher-made tests. A reader might want to know what an A and a C student essay looked like and the kind of comments the teacher made on each.

If the subject of a study is, say, a textbook, its visual quality and the character of its prose would be important for the reader to see, and examples of pages and text would be helpful. Examples might very well be located in the appendix. An appendix can also contain something of the writer's background and view of education as it is relevant to the study.

Cognitive or behavioral psychologists typically are not expected to provide a biographical statement in the appendices of their works, since it is assumed that their methods are so procedurally objective that their subjective life has no point of entry as a "contaminant." In qualitative work the researcher's background can influence the way in which the situation is described, interpreted, and appraised; hence knowing who the researcher is and where he or she has come from is not altogether irrelevant. The point here—the deep point—is that in the kind of work described in this book personal biography is one of the tools researchers work with; it is the major instrument through which meaning is made and interpretation expressed. It is not an interference, it is a necessity. And because we recognize that the nature of this biography influences how things will be seen and described, information about the author is quite appropriate.

An appendix can also describe the research methods employed in the study. Probably one of the best examples of such a description is found in the second edition of William Foote Whyte's *Street Corner Society* (1961). Here Whyte steps back from the story he tells about working-class Italians in Boston, a story that has become a classic in the literature of qualitative research, and lets the reader in on the background of his study, how he began it, and how he obtained the data he used to write the work. Whyte's appendix is a very useful portrait of method.

In some ways an appendix can be regarded as a way of displaying the ingredients and the tools used to build the narrative that the reader has read. Here are my hooks, my net, my rod; here are samples of the wheat, the chaff, and the fruit I used to create the meal you have just eaten. Here is a vignette of my background—it says something about where I come from and what I care about. All of these resources were important in doing the study. I display them to you so that you can gain a better understanding of what I did and how.

Given the skilled use of the methods described so far, does the study of cases provide only local knowledge, or does such study have larger, more general lessons to teach? It is to that question that we now turn.

Notes

1. Donald Schoen (1983) has written eloquently about the kind of flexibility and intuitive grasp of process and context reflective practitioners employ in the wide variety of situations in which they function. Jazz musicians and athletes, as well as business executives and teachers, seldom follow a plan of action as though it were a blueprint. On the contrary, flexible purposing and sensitivity to the context are the hallmarks of qualitative intelligence in action.

2. I believe that one of the most important recent developments in American education is the growing interest in giving teachers a voice in policies and practices affecting their work. Both the Carnegie Commission's report on teaching and the Holmes Report underscore the importance of increasing the professional esteem and autonomy of teachers. One potential consequence of this development may be the increased sense of parity among university researchers and public school teachers. As such parity grows, access to schools and classrooms will be the result of a negotiation between those working in universities and those working in the schools. Even more, we are likely to see greater collaboration between researchers and teachers. Ultimately, teachers themselves may very well assume major responsibility for their own research agenda and, hopefully, schools will make it possible for teachers, as professionals, to pursue those agendas.

3. Some researchers, such as MacDonald (1977) and Donmoyer (1990), have advocated something approaching "democratic" evaluation. In this model everyone's voice is given a chance to speak, and the final evaluation product is the result of negotiation among those involved in deliberation. Clearly, there are merits to such an approach. However, I believe that there is something called expertise and that not everyone has it. We may all be experts at some things, but not at everything. I believe that there needs to be a place in education for someone with expertise in describing, interpreting, and appraising educational practice. I do not regard reliance on expertise as antidemocratic or elitist; I regard it as the result of recognizing different kinds of competencies and utilizing them appropriately.

4. I am indebted to Alan Peshkin for his keen observations about the importance of leaving the site clean.

5. There are other ways to formulate the major dimensions of schooling, but these for me address the most important ones. For a study that has utilized these dimensions in the analysis of schooling, see Uhrmacher (1990).

6. Counting the incidence of events is, of course, a much easier task than appreciating relationships among events. Yet, the presence of something,

independent of its relationship to the features of the whole in which it participates, is hardly ever informative about its meaning or its value. Learning how to appreciate these relationships is a major aspect of connoisseurship, and leaning how to create them, a major achievement of artistry.

7. One of the keenest insights of progressive educators was their recognition of the intellectual importance of helping children see the connections between means and ends. Rote learning fails to assist children in making these connections, and, as a result, the meaningfulness of what has been learned is substantially eviscerated. Indeed, one can argue that unless children understand how conclusions are reached, they are not likely to have an understanding of the meaning of those conclusions.

8. The equity issues here are of substantial importance. When school programs withhold from students the opportunities to use important forms of representation, they deny students access to meanings that might otherwise be theirs. In addition, they deny opportunities to shine to those students whose aptitudes and interests reside in the areas addressed by those neglected forms. Such practices are profoundly inequitable, as is the common practice that universities impose upon students whose aptitudes, interests, and efforts reside in the arts. Many universities give students no credit for the grades they received in the fine arts when they calculate the student's grade-point average. This is especially ironic because the very institutions that withhold credit from students whose work and talents are in the arts offer arts courses on their own campus for which they give not only credit, but an academic degree.

9. In an interesting and important edited book on the effects of reward on children, titled *The Hidden Cost of Reward*, Mark Lepper and David Greene point out that children who are given extrinsic rewards for activities that would be otherwise intrinsically satisfying, such as easel painting, are less likely to engage voluntarily in such activity than are children who receive no extrinsic rewards for the same activity. We have not yet begun, I think, to estimate adequately the side effects of reward systems that habituate students to external rewards for their work in school.

10. For the full report of this study, see Elliot W. Eisner (1985c). Also, see Eisner (1985b), particularly pages 256–74, "Playing the School System: The Low Achievers Game," by Barbara Porro.

11. Theory, of necessity, cannot adequately encompass particularity. Particulars are specific and idiosyncratic, and theory is general and ideal. Theory is useful as a guide, a rule of thumb, but will inevitably fail to provide a perfect fit between generalized notions and relationships and the individual classrooms, teachers, and events with which teachers and researchers must deal.

Chapter IX

Do Qualitative Case Studies Have Lessons to Teach?

Poetry is something more philosophic and of graver import than history since its statements are of the nature rather of universals.

Aristotle

The particular is always more than a match for the universal; the universal always has to accommodate itself to the particular.

Goethe

The Canonical Image

It is common knowledge that in research the ability to generalize depends upon a statistical process through which a sample is randomly selected from a population. The idea is that if the selection is genuinely random, then whatever is true of the sample will also be true, within certain limits of probability, of the population from which the sample was drawn. Through the development of inferential statistics, truly elegant procedures are available for selecting and analyzing samples in ways that allow researchers to extend what they have learned to a larger world. Most research training programs teach students the logic of such methods and how to employ them. Not just sampling, but *random* sampling is the cornerstone on which statistical inferences are built. Such inferences, in general, become more reliable as the size of the random sample is increased and the parameters of the population from which it is drawn better understood. Given such assumptions about generalization, what are we to do with the case of $N=1$? If samples must be random and if the size of the sample makes a difference, how shall we regard studies whose subjects are neither randomly selected nor very large? The individual case study, after all, could not be any smaller.

Although the logic of random sampling is impeccable, it is also apparent that in our daily lives we do not randomly sample in order to generalize. Yet, we do, in fact, learn lessons "from life," from events that are about as far from random as they can be. Furthermore, these lessons learned from the ad hoc are, so to speak, single-shot case studies, not units constituting a random sample. On what basis do we make generalizations and learn lessons? And what lessons can we learn from the nonrandom, $N=1$ experiences that we have daily?

To answer these questions we need to examine the meaning of "lesson learning," the meaning of generalization, and the meaning of that old and venerable concept so dear to the hearts of both learning theorists and educators: *transfer*.

What Does It Mean to Generalize?

Generalizing can be regarded not only as going beyond the information given (Bruner, 1973), but also as transferring what has been learned from one situation or task to another. I conflate generalization and transfer because transfer always requires more than the mechanical application of a set of skills, images, or ideas from one situation to another. If two situations or tasks were identical, the need to generalize would be zero. One would need only to transfer lock, stock, and barrel what one had learned from Situation A to Situation B, something like moving a truckload of furniture from one place to another. But this is not the case. Skills, images, or ideas are applied to situations that are never identical; some features of the situations always differ. Hence transfer is a process that has generalizing features.[1] A person must recognize the similarity—but not identity—between one situation and the next and then make the appropriate inference. In fact, we can even think of learning itself as *requiring* transfer, since we would be unlikely to say that someone had learned something unless the person could, in fact, demonstrate that learning had occurred by displaying it in situations other than the one in which the learning initially took place.

One necessary difference between two situations is, of course, time. But almost always there are significantly more complex and subtle differences with which individuals must deal. The ability to generalize skills, images, and ideas across situations appropriately represents one form of human intelligence. Some situations look alike but are not, and some that do not look alike, are. All of this, of course, depends upon the perspective one brings to the scene. Knowing which perspective to adopt for what purposes is part of the generalizing process, and this human ability is particularly relevant in assessing the utilities of qualitative case studies.

This line of reasoning suggests that statistical generalization based upon random selection is a special case of a more general process, one that makes possible the adaptation of the organism to its environment. If each new situation required a wholly new repertoire, it is unlikely that humans could survive.

The Content of Generalization

We can think not only about the process of generalization, but also about the "content" generalized. Just what is it that one learns and uses? Here I will identify three important forms of learning that have been discussed by developmental psychologists such as Jean Piaget (Piaget & Inhelder, 1964) and Jerome Bruner (1964). Despite implications to the contrary, these forms of learning are by no means either hierarchical in cognitive import or restricted to the young.

What generalizes is what one learns, and for our purposes these can be regarded as (1) skills, (2) images, and (3) ideas. In Brunerian (Bruner, 1961) terms they correspond to the *enactive,* the *iconic,* and the *symbolic* aspects of human cognition.

Skills generalize as they are applied. These skills may be rooted in forms of performance we sometimes, too simply, refer to as "manual" and to those skills that allow us to make fine-grained discriminations among the qualities that constitute a complex and subtle perceptual field. A skill is not simply something we do physically, it is something that requires thought in the doing. Nothing can be done skillfully without thought.[2]

I use the term *skill* in this context for analytic purposes. We need to be mindful that acting and imaging are both manifestations of thinking and that the level of competence with which they are used reflects the kind and quality of thinking that has brought them into being. For our purposes, learning to see and learning to write about what we have seen are important generalizable skills (hence, forms of thinking).

Images also generalize. Images are constructed from our transaction with empirical qualities. These qualities emerge in cinema, photography, painting, diagrams, melodies, movements, and the like. Images also emerge from words whose form and content have the ability to generate images. Thus, for example, our personal images of feminine beauty, masculinity, patriotism, or moral weakness are influenced by the public images we encounter. We appropriate images as well as generate them, and these images, once internalized, not only exemplify, they also provide the parameters for seeing and classifying (Neisser, 1976). In short, images have a powerful instrumental function. This function is an expression of their generalizing capacity.

It is the generalizing capacity of the image that leads us to look for certain qualities of classroom life, features in teaching, or aspects of discussion, rather than others. Once we secure images of excellence in these realms, we apply them to other aspects of the world to which we believe them to be relevant.[3]

For qualitative research, this means that the creation of an image—a vivid portrait of excellent teaching, for example—can become a prototype that can be used in the education of teachers or for the appraisal of teaching. Because qualitative writing is often vivid and concrete, its capacity for generating images is particularly strong. But even theoretical ideas are image-based. The ideas developed by Max Weber (1968)—of authoritarian, democratic, and charismatic styles of leadership, for example—are imagic in character. In a telling passage that adumbrates the contents of his book *Sociology as an Art Form*, Robert Nisbet (1976) describes the power of "forms" and themes created by theoretical sociologists "to set forth the cultural landscape."

> It is with no violation of context or content whatever that I have chosen to describe sociology in its great formative age, the age that reaches from Tocqueville and Marx through Weber, Durkheim, and Simmel, in the terms "social landscape," "portrait," the "illusion of motion," and what I have called "the rust of progress." Precisely as painting or literature may be, and of course often has been, seen in the terms of landscape, portrait, and so on, so may sociology be seen thus. To set forth the cultural and social landscape of Western Europe, to identify distinctly the dominant role-types, to seek to derive dynamic strength, motion, or movement from structure and setting, and to assess the costs to community and individuality of modernity—all this is as much the objective of a Marx or Simmel as it is of a Blake, Coleridge, Balzac, or Dickens among writers and of a Hogarth, David, Millet, or Daumier among those who made line, light, and shadow serve the cause of illuminating reality. And, whether an artist as such or a sociologist, the influence of the themes I have mentioned—*community, authority, status, the sacred,* and *alienation*—is unmistakable. (pp. 40–41)

Nisbet characterized the formative period of sociology as a time populated by theoreticians who made forms similar in function to the ones artists create. For Nisbet, the seminal concepts of sociology are embedded in themes that have imagic features. Once internalized, those images became the most important weapon in the sociologists' theoretical arsenal. Once a portrait of the authoritarian personality was painted, we acquired a means through which it could be found. Furthermore, we tend to seek what we know how to find. Thus the hunt is influenced by the tools we have and know how to use. The great images of science, often initially expressed as metaphors (Langer, 1976), are among the most generalizable conceptual devices we possess.

Although skills and images are two of the modes that enable us to generalize, they are not the ones we usually think about first. A generalization is usually thought of as a statement about a state of affairs, some claim or proposition that purports to be a true statement about something. Thus when social science research yields generalizations, we usually regard them as the major product of the inquiry because they allow us to make predictions, or at least to have expectations, about the future. The statement that there is a significant positive correlation between social class and IQ measured on a Stanford-Binet scale describes a state of affairs, is a generalization, and provides a structure for framing expectations. Although such a generalization has basic theoretical problems, and although it might not be true in every case we encounter, it is, more often than not, what we would expect to find if we were guided by it. When we conduct research, we hope we can arrive at useful generalizations and have a good theory that provides an explanation of why they work.

So far I have highlighted the fact that the content we generalize is ideas couched not only in linguistic form, but also in skills and images. We generalize skills when we know how to apply them in situations other than the ones in which they were initially learned, and we generalize images when we use them to search for and find features of the world that match or approximate the images we have acquired. Images can function, just as propositions can, as categories that enable us to seek and sort the world we encounter. They are devices through which our experience is construed.

The Means Through Which Generalizations Are Applied

Once we recognize the variety of modes through which generalizations occur—skills, images, ideas—we can ask more specifically about the means through which they are applied. As I have already indicated, formal inference is the ideal for generalizing within scientific inquiry. Random selection is used to make formal inference possible. Other means are *attribute analysis* and *image matching*. In attribute analysis our image of the specific attributes that mark a particular class of objects or processes—say an eagle or an inductively taught lesson—can be used to identify their presence in our experience. We can and do make inferences on the basis of partial information. With enough partial information, we make classifications and judgments in which we have some confidence. In some cases, the amount of information we need to make confident judgments and inferences is minimal, if the information we have defines a unique attribute. For example, if we are asked to meet someone at an airport gate whom we do not know but who we know will be wearing a purple rose in his lapel, we are unlikely to need more information to make an accurate identification of the individual. In this case we look for a specific attribute, which is enough to tell us how to recognize what, or whom, we seek.

In other cases we have a generalized image, a *gestalt*, and find what we are seeking not by looking for specific attributes, but by matching a pattern seen with an image remembered. Deciding whether or not it is our friend Joe who is walking a half-block ahead of us is not usually a function of counting attributes, but of matching the general conformation of the person we see with Joe's image as we remember it. In fact, attributes considered individually may be right, but their pattern may be wrong. I believe we tend to trust the pattern or overall quality more than the individual attributes. In a good caricature, each of the attributes is likely to be wrong—they are typically gross exaggerations—but the overall pattern works. Conversely, a poor caricaturist might get the individual attributes right, but the overall pattern might be wrong—in such a case, the caricature would not work.

So far, we have examined the idea that all learning involves generalization. Since the test of someone's learning is the person's ability to display what has been learned in new situations, and since no two situations are identical, generalization must occur.

Further, we have examined the idea that the content of generalizations is not only ideas, but also skills and images. The content of generalizations varies, as does the means through which generalizations occur. We generalize through *formal inference*, through *attribute analysis*, and through *image matching*. Some generalizations are so formalized that they can be converted into systems such as symbolic logic, others require only partial information from which inferences can be made, and still others involve matching overall patterns.

The Sources of Generalization

As I have already indicated, most generalizations are derived from life itself. A young child who touches a hot teapot generalizes, whether correctly or not, to the potential consequences of touching other teapots. When we think about teaching, we tend to believe that teaching experience is a good teacher. Indeed we often say that some things can be learned only through experience, meaning that they cannot be taught by declaration, whether through talk or text. Some things need to be learned by recognizing the connection between act and consequence, and by experiencing the qualities of an object, process, or situation. We know we are drinking orange juice if we have tasted orange juice before and know that we have done so.

Direct contact with the qualitative world is one of our most important sources of generalization. But another extremely important source is secured vicariously through parables, pictures, and precepts. One of the most useful of human abilities is the ability to learn from the experience of others. We do not need to learn everything first-hand. We listen to story-tellers and learn about how things were, and we use what we have been told to make decisions about what will be. We see photos and learn what to expect on our forthcoming trip to Spain. We see the play *On the Waterfront* and learn something about corruption in the shipping industry and, more important, about the conflicts and tensions between two brothers taking vastly different roads in life. We see the film *One Flew over the Cuckoo's Nest* and understand a bit more about how people survive in an institution that is hell-bent on their domestication. All of these narratives are potentially rich sources of generalization; all contribute significantly to our lesson learning. All are, in a sense, one-shot case studies.

Several features of stories and of educational criticism contribute to their importance as generalizing vehicles. First, when we limit the content of generalization to what can be said in a literal mode, we limit what can be said. The epistemological utility of the literary narrative or the metaphorical characterization is precisely that such forms convey what literal language cannot represent—or at least cannot represent as well. The form of a text is a part of its meaning, and when meaning is restricted to the literal, those meanings that require other forms must remain voiceless.

Second, attention to the particular, to the case, is descriptive not only of the case, but of other cases like it. When Sarah Lawrence Lightfoot (1983) writes about the Brookline High School or the George Washington Carver High School or the John F. Kennedy High School, she tells us more than just what those particular schools are like; we learn something about what makes a good high school. Do all high schools have to be good in the same way? No. Can some high schools share some of their characteristics? Yes. Can we learn from Lightfoot what to look for? Certainly.

When Ted Sizer (1984) creates a fictional character named Horace Smith to reveal a teacher's day—and life—does the fact that the portrait is a fiction mean it is not real? I think not. As Nelson Goodman (1978) has pointed out, some of the most real people we have ever known weren't: Robin Hood, Mr. Chips, Don Juan.

The use of the particular to say something about the general is called in philosophical circles 'the concrete universal'. The concrete universal is regarded as a true rendering of universal features through 'exemplification'. When Aristotle (McKeon, 1941) writes that poetry is more philosophic than history, he makes the point clear. The ancients were interested in ideals and essences. Poetry was one way to reveal them.

Who Generalizes?

We turn now to the question of who generalizes or who learns the lessons that qualitative case studies have to teach.

In conventional statistical studies in the social sciences, the construction of a generalization is left to the researcher. Given a certain set of procedures, a certain set of findings, and a hypothesis that when tested enables one not to reject the theory from which it was derived, the researcher makes an inference or generalization to the population from which the sample was drawn. The logic is straightforward, once the necessary procedures are in place. In conventional statistical research, however, such procedures are seldom in place. More often than not, inferences are made to larger populations not because of impeccable statistical logic, but because it makes good sense to do so. The vast majority of conventional research studies in education generalize from nonrandom samples. Thus, *it is the investigator* who makes the claim that the study yields particular generalizations or that there are no grounds as yet to reject the theory that was used to generate the findings.

In qualitative case studies the researcher can also generalize, but it is more likely that readers will determine whether the research findings fit the situation in which they work. The researcher might say something like this: "This is what I did and this is what I think it means. Does it have any bearing on your situation? If it does and if your situation is troublesome or problematic, how did it get that way and what can be done to improve it?"[4] The logic in qualitative studies is softer—it's more analogical.

The conception of generalization in the context of educational research clearly implies that what we learn from an inquiry will be used in other settings or is to be applied to them. This concept has a long tradition and certain obvious utilities. If we are unable to use what we learn, learning has no instrumental utility. Yet the idea of applying generalizations to practice has some problematic features. As I have indicated, one of these is the implication that information proceeds from the top down, that what researchers learn, teachers—at least professional teachers—should employ. Teachers are sometimes regarded as farmers in the field and researchers as the agricultural scientists who find out what really works. In the field of agriculture, an agricultural extension officer carries the products of science to the farmers, who learn what research has produced and then proceed to modify their behavior in light of their new-found research-based knowledge. The paradigm moves from basic research, to applied research, to implementation in the practical world. In the field of education, a field more complex and context-sensitive than farming, a harder term is often used: *installation*, a word that conjures up something akin to hooking up a refrigerator in a kitchen. As a result of "installing" a new curriculum, it is expected that schools will produce better products. Once the curriculum is installed, we want it to be "aligned" at each grade level.[5]

This conception of school improvement was once believable, but no longer. Teaching and farming are not the same, and creating good schools is not like growing better corn. Educational virtue is not uniform. What makes for educationally sturdy students depends not only on the conditions, but on the students themselves. What might work at one time might not work at another. What is effective in one area of the country might be inappropriate in another. What some teachers can do others cannot. What some communities want done others reject. And so on.

The conditional quality of educational life, its high degree of context specificity, is formidable. What this means for practice and for the uses of research is that in most settings generalizations derived from research are not likely to be taken as gospel. Researchers are not the ones to provide rules of procedure to practitioners; there are no sacred seven steps to effective teaching. We offer considerations to be shared and discussed, reflected upon, and debated. If one looks at research as an effort that is intended to increase, as Clifford Geertz once said about the aims of ethnography, "the precision through which we vex each other" (1973, p. 29), then the relationship between researcher and teacher, between the products of research and their use in schools, is one of mutual inquiry and negotiation. Their generalizing qualities are not so much located in Truth, as in their ability to refine perception and to deepen conversation (Rorty, 1979).

Such a conception of generalization lightens the burden. This lightened burden is not to be regarded as an invitation to irresponsible description, interpretation, or evaluation, but rather as a reflection of the recognition that generalizations are tools with which we work and are to be shaped in context. They are a part of the substantive exchange between professionals with their own expertise, not prescriptions from the doctor.[6]

Where Generalizations Are Focused

Generalization is usually thought of as focusing upon the future; that is, we use what we learn from some state of affairs to think about other future states of affairs to which the generalization is relevant. If we find that some experimental treatment has an effect on a randomly selected group, we expect that groups like the sample would be similarly influenced if we employed the same treatment. In this sense, the utility of a generalization is determined by whether it helps us know what to anticipate under particular circumstances. The validity of the generalization is determined by the extent to which what we have come to expect is borne out as we use it. Generalizations of this kind, the most common type, may be called *anticipatory*.

But generalizations emerge through another process, what I call *retrospective generalization*. It is developed not by randomly sampling and using findings to anticipate the future, but by encountering or formulating an idea that allows us to see our past experience in a new light. Retrospective generalizations find their subject matter by examining history rather than by anticipating the future. Consider the following example.

It has been observed in the study of classroom practice that in the elementary grades, teachers working with individual children at the teacher's desk will, at regular intervals, look up and survey the room in order to monitor the behavior of the rest of the class. This observation, not often noticed until it was described, provides a description whose validity we can check by consulting our own experience. Once the phenomenon has been mentioned, most readers are able to recall experiences in which their teachers behaved this way.

What other forms of monitoring do teachers use? Jack Kounin, a long-time student of classroom practice, coined a term that characterizes such teaching skills. He called it "withitness" (1970). According to Kounin, a teacher who was "with it" had eyes in the back of her head and didn't miss a trick even when writing on the blackboard. Kounin's concept of "withitness" was developed from a fresh perception of the familiar so that once it was named, consciousness of the particular was raised. In *Among Schoolchildren,* Tracy Kidder (1989) describes Mrs. Zajac's ability to see everything this way. The generalizing process occurs through the power of the concept to enable one to recall and to find significance in an array of prior experiences. The generalization is retrospective.

Consider another example. A few years ago I was providing consultation for the National Humanities Faculty to a group of middle school teachers. At the end of the day, I met with a school principal, and we became engaged in an animated discussion of American schooling. In the course of our discussion, the principal commented, "Schools are places with very few soft surfaces." When I heard his comment, made off-handedly in the course of a conversation, I felt a certain flash of insight. "Of course!" I said to myself as I used his comment to consult my prior experience and to validate what he had said. All of the schools I had known as a student and as an elementary and high school teacher had wood, linoleum, Formica, and metal surfaces: the entire environment conveyed a sense of industrial efficiency. Schools were designed to make the janitor's life easier and to be sturdy enough to withstand the wear and tear of children and adolescents. But they contributed little to creature comforts; they were not designed to encourage one to linger.

Most schools and classrooms are right-angled places, brittle rather than flexible, hard rather than soft, spare rather than elaborate, standard-ized rather than unique, lean rather than fat. They reflect and express a way of life, and they provide a certain way to be alive. The principal's casual comment opened up a fresh set of considerations, considerations that had theoretical impact and raised some new questions. Why are schools designed that way? What do hard surfaces imply for teachers and students? What other aspects of the institution have similar features; that is, is the hard-surfaced quality of schools part of a pervasive hardness that expresses itself in nonarchitectural dimensions, such as testing, teaching, the schedule of the school day, policies about behavior, and so forth? Or is the hard-surfaced classroom incongruent with the rest of the enterprise? And if so, why?

These examples are intended to illustrate how we find a fit between a general statement and our personal histories. New ideas can reconstruct our past. Indeed, Dewey regarded the most powerful aspects of learning as those resulting in the reconstruction of experience (1938). Once a Darwinian idea emerges, for example, the past never appears the same. Nor does the future. We have acquired a new perspective for making sense. When we make sense of experience we already have, the generalization can be regarded as retrospective.

Retrospective generalizations, born by examining our prior experience, also perform an anticipatory function. Once we recall the absence of soft surfaces in the schools and classrooms we have experienced, we can look for similar features in the schools and classrooms we have yet to see. In this sense, the generalization has a lesson to teach: If we look for such qualities, we may very well find them. The idea or concept functions as a guide through which experience that might otherwise not be achieved can, in fact, be secured. Like a guidebook, the generalization sensitizes readers to what is likely to be found, if they know where and how to look.

Qualitative case studies are full of opportunities for generalization. Such studies are typically nonrandom, and as case studies they focus on the particular. But, as Lee Shulman says, every case is a case of something, just as every sample—whether random or not—is a sample of something. If we learn something about a case that we did not know at the outset of the study, not only have we achieved consciousness of that quality or feature, but also we learn to look for that quality or feature in other places. J. M. Stephens (1967) once wrote about the concept of "spontaneous schooling." He said that if you teach a group of students the names of half of the state capitals, a few weeks later, even without further instruction, they will know the other half. Knowing the names of the state capitals implies not only knowing the names of some particular state capitals, but knowing that state capitals have names and that they can be known. The lead is enough to take care of the rest.

Formulating generalizations that approximate the laws formulated within the physical sciences has, for some researchers, been a long-standing ideal in educational research. In that ideal, educational research would eventually build an edifice of knowledge, brick by brick, that would provide information to practitioners with the same kind of precision that the laws of physics provide for engineers. Educational research has been regarded as foundational to educational practice. Once the laws of learning were discovered, their application would be the responsibility of those professional teachers who understood them.

This ideal arose early in the history of educational research. Edward L. Thorndike (1910), one of the two major pillars of American education, and the most influential of early researchers in education, described the prospects for educational research in the lead article of the first issue of *Educational Psychology*, published in 1910:

A complete science of psychology would tell every fact about everyone's intellect and character and behavior, would tell the cause of every change in human nature, would tell the result which every educational force—every act of every person that changed any other or the agent himself—would have. It would aid us to use human beings for the world's welfare with the same surety of the result that we now have when we use falling bodies or chemical elements. In proportion as we get such a science we shall become masters of our own souls as we now are masters of heat and light. Progress toward such a science is being made. (pp. 6, 8)

Our ideas about research in education have become appropriately more modest in recent years. It is not likely that we shall get statements such as "if you have x, as measured by y, under conditions k, apply q, and you will get z." In almost no case do we know the parameters under which a treatment's effect will hold. What we do know is that conditions and contexts vary. Conditions vary because human teachers interpret and give their distinctive stamp to what they teach. Experimental treatments cannot be literally replicated when a human teacher mediates the treatment. Contexts vary because no group of students is identical to another, nor are classrooms. What students bring to the scene and how they respond vary, hence teachers always need to mediate their teaching *artistically* so that it is relevant and appropriate to the students being taught. The kind of generalizations that once functioned as ideals of educational research have been modified so that they are more suitable for the phenomena with which teachers deal—thinking and feeling students and classrooms that change in unpredictable ways within short periods of time. Given this newer, more modest, and more realistic view, generalizations are regarded, even by those previously committed to a "harder" view, as propaedeutic to the art of teaching. Gage, for example, acknowledges that scientific generalizations provide a scientific basis for what, in practice, depends upon art (1978).

It should be pointed out that the art of teaching *is not*, in its most important respects, like the practice of medicine or engineering. In both medicine and engineering a body of knowledge exists that is far less context-dependent and far less subject to idiosyncratic application than is teaching. The use of the Salk vaccine or thermometer, the removal of an appendix, the application of a cast to a broken leg, the identification of breast cancer, and so forth have a procedural standardization that has no counterpart in education. This is *not* to say that the medical practices identified above are uniform, only that educational research has been unable to provide any comparable standard operating procedure to practitioners.

The reasons, I think, are clear. The goal in identifying breast cancer is always the same: to find breast cancer, if it is present. On average, mammograms are thought to be about 85 percent effective (Feig &

McLelland, 1983). The goals for teaching are not always the same, nor will the "route" that proved effective with one group of students necessarily be effective with another group living and working in other situations. Generalizations in education, whether produced through statistical studies or through case studies, need to be treated as tentative guides, as ideas to be considered, not as prescriptions to follow. "It all depends" is probably the most useful qualifier to attach to answers to questions about the efficacy of particular educational methods.

On "Knowledge Accumulation" in Qualitative Research

One of the putative weaknesses of qualitative research is its limited ability to contribute to the accumulation of knowledge. Since the situations qualitative researchers study are unique and the methods they employ are so heavily dependent upon their own personal aptitudes, the task of providing knowledge that accumulates is thought to be particularly difficult. In fact, some believe that qualitative research is noncumulative.

The concept of accumulation is, upon reflection, an interesting metaphor. It conjures up an image of something that grows—dollars can accumulate, so can garbage. Dollars accumulate because they participate in a common system of currency or because there are transformation rules for calculating equivalences. Garbage accumulates because its volume increases, but there is no order in garbage comparable to the order found in currency.

Which image of accumulation best fits research, whether conventional or qualitative? It seems clear to me that given the diversity of theories, concepts, and methods employed within any particular field—say, psychology—let alone among different fields, we cannot use the term *accumulation* to mean what we mean when we say that dollars accumulate. Variables, even by the same name, mean different things when different tests are used to measure them. The interpretation of findings emanating from attribution theory, for example, will differ if a reinforcement model is used to explain why people assign attributes to others to account for their behavior. Piagetians and Eriksonians provide different perspectives on the development of competence, as do those following a Freudian model of human development. Sternberg (1988) and Jensen (1969) conceptualize intelligence in radically different ways, as do Hunt (1961) and Gardner (1983).

Is it reasonable to expect the findings of research to accumulate when the research is conducted under the aegis of different theories, using different core concepts and different instruments to measure or describe key variables? In what sense can such accumulation occur? Certainly not in the sense of accumulating dollars. Yet garbage is not a felicitous metaphor. Is there some way to conceptualize knowledge accumulation that is more realistic than the way we accumulate money and less repugnant than the way we accumulate garbage? I think there is.

First, the idea that knowledge accumulates suggests that knowledge is an inert material that one can collect, store, and stockpile. To regard knowledge as inert is to reify it. Knowledge is not an inert material discovered through research, it is a functioning aspect of human cognition, a resource that lives in the biographies, thoughts, and actions of individuals, not something that one can stockpile and point to. For knowledge to be, it must be known. To be known, someone must act upon it. In short, knowledge is a verb.

Second, if knowledge can be said to accumulate, its growth in both education and in the other social sciences is more horizontal than vertical. By horizontal I mean that what we generate through inquiry into educational matters are ideas that contribute to the development or refinement of conceptual frameworks, perspectives, or metaphors through which the world is viewed. We learn—or we can learn—to work with and shift those perspectives, to examine situations from multiple perspectives, to use what others have found as cues or as clues with which to search and see. If we look at human development from an Eriksonian perspective (Erikson, 1963), what comes into focus is dependency, autonomy, and group identity. If we look at human development from a rational-choice perspective (Raiffa, 1970), we think about opportunity costs, long- and short-term benefits, and risk. Given this latter view, the human being is regarded as a reflective and rational actor, almost, it seems, driven by a set of economic criteria: the rational actor calculates the probable net gain from each possible option and weighs it against its potential costs. If we view curriculum choices from the value perspective of academic rationalism (Eisner, 1985b), we will try to introduce the young to those eternal verities residing in the great books and in other great human works. If we think of educationally virtuous curricula as aimed at the development of students' particular aptitudes or as increasing the personal relevance of their studies in school, we will make other curricular choices.

It is not clear that an Eriksonian perspective of the child can rest comfortably upon a Skinnerian view. Knowledge accumulation is not like building with blocks. But both Erikson and Skinner can help us attend to aspects of human development that are potentially useful. Thus, what may be said to occur in conducting research is the creation of resources that others can use to think about the situations in which they are interested. Multiple perspectives need not lead to a fight between paradigms to determine which one is correct; a more constructive function is to determine which perspective is useful for what ends.

Given this view, the claim that qualitative research does not accumulate is mistaken. It does accumulate, but it is more of a horizontal accumulation than a vertical one. It is an expansion of our kit of conceptual tools. This view regards as mistaken the expectation that there can be a single theory that unifies the social sciences or a single language that will do what a multiplicity of tongues cannot achieve. Paradigm plurality is worrisome to some. Yet what could be more enslaving than having to use one framework, one language, one set of criteria for appraising everything? I believe the world profits when there is more than one drummer to whom scholars and teachers with different aptitudes, values, and interests can listen.

My point here is not to claim that the products of research have no bearing upon each other, or that they do not connect in any way. It is, rather, to challenge the notion that all researchers must use a common intellectual currency whose profits are additive in the same way in which money accumulates in the bank. Research studies, even in related areas in the same field, create their own interpretive universe. Connections have to be built by readers, who must also make generalizations by analogy and extrapolation, not by a watertight logic applied to a common language. Problems in the social sciences are more complex than putting the pieces of a puzzle together to create a single, unified picture. Given the diversity of methods, concepts, and theories, it's more a matter of seeing what works, what appears right for particular settings, and creating different perspectives from which the situation can be construed.

This conception of the accumulation of knowledge suggests that even in the social sciences, learning from research is closer to the naturalistic forms of generalization Donmoyer (1980) and others have described than to fitting puzzle pieces to complete a picture. Human beings have the spectacular capacity to go beyond the information given, to fill in gaps, to generate interpretations, to extrapolate, and to make inferences in order to construe meanings. Through this process knowledge is accumulated, perception refined, and meaning deepened. This model of knowledge accumulation is less like making deposits to a bank account than preparing a fine meal. Indeed, a fine meal is much more apt an image than either the tidy rationality of a bank account or the redolence of a garbage dump. In the meal, each course connects with and complements the others. Such an image is not a bad model for knowledge accumulation in qualitative research.

Notes

1. David Berliner was the first to suggest to me that the process of generalization is inherent in all learning. I am indebted to him for his keen insight, which has provided the basis for this section of this chapter.

2. It often appears that skilled performance occurs without reflection. This, it seems to me, cannot be the case. Even in the most rapid forms of information processing, cognition is at work. Without the engagement of mind, choices

cannot be made and action deteriorates into mere behavior. Mind mediates activity even in its swiftest form.

3. The importance of images in the process of holistic evaluation cannot be overestimated. Our ability to appraise the quality of objects and events without engaging in a complex componential analysis is displayed by connoisseurs in a wide variety of realms. Particularly in the visual arts, rapid holistic judgments are made on the basis of the relationship of images encountered to those images of virtue within the genre of the work being evaluated.

4. These questions are only slightly different from those posed by Mike Atkin during his leadership in the Stanford and the Schools Study. See Atkin, Kennedy & Patrick (1989).

5. In addition to "installing" curricula, and aligning them among grade levels, we "in service" teachers almost, it seems, every 6,000 miles. What is significant about these terms is the images they conjure up and the premises on which they rest. As long as we continue to use automotive metaphors we are likely to treat teachers, teaching, children, and learning as something akin to automotive maintenance and repair.

6. By regarding generalizations derived from educational criticism and other qualitative forms of inquiry as intellectual resources with which one works, the kind of dogmatic assurance that sometimes accompanies "what research tells us" is softened. Since no generalization can fit an individual context perfectly, modification is always necessary. This modification requires judgment on the part of intelligent practitioners. Hence, they are the ones who must act upon the situation after researchers have finished their work. In the end, it is practitioners, the users of ideas, who must determine whether the ideas that are available are appropriate to their situation.

Chapter X

Ethical Tensions, Controversies, and Dilemmas in Qualitative Research

The heart has its reasons, which reason does not know.

Pascal

Knowing the Right Thing to Do

In this chapter I turn to a sticky, complex, and, at times, a "dangerous" and potentially harmful aspect of qualitative research and evaluation. I turn to the ethical tensions, controversies, and dilemmas that accompany qualitative research.

There is unanimous agreement among researchers and evaluators that their work and behavior should be ethical. There is unanimous agreement that researchers should avoid unethical behavior and that doing good is better than doing harm. Virtually all agree that deception is bad and that honesty is good. All of us prefer a virtuous relationship with others, even those we study, and the idea of deceiving others violates our personal moral code. Let us settle the issue without further ado. Unethical behavior has no place in qualitative research or evaluation of any kind. We are to be ethical at all times—paragons of virtue, if possible—thereby ensuring not only the good opinion of others, but access to a better life later.

If the matter was quite so simple, the need for books, chapters in books, and scholarly articles on ethical issues in social research would be unnecessary. If there were simple rules to apply, we could easily be taught to follow them and in so doing to feel confident that we were doing the right thing all of the time. Alas, there are no such rules, at least not any I know. There are principles, concepts, considerations. And there are genuine dilemmas. My aim in this chapter is not to provide a set of rules, for none can be provided, but to explore the issues, to share some tales from my own experience—a kind of confession of mistakes I have made—and to develop a more complex appreciation of ethical considerations in qualitative research.

213

Chapter X

Can Consent Be Informed?

I start with the assumption that the aim of educational research and evaluation is the achievement of a virtue: the creation of knowledge, thus enlarging our understanding of education and leading to its improvement. That is, researchers in education, whether they are conducting qualitative or statistical studies, are attempting to do something that is socially useful. Although research may further the careers of researchers, its public aim is to further the public good.

The doing of a social good, however, can involve harming others in order to achieve that good. This is most clearly illustrated in the biomedical field. In 1932 the U.S. Health Service conducted what has come to be called the "Tuskegee study." During the course of this study, 399 black men who had syphilis were denied treatment for this disease in order for the Centers for Disease Control in Atlanta to study the course of its development. The study was continued into the 1940s when penicillin was available and could probably have been curative (Jones, 1981). This unmitigated evil might have provided some useful medical knowledge, but only by violating the rights of the patients. In Nazi Germany concentration camp inmates were immersed in ice water to study its effects on human beings (Shirer, 1959; Lifton, 1986). The aim was to enable the German Air Force to help its pilots survive the frigid sea if they had to ditch their planes in the Atlantic. The results of these Nazi experiments have recently become public (Shabecoff, 1988). Should these results be used to increase our understanding? On this issue there are heated debates and wide differences of opinion. What principles should be appealed to?

Social science research seldom produces horror stories of the magnitude just described. Even Stanley Milgram's research (1974) on obedience is qualitatively different from the examples I have cited. The concept of *informed consent* was invented to prevent experimental practices in the biomedical field that violated individual rights (Beauchamp et al., 1982). In turn, it has been used and is currently applied to research in the social sciences. Whether the concept of informed consent is appropriate in the social sciences and just what it means for the conduct of qualitative research are not entirely clear. The concept of informed consent implies that the researcher knows *before* the event that is to be observed what the event will be and its possible effects. Just how does one get such knowledge? Is being observed surreptitiously an invasion of privacy, like taking pictures of people who have not been asked for their permission? Some people might object. What obligations do researchers have to those who might object, and how can researchers know without asking? And if researchers ask for and receive consent, should the study be done? Will not knowledge that they are being observed change people's behavior? Will some refuse, and if so will that undermine the study by biasing the sample?

What about observing classrooms? Some experimental schools have one-way mirrors for purposes of covert observation. Are the children's rights being violated by such a practice? What about the teachers? Is it okay to observe children surreptitiously, but not their teachers? Do adults have rights that provide them with more protection than children? Typically the opposite case is true. Does it make moral or practical sense to ask a seven-year-old for permission? Answers to these and other questions are not simple, and, as we shall see, the ethical principles to which one can appeal are abstract and general, rather than concrete and specific.

As I have indicated, the notion of informed consent implies that researchers are able to anticipate the events that will emerge in the field about which those to be observed are to be informed. This is hardly a characteristic feature of field research. Researchers usually do not know what will emerge, except perhaps general themes, and therefore are not in a good position to inform those to be observed about what to expect.

One of the typical tactics of field research is to follow up on leads that could not have been formulated or anticipated—researchers often follow their noses, and if their noses are good, what they write about is both interesting and important. Who knew that students would pass around last year's test for a course in which they are currently enrolled as a way of coping with the demands of a chemistry course? Who knew that Bill would develop really clever ways of cutting class by forging notes from other teachers? Who knew that the course in Italian language would be taught by a teacher who spoke virtually no Italian and whose conception of Italian culture extended not much beyond "Italians love red wine"? Who knew that the principal often gave up on weak teachers whom she believed she could not influence and in so doing indirectly deprived students of meaningful engagement in potentially important subjects? Do such surprises impose any obligations on the researcher?

Are researchers to tell teachers what they really think of their teaching? Are they to talk to the principal about grossly incompetent teachers, thereby violating confidentiality? If they do not, how many more students will have their educational rights violated by having to suffer through such teaching?

Thus we all like the idea of informed consent, but we are less sure just who is to provide that consent, just how much consent is needed, and how we can inform others so as to obtain consent when we have such a hard time predicting what we need to get consent about.

Consider further the practice of providing those who are going to be observed with a description and rationale for the study we wish to undertake. For example, we ask the principal of a school or the superintendent of a school district to gather together teachers or principals who might wish to participate in a study we want to conduct. The study requires observation of classes, every day, all day, for two weeks. A report will be prepared that describes and appraises what has been seen (Eisner, 1985c). The aim of the study is to further our understanding of the conditions under which high school students and teachers work and the way in which those conditions influence what takes place in classrooms. This is important, the teachers are told, because the public has placed too much reliance on standardized test scores as a way of assessing the quality of schools. Those tests capture too little of what is taught and learned and sometimes obscure the very important contributions that teachers make to the educational development of their students. Furthermore, the deeper problems of schools might be due to factors that cannot be overcome by "more time on task," more required courses, higher standards, more testing, or more homework. The problems of schools that beset both teachers and students might very well be both more complex and more subtle.

Furthermore, the teachers are told that the most important contributions they make to their students might be located in interactions that achievement tests don't measure. Hence it is possible that much really excellent teaching never is given the visibility it deserves. Yet the public needs to know what is happening in order to make a fair assessment of its schools. We want to understand what is going on in schools by looking directly at real classrooms for comparatively long periods of time in order to provide the profession and the public with a more comprehensive analysis of at least a few schools in the area. We say to the teachers, "We hope we can secure your permission to visit your classrooms for a two-week period. At the end of the two weeks, if you wish, we will be happy to give you some feedback on what we have seen and what we think it means."

With little discussion the teachers and the administrative staff agree to participate. Participation means that we can have access to their classrooms and, if they want feedback at the end of the study, we will provide it to them.

Is this an example of informed consent? We worked only with volunteers. We described the aims and significance of our study. Everyone knew just how long we would be in the classroom. We promised feedback if they wanted it when the study was completed. What more could be provided? Plenty.

The teachers did not know if they would have the opportunity to read and comment on the study before it was published. They did not know whether their comments would be included if they thought a gross misunderstanding had occurred or if they believed they were described unfairly. They did not know if we would interview students to determine how they felt about their classes or if we would consult with teachers themselves during the course of the study. They did not know how we would conduct ourselves once in their classrooms or if we would provide assistance to students if students asked us for it. They did not ask about the degree of anonymity they could expect or if we would talk with the principal about what we had seen. They didn't ask us if they would need to spend additional time in school on tasks relevant to our aims as researchers, and so forth.

Now the question that must be addressed is this: Is a person and/or group adequately informed if they do not have the technical sophistication or expertise to raise questions that someone more sophisticated would raise? Do researchers have an ethical responsibility to serve in a dual role: first, as researchers with a project aimed at satisfying their research purposes, and second, advocates for the practitioners, raising questions that the researchers know should be raised in order for practitioners to make a competent assessment of the risks?

We all know by experience that providing partial information can be as misleading as withholding information. We also know that people are not always competent to appraise the information they are given, particularly in technical matters in which they have little or no expertise and therefore little foresight. Is the withholding of information that might jeopardize our interests a form of deception? Is it deceptive to cultivate rapport, and even more, to express more friendship than we actually feel, in order to inspire confidence that furthers our own ends? Put another way, can we ever live social lives without minor deceptions, incomplete stories, false enthusiasms? How many times have we said to colleagues, "I was really impressed by your paper," when we really weren't? Is this a form of deception? Does the answer depend on whether we are trying to make our colleagues feel good or whether we have a self-serving private motive?

When qualitative researchers work in the field, they are always "on." But by this I mean that qualitative researchers make use of anything they can: comments made casually by a student, teacher, or parent; something seen on a classroom bulletin board; the way in which teachers speak to the school principal; who sits next to whom at lunch. All of this and much more is grist for the research mill. In addition, establishing rapport means making people feel psychologically comfortable. A sense of comfort is important so that people will be more likely to reveal to researchers what they really think. The aims served are those of researchers, not primarily of those researched.

Furthermore, many people seldom encounter others who are willing to listen carefully to what they have to say over long periods of time. In this sense, qualitative researchers who convey to teachers or students a sincere interest in their opinions and ideas are likely to elicit a great deal of information that individuals may not even know they are providing. In addition, the person interviewed often receives a kind of therapeutic experience in the process, the kind that comes from being able to "unload."

On the one hand, to be able to create the psychological comfort that makes it possible for people to reveal what they think, feel, and fear is the mark of a good field researcher. On the other hand, the people interviewed might have regrets later about what they have said. They might feel vulnerable. In itself such a practice does not appear to violate any of the norms I have discussed, but it can slide over the edge of such norms if researchers allow themselves to play the role of therapist for someone more than ready to share intimacies. In short, researchers can take advantage of a quasi-therapeutic relationship because of the attractiveness of one of our most treasured gifts to others—the gift of lending serious attention and a sympathetic ear to what someone has to tell us.

Confidentiality

Consider again the matter of confidentiality. We promise confidentiality to those whom we study. Is it ever right to break our promise? Are there times when it is acceptable, indeed just, to go back on our word? Breaking promises made to fellow professionals and deceiving others are ugly notions. We do not like to think of ourselves as succumbing to such practices. But consider the following scenario. A researcher makes the following promises to a teacher he has asked to observe: first, that his observations will be kept confidential, and second, that if and when a report is written, its contents will be so disguised that no one will be able to tell who had been observed. The observer begins a course of observation and one day notices the teacher, a thirty-eight-year-old male, fondling one of his seven-year-old female students. What should the researcher do? Should he keep his promise to the teacher not to divulge what he has seen, or should he make a beeline to the principal to report it? Here the answer seems clear. A crime has been committed, and the obligation to report a crime supersedes a promise made to the perpetrator. Indeed, not to report what had occurred, if the observer was certain, would itself be a crime.

But suppose what is observed is not so egregious or flagrant and not a crime. Suppose a researcher observes a teacher who is incompetent. It is beyond a reasonable doubt that the students are learning to abhor the class and the subject matter. They are wasting their time in this class and wasting opportunities to study with a teacher who has something to offer. How bad does teaching need to be before the researcher should say something to the principal? Or does the researcher never say anything to anyone if he or she has made a promise not to divulge to others what has been observed? Perhaps the principal knows the teacher to be incompetent, but does not or cannot do anything about it. What is the researcher's responsibility?

What if a researcher sees a racially bigoted teacher subtly encouraging children to be bigots? Should the researcher tell someone and break the promise of confidentiality? Is the pursuit of knowledge so important that it overrides the immediate interests of children?

The examples I have given pertain to problem areas, areas in which teacher incompetence is displayed. It is seldom an ethical problem to deal with high levels of competent behavior. Yet what obligation, if any, does the researcher have to share the stellar but unrecognized accomplishments of a teacher he or she observes? Putting the shoe on the other foot, do researchers have a responsibility to correct misconceptions of teachers who are really superlative in their work but are regarded as average or below average by their colleagues or by the administration? In other words, is the obligation, if it is an obligation, to commend as important as to give negative criticism? I have put the case too strongly, but readers will know what I mean. Someone who does good but whose good goes unrecognized is being treated unfairly. Do researchers have an ethical responsibility to foster the fair treatment of those they observe?

Can Those Studied Opt Out?

Should researchers inform those observed—say, teachers—that they have a right to withdraw from a study at any time they wish? Will such an invitation increase the probability that some teachers will exercise that right, and if they do, what will that do to the study? Yet, if they are not given that option at the beginning, they might not realize that they have the right to withdraw. After all, few researchers sign written contracts with those whom they study. Teachers or school administrators could decide that the study is an imposition, or that they feel uncomfortable, or that they have other things to do with their time. In fact, those observed can decide at any time that they do not wish to be observed any longer. Should they be informed at the outset that this is an option, or should that bridge be crossed only if and when they come to it?

One way of resolving such problems is to try to appeal to some principle that guides ethical conduct. If a defensible principle can be found or formulated, and if the ethical decisions researchers make are consistent with such a principle, it seems reasonable to assume that the decisions guided by the principle will be ethical. But there can be more than one defensible principle, and at times such principles may conflict.

Consider, for example, withholding information that would otherwise allow the observed to make a decision adverse to the interests of the researcher and hence to the research. Upon analysis of the potential consequences of withholding information, the researcher reasonably concludes that there would be no likely adverse effects on the observed. In addition, the potential benefits of the study to others are unarguable.

Now this looks like a rather straightforward case. By withholding some information one increases the probability that a socially beneficial study will go forward. One also believes that the information withheld will cause no harm to those studied. Why not withhold information? The potential gains far outweigh the potential harm. In fact, the probability of harm is quite small.

One qualitative researcher, Lincoln (1990), relies upon Kant's categorical imperative that states, "Act as if the maxim of thy act were to become by thy will a universal law of nature." A "rights" position is embraced, so that there is no room for contextual ethics. People should never be used solely as a means to another's ends, regardless of context. Yet there is another principle, a utilitarian principle, that leads one to ask whether more good than harm is likely to be produced by a decision. A decision guided by the former rule might lead to one course of action, a decision guided by the latter to quite another.

The categorical imperative and its derivations would reject the utilitarian principle on the basis that although it is a relevant consideration, it is utterly inadequate. Humans, it would be argued, have rights that should not be compromised. The right to autonomy is one of them. Not to be used solely for the purposes of another is a second. Even if one were confident that no harm would come to the observed and that the public would benefit, withholding information that the observed needed in order to act would diminish the observed's right to autonomy, and hence would restrict the individual's freedom.

The counter to this argument is that the principle of rights rigidly defined undermines social progress and harms the larger good by unreasonably impeding the growth of knowledge. Social life cannot be lived fully under a yoke of rigid rules; different contexts and situations require intelligent judgment, not simple strictures. Indeed, we frequently embrace social norms that recognize the need *not* to ask for consent from others we observe because if we asked for such consent, we could not secure the information we need, information that serves the public good. Department stores use hidden surveillance cameras, thereby protecting their interests but invading the privacy of others. The police shadow suspects who have not yet been formally accused of a crime. One-way mirrors are sometimes used to observe classes in action. Those observed might not know they are being observed. Should they know? Should the teacher know? How old should students be before they are asked, if they are to be asked?

The point of these examples is simply to demonstrate the fact that we have, as a society, a long history of covert surveillance justified by the ends we seek to attain.[1] We do not inform others that they are being watched, for several reasons. First, we may believe it is unnecessary, *if* we believe the practice is inconsequential to those observed. Second, we fear that if we were to ask for permission to observe the behavior in which we are interested, the research we wish to conduct might be rendered impossible. Third, we may believe that even if there is some invasion of privacy, ethical judgments must sometimes be made on broader, more general social grounds and that substantial contributions to the public good warrant a "minor" invasion of individuals' privacy.

Each of the foregoing justifications for not informing "subjects" would be rejected by those embracing a "rights" perspective on ethics. I must confess that I do not know how to resolve such differences so as to satisfy all parties. Like many of life's problems, this one does not always have a single satisfying solution. Indeed, many of life's problems are not problems but dilemmas, and, similarly, many of the ethical problems in qualitative research are not problems but dilemmas; one cannot get away unscathed.

The need to pay special attention to ethical considerations in qualitative research is especially important, for very good reasons. Their neglect can cause serious problems for both the researcher and those researched. In conventional quantitative studies the data are usually secured during brief periods of time; a standardized test is administered to students, or someone with an observation schedule spends an hour or two in a classroom. Qualitative researchers hang around. They get to know the players, sometimes they become friends of those whom they study, and they learn about things that neither researcher nor researched could anticipate; they try to secure an intimate view of the classroom or school. Furthermore, the form of reporting is far more detailed and concrete than it is general and abstract. In a good educational criticism, for example, the people described become real, and even if no one else can identify the situations or people studied, those studied can; hence, the potential for pain as well as elation is always there.[2]

Quantitative studies usually report means, variances, and probabilities and do so on the basis of data secured quickly and reported abstractly. Although low test scores can jeopardize a school's reputation if the school—or the teacher—is identified, such data are seldom as personal as the kind of information found in qualitative research.

This potential creates, I believe, the need to be particularly careful in doing qualitative research. The following account, a "real life" description of my own experience, illustrates how my good intentions and naivete caused difficulty in one school. I have already alluded to this example, but I provide it here in more detail.

Some Real-Life Mistakes

The study focused on six high schools in the San Francisco Bay area of California (Eisner, 1985c, Atkin, Kennedy & Patrick, 1989). My aim was to understand the ways in which the organization of a school, the school's reward system, and the climate of the school as a whole influenced the students' educational experience and the way in which teaching occurred. In addition, I hoped that examples of stellar teaching would be identified during the course of observation and that when they were described, the report would help the public become aware that there were places of pedagogical excellence in secondary schools, at least in this area of California. I hoped that this study would counteract some of the gloomy analyses of American secondary education that were reported in *A Nation at Risk* (USA Research, 1984) and in other publications that had appeared shortly before the study was begun.

One major part of the study required graduate students to shadow students in each of the six high schools for two weeks. This procedure would give them access to the school and to individual classes, and would provide them with a teen-age guide whose comments and general conversation would make it easier to understand what was going on. During the course of shadowing students from 8 A.M. to 3 P.M. daily for two weeks, the graduate students would compile field notes and prepare an educational criticism for each school.

Since six schools would be studied, we would review all of the educational criticisms that were written and then do a content analysis of each in order to locate important common themes. We would then illustrate these themes through concrete examples. We would eventually write a report using the twenty-four educational criticisms as sources. We promised schools, teachers, and students anonymity in our final report.

We contacted the superintendent of each of the six districts, described the study, and made a request to speak to high school principals in their district. In all cases they granted permission. We followed the same procedure with principals, except that here we asked to speak with the entire school faculty in order to seek their permission to conduct the study in their school. Again, after we described the aims and method of the study, both principals and faculties granted permission.

We then asked the English teachers in each school to ask students in their classes if they would like to be shadowed for two weeks by a Stanford graduate student. The teachers described the aims of the study to their students. We secured a list of students who had volunteered to be shadowed, reviewed their programs and cumulative folders, and identified those suitable for our purposes. From the pool of students we had identified, the principal selected those whom he or she thought particularly suitable for the study. We then selected the students we would shadow from the list suggested by the principal. Each student was telephoned by the Stanford graduate student who was to shadow him or her, and a time and place to meet were determined so that the shadowing could begin.

At the end of the two-week shadowing period (which actually took three weeks: one week of shadowing, one week off, another week of shadowing) each researcher wrote an educational criticism, and we moved on to the next school repeating the same procedures. When all of the shadowing in all of the schools had been completed and all the educational criticisms written, we conducted a content analysis of the twenty-four educational criticisms to identify the common themes that would guide the writing of the final report.

Before we prepared the final report, we offered feedback sessions to each of the principals. Of the six principals whose schools were studied, four wanted feedback. The plan was to provide oral feedback to them and the teachers who wished to attend, and then, during the following academic year, to prepare a final written report. Since I was to be in Europe the following academic year, I would have the time to write the report and to share it with the dean of the School of Education under whose leadership the study had been undertaken.

I have identified earlier in this chapter some of the errors I made regarding informed consent: I did not inform either teachers or administrators that they would not have an opportunity to review the written report or to comment upon it before its release. I did not specify the responsibilities teachers would assume or whether they would be required to devote time to the study beyond their own teaching, and so forth. But these errors of omission were not the only ones made, nor were they the most serious.

The superintendent of one of the school districts made the inspired suggestion that four experienced teachers from the high school in his district shadow four high school students for three full days as a kind of supplement to the observations that the Stanford graduate students were making. I readily agreed. The principal of the high school selected the four teachers, whom I then briefed on method and asked to prepare a brief educational criticism, or something close to it, after they had concluded their observations.

It is important to remember that one aim of the study was to identify excellent teaching and to present to the public through the study something of the unappreciated achievements of secondary schools. In fact, I hoped we would find much to boast about in order to counter the spate of negative criticisms that teachers and schools had been subjected to in the public press.

My aspiration was not fulfilled as I had hoped. We saw little to boast about in any of the schools we observed. We did find some remarkable teaching, but it was clear that these teachers were exceptional. The norm for the group of teachers we observed was not very high, for many reasons. Some of the reasons had to do with the structure of the school, with the use of shortsighted reward systems that undermined intrinsic motivation, with the paucity of feedback on teaching, and with the too-frequent feeling among teachers that no one really cared about their work. I described these issues in the report. In short, we did not find what we had hoped to find, except in some rare cases.

But perhaps our observations were a function of coming to the schools with a university "bias," perhaps our expectations were too high, or perhaps we misinterpreted what we had seen. The observations of the experienced teachers who shadowed students in their own school, however, were in line with what we had seen, and their reports were congruent with ours. Although the picture of high schools that emerged from the study had its high moments, on the whole it was not very flattering.[3]

As I indicated earlier, I wrote the report while I was in Europe and sent it airmail to Stanford. While I was still in Europe, the report was duplicated and released to the schools and to the press before the schools had a chance to comment. To make matters worse, a reporter found out which high school teacher was the author of a statement I included in the report that described in rather negative terms the life of students in the school in which she taught. Next, a picture of this teacher appeared in the local newspaper, the teacher was interviewed, and the school, the school's principal, and the district's superintendent lost the anonymity I had promised.

The results were predictable. The principal was extremely upset. The superintendent, a wise and rare educator, wanted further information and visited the school himself to see what was going on. I met with the superintendent, the principal, and some of his administrative staff, as did some of the teachers who had shadowed students in the school. The teachers did not take issue with most of what the report had to say; their own written material was not unlike our own comments, albeit much briefer. The problem was never fully resolved. The principal felt betrayed. I felt very bad about the report being sent out without my permission, and to this day, it would be difficult, perhaps impossible, for any researcher to conduct another study in that school. This is a first-hand example of not leaving the site clean.

All of the mistakes in this case were made by well-meaning but naive people who did not foresee the errors of omission and commission they were making. I had not adequately informed the faculty of the school about the study or their rights and responsibilities simply because I had not thought deeply enough about my own obligations. Someone in the School of Education at Stanford distributed the study without my permission, thinking it would be good to do so. Someone gave the newspaper reporter the name of the teacher whose excerpt appeared in the report I wrote because he or she wanted to be helpful (perhaps to secure publicity for the research).

This story illustrates not malevolent behavior, but good intentions gone wrong and ignorance due to inexperience. Ethical considerations were simply not particularly high on the agenda of my interests or concerns. This has now changed.

To Sum Up

The aim of this chapter is to *identify* some of the ethical tensions, controversies, and dilemmas in qualitative research, not to resolve those ethical tensions. I have attempted to illuminate some of them and to describe the situations in which principles come into conflict. We all want to act virtuously and to secure informed consent from those we study, but it is clear that we cannot always inform others about the course of our research, not only because we often cannot predict its course, but because at times we cannot predict our aims. We can, of course, enter the field with certain general questions in mind, but whether these questions will remain dominant depends on what sense we make of the situations we experience once on the site. Furthermore, we cannot get consent from everyone who contributes information to our work because to do so would make our work impossible. Thus, to some extent, we do invade the privacy of others. We will be using others for our own purposes. How should we conduct ourselves? What do we owe those whom we study? What principles can we appeal to for guidance?

Even at the abstract and general level there can be conflicts between two arguable ethical positions. If we embrace the concept of rights—a kind of categorical imperative—we guide our professional life by certain rules in a way not unlike those who are guided by orthodox religious principles. To the religiously orthodox, compromise or contextual ethics are *generally* unattractive and often unacceptable options. If, however, we believe that wisdom requires judgment of the consequences of an act, then we try to anticipate the consequences, not only to those we study, but to those who might benefit from what we have learned. If we are epistemological realists and assume we are searching for Truth, the justification for compromising the interests of those we study might be greater than if we believe that we are not primarily after Truth, but after fallible versions of the world that we can use. What we have in the Ten Commandments is a categorical imperative: No ifs, ands, or buts. What we have in consequentialism or utilitarianism is assessment of context and the exercise of judgment. But in consequentialism we introduce the thin edge of a wedge that eventually could be used to justify what we believe ought not to be justified.

What then do we have? We might like to secure consent that is informed, but we know we can't always inform because we don't always know. We would like to protect personal privacy and guarantee confidentiality, but we know that we cannot always fulfill such guarantees. We would like to be candid, but sometimes candor is inappropriate. We do not like to think of ourselves as using others as a means to our own professional ends, but if we embark upon a research study that we conceptualize, direct, and write, we virtually assure that we will use others for our purposes.

What all of this means for me personally is that I do not believe we can, in practice, meet all of the categorical imperatives that function as ideals for our work. Ideals, in any realm, are always somewhat out of reach. Similarly, I would not be happy with an approach to qualitative research that appealed to a utilitarian or consequentialist position that made virtually any action justifiable.

This leaves us with the tensions, controversies, and dilemmas with which we started. I hope, though, we now have a somewhat greater consciousness of the issues and considerations we can take into account. With such consciousness we are in a better position to exercise sensibility, taste, and that most precious human capacity, rational judgment. We are, I believe, destined to remain without rules in matters of ethics. Perhaps that is as it should be, a certain sign that all of us are "condemned" to a significant measure of freedom.

Notes

1. A recent illuminating analysis of surveillance methods and their impact in modern society can be found in Gary T. Marx's *Undercover: Police Surveillance in America* (1988).

2. Nancy Schepper-Hughes indicates that townsfolk in the Irish village she studied were able to identify themselves in her book, *Saints, Scholars, and Schizophrenics: Mental Illness in Rural Ireland* (1979). In many ways this is not surprising, particularly if the writer has done a good job in portraying the world or some aspect of it as vividly as is desirable.

3. I must confess that this was a disappointment to me since I wanted to be able to portray features of schooling that were admirable and that might have provided a new set of perspectives that other studies of secondary schools had missed. Given what we had found, my aspiration for such a perspective was not fulfilled.

Chapter XI

Looking Ahead: Preparing Qualitative Researchers

Those who refuse to speculate are traitors to the future.
Alfred North Whitehead

Inventing the Future

The growing interest in qualitative inquiry in education represents more than a mere refinement of existing modes of inquiry. It represents the beginning of a new way of thinking about the nature of knowledge and how it can be created. Further, the entry of qualitative considerations into educational research makes it possible to understand more clearly the assumptions upon which conventional approaches to research are based. It therefore contributes not only to a new appreciation of qualitative methods, but to a deeper understanding of conventional forms of research as well.

Readers might worry that in writing about qualitative modes of inquiry and their more conventional counterparts—say, the experiment whose effects are determined through analysis of variance—I have created a false dichotomy, an either/or representation, or a set of methodological polarities that do not match the real world. What we really have, they might claim, is not a difference in kind between qualitative approaches and the quantitatively reported experiment, but a difference in where research methods fall upon a continuum. My response is that while the concept of "continuum" is an ecumenical one, given the appropriate frame of reference, virtually anything—even sex—can be put on a continuum. To dismiss or underestimate the basic differences in method and epistemology between a laboratory experiment, and an educational criticism is to miss the unique contributions of each genre of work. There are differences between such works that even if put on some imaginary continuum would still not obliterate their fundamentally different features.[1] I agree with Smith and Heshusius (1986) that it is better to recognize differences and to exploit plurality than to try to gloss over them in the name of unity. We can

227

have plurality of procedure and epistemological diversity in the field and still speak to each other and work toward common ends. In fact, plurality of method is much more hopeful than fealty to a single model of legitimate inquiry. What we need is excellent work, whatever the genre, and scholars who are capable of shifting perspectives and sufficiently flexible to know what questions and criteria to put to a study.

How do we get excellent qualitative research? What kinds of programs might be useful in preparing young scholars capable of creating such work? This chapter addresses these questions and the future of qualitative inquiry in education.

Preparing Qualitative Researchers

The readers for whom I write are those who wish to learn to conduct qualitative research in education, particularly that form called educational criticism. These include practicing teachers and school administrators, but most especially doctoral students in the field of education.

In many ways the preparation of qualitative researchers is easier now than it was in the early 1970s. First, qualitative methods in educational research are far more acceptable today than they were then. Major research universities have schools and departments of education in which courses on qualitative methods are taught—places like Stanford, Harvard, Chicago, Columbia Teachers College, Michigan State, and the University of Illinois, to mention only a few. Second, we have models of qualitative work in education that did not exist in the early 1970s, as well as increasing attention to such work in the American Educational Research Association. A new journal, the *International Journal of Qualitative Studies in Education*, founded in 1988, publishes articles devoted to qualitative methods and the results of their use. Indeed, even the *Educational Researcher* in the past five years has devoted about 10 percent of all of the articles it has published to qualitative research issues. Considering the broad diversity of interests in the educational research community, this degree of attention is impressive.

In order for students in the 1970s to undertake a doctoral dissertation in the School of Education at Stanford using qualitative methods, they had to write long introductions to their proposals, and then to their dissertations, justifying the use of such methods; one dissertation I directed contained a seventy-page chapter justifying the use of educational criticism. The picture today is different. At Stanford's School of Education qualitative methods have joined the methodological requirements graduate students must study.

There is, though, one tendency that is troublesome: the tendency to reduce qualitative inquiry to ethnography. Ethnography is qualitative in character, but not all qualitative research is ethnographic. I wish to address this point here before laying out an agenda for the preparation of qualitative researchers in education.

Ethnography is a branch of anthropology, which is a discipline concerned with the study of culture. Physical anthropologists often study cultural evolution through the measurement and analysis of artifacts. Cultural anthropologists typically try to understand the meanings shared by those who participate in the culture. Since qualitative researchers in education typically study communities, schools, and classrooms in order to understand what makes them tick, the tendency to look to ethnography—the branch of anthropology that, according to Geertz (1973), is concerned with inscription—is understandable. Yet anthropology is not only characterized by a set of methods—field study, the use of informants, inscription, the analysis of artifacts, and so forth—it also is characterized by a set of concepts and theories through which focus is secured and interpretation achieved. These concepts and theories—adaptation, culture, kinship, taboo, totemism, incest, community—and theories such as the structuralism of Lévi-Strauss, the functionalism of Malinowski, the structural-functionalism of Radcliffe-Brown, and the configurationalism of Ruth Benedict are not intellectually indifferent. Each in its own way shapes perspective and imposes its own interpretive frame. These concepts and theories are important, even when they operate only tacitly in field work. In the end, they give focus to the work; the questions Benedict asks about what fits within a culture and what contributes to its unique order, pattern, and texture are different from Malinowski's functionalism. Malinowski is more focused on the utility of, for example, a rite of passage for enabling a culture to survive within its particular environment. Each theory, so to speak, puts to the world its own questions and gets, therefore, its own answers.

Yet the questions raised by these cultural theorists, even when considered collectively, do not exhaust the questions that could have been put or the theories that could have been used to explain what was seen. Ethnography, even taken as a whole, constitutes a limited repertoire of meaning structures. Thus, to regard qualitative research as solely ethnographic is to limit what qualitative work can be.

If concepts, theories, and the questions that different theories suggest are important in shaping focus and explaining what one sees, then using different concepts and theories is important for revealing the richness of social phenomena. Where do we find such concepts and theories? At least one place is in the social science disciplines, and especially in those concepts and theories that have been developed in the field of education. We can look at a school as a culture in a way that is not unlike the way in which Margaret Mead (1928) looked at Samoan life. But we can also look at schools through the perspectives of political science: as power structures, as institutions that foster particular ideologies, and as loci for negotiation, treaties, and political coalitions.

We can observe a classroom as an arena in which educational philosophies are played out, as a place for "turn-taking," as a race for scarce resources—high grades—and as a situation in which teachers surreptitiously create ways to actualize their own deeply held professional values while meeting institutional norms. We can examine the school from sociological perspectives and ask about matters of status, gender, and social structure and their relevance for initiating the young into implied social norms. Each of these concepts is derived from a social science discipline and can serve as the interpretive heart of qualitative research. What defines such research is threefold: (1) what one attends to in the setting, (2) how one secures information about what one has observed, and (3) the way in which what has been observed is integrated and made significant. Anthropological perspectives generate studies in which the terms of description and interpretation are cultural in the anthropological sense. The focus of the study will be shaped by a tradition and by theoretical interests functioning within the field of anthropology. If one has other interests and other concepts—say, power—political science is the more appropriate resource.

Qualitative inquiry is marked by the way in which the world is viewed and portrayed, and by the conceptual orientation used to see and to make sense of what one has seen. Qualitative inquiry can be historical, sociological, political, or educational, and more. Indeed its character can be derived from any of the disciplines from which its focus, description, and explanation have been secured. The early efforts in biology to classify and to create taxonomies were qualitative efforts. All of the social sciences have in common the search for pattern in the qualities they observe, the effort to illuminate and display what has not been previously noticed, and the attempt to account for what has been seen; this explains the invention and use of concepts and theories relevant to particular disciplinary aims.

Since our task is to conceptualize the features of a program that would be useful in preparing skilled qualitative researchers, we turn first to the heart of any form of qualitative inquiry: the development of perceptivity.

The development of perceptivity, or what I have called connoisseurship, is critical for qualitative work of any kind because it is the achievement of experience of a classroom, school, community, textbook, set of instructional materials, or student essay that provides the material from which patterns are perceived and interpretations are made. If researchers have no consciousness of what is significant in a setting, it is unlikely that anything subsequent will occur that is of interest. The teacher needs to experience the qualities of a class to have a basis for action. The qualitative researcher must experience the qualities that pervade a classroom to have a basis for any kind of theoretical interpretation.

Theories and concepts, schema and categories, provide cues with which to look, but cues are only pointers—one still must be able to experience the qualities pointed to. In this sense, theoretical language—indeed, any language—can act as a heuristic that makes the search more efficient, but it is in the refinement of the sensibilities that the phenomena themselves are made real in experience.

The major resources for such experience, aside from and more significant than concepts and theories, are refined sensibilities related to a domain of interest. I say "a domain of interest" in order to emphasize that there are limits to the generalization of sensibility. Experiencing the nuances of a lesson in algebra is not the same as experiencing the nuances of a lesson in art. Thus learning to see—or more broadly, learning to experience—functions within parameters that have limits. Connoisseurs of African art may be insensitive to the art of the French Baroque. People who are competent at appraising the teaching of physics may be out of touch with the teaching of history. As Stodolsky (1988) says, "the subject matters."[2]

The perception of a set of phenomena clearly depends upon visual differentiation. Visual differentiation not only requires refined sensibilities—indeed, that is what is meant by differentiation—it also requires a schema against which to compare and with which to conduct what might be called a perceptual search. In fact, the development of connoisseurship in a domain implies a stock of schemata whose use often looks not like a search, but more like the seamless, almost effortless moves of a skilled practitioner. Those with refined sensibilities and an appropriate schema see quickly. Furthermore, they understand the significance of what they see. Their rendering of, say, a discussion in the social studies is much more likely to zero in on what is important within some educational frame of reference (Berliner, 1988).

How Do People Become Connoisseurs?

The problem we face is how the skills of perception or connoisseurship can be developed. One requirement is guided practice in the analysis of the phenomena one wishes to learn about. To develop perceptivity in teaching social studies, for example, one must observe many social studies classes. Now it might be said that the doctoral student or teacher already has a great deal of experience observing classrooms. After all, unlike those who choose other fields, those who go into education have lived in classrooms since they were five. It would seem that they have a vast body of experience to draw upon.

Things are not quite so simple. One can spend a lifetime in a community and still experience only a small portion of what is there. It often takes perceptive and articulate writers to point out what one missed.

Someone can spend a great deal of time in a classroom, indeed the better part of a childhood, and still miss many of its major features. Being in the role of student in a school is not the same as being in the role of a student of schooling. The perceptual attitudes associated with each role differ. The implication of this is that students wishing to conduct qualitative research need to have practice in learning to see. They can secure this in several ways.

First, videotapes of classrooms in real time can serve as the subject matter for analysis. There is no reason why schools and departments of education cannot have, as a part of their instructional resources, a variety of tapes displaying teaching in a range of fields and grade levels. Videotapes are relatively easy to make as long as classroom teachers are willing to grant permission. Tapes can be made in classrooms in schools in various parts of the state or country and shared through cooperative relationships with other institutions.

While there are very important differences between watching a videotape of a teacher or class and being present in the classroom—the aperture and focus of a video camera is not nearly as flexible or as swift as the human eye—using videotape has very important advantages. Tapes can be replayed. The importance of playback is related to one "rule" that I impose on those who analyze videotapes: students must be able to refer to the qualities on the tape that support their descriptions, interpretations, or evaluations of what they have seen.

The function of this rule is not to accommodate behaviorist criteria, but to increase caution and reflectivity, to encourage students not to use the tape as a Rorschach test or as a license to say whatever they please, regardless of what is there to be seen. Of course, much of what is seen is open to interpretation. For example, was the student's rapt attention to the teacher real or feigned? Differences in interpretation, even in description, create a context for deliberation, debate, and precisely the kind of mustering of evidence that contributes to the development of educational connoisseurship. In my experience, students are impressed with both the complexity of teaching and the apparent inexhaustibility of what can be said about a forty-minute videotape. As discussion and analysis proceed, more and more is seen as more and more is said. Sometimes first impressions are sustained; often they are revised. The aim is not to exhaust the tape, but to provide the conditions through which students can learn that there is much more to see. They learn from their peers' comments and from their own growing awareness.

It is important that these tapes not be edited. The gray, sometimes dull aspects of classroom life are important and perform significant psychological functions. To edit out such material might make the tape more interesting, but it would significantly alter the conditions that students of schooling need to understand.

Some students might comment after the first four or five minutes of analysis of a forty-minute tape that such a limited snippet is not a fair sample of the teacher's work. They are, of course, correct. They need to be reassured that their analysis is not going to be taken as the last word on the teacher's work. It is an exercise from which to learn, not a report about a particular teacher. Neither forty minutes of observation nor a videotape is an adequate resource for making dependable judgments about individual teachers or their classrooms.

Because the teacher is typically the center of the stage in the classroom, the video camera is often focused almost exclusively on what the teacher is doing. This should be avoided. The problem here is that the students' reactions are often neglected. A good camera operator will focus not only on the teacher but also on the students and will try to provide a wide-angle view of the entire classroom at the outset so that viewers have some sense of the scene as a whole—the number of males and females, the layout of the room, and so forth. At the initial stages it is important to get a sense of the context, so that students can feel almost as if they had been there in person. I do not wish to go into the technical details of videotaping classrooms, except to say that the teacher should wear a wireless mike and that someone besides the camera operator will need to use a rifle microphone to pick up students' comments. My point in this section is to underscore the usefulness of videotape in developing educational connoisseurship.

Describing, interpreting, and evaluating videotapes are boot camp for the real thing—the live classroom and functioning school. Nothing replaces being there. Being there means that novice researchers can talk to the teacher and to the students about their work, their aims, their satisfactions, and their frustrations. Being there enables them to pick up information that eludes even the most skillfully produced videotape. Being there means they act as their own editor, something that is sacrificed when someone else decides where to point the camera and what to pick up on the audio. Our ability to tune in and out, to receive information through peripheral vision, to process on a multiplicity of channels, and to cope with complex speech and action, become vivid when we compare being there with watching a videotape. Playbacks are, of course, not possible in the classroom. Time cannot be stopped. Videotapes have unique utilities, and their use in developing connoisseurship is invaluable. But the textures and smells of classrooms, the experience of having to cope with one's own intrusiveness in a class filled with children or adolescents simply do not exist when one watches a videotape in a university classroom. Hence, the second major training resource, and the most important, is access to real classrooms and schools. It is through such access and the guided practice and analysis of what is seen that the skills of connoisseurship are cultivated.

Perceptual differentiation is fostered by having opportunities to compare and contrast qualities and configurations; watching videotapes or observing classrooms in which, say, two teachers teach the same subject, preferably the same topic, to comparable groups of children provides a rich resource for developing an awareness of similarities and differences. McCutcheon (1976) produced precisely such materials in her study of three male teachers teaching children at the same grade the same topic within a science lesson in three elementary schools within the same school district. What such material teaches, in addition to the refinement of perception, is the important lesson that each teacher inscribes his or her own signature on a class and that at one level there is no common curriculum, even when teachers use the same curriculum syllabus and textbook.

Some differences in the perception and interpretation of classrooms are inevitable, and beginning researchers should anticipate that some of these differences will be unresolvable. The unresolved differences among observers can be set aside for a time—indeed, they may occupy a permanent place on the back burner. At other times what appears unresolvable may generate very useful discussion and provide a stimulus for deeper analysis.

It is difficult to overestimate the importance of perceptivity in the conduct of qualitative inquiry. The practical implication of this point is that methodological training ought to focus as much on refining the skills of perception as it now focuses on developing competence in research design and skills in statistical analysis. We seem to assume that the sensibilities need no cultivation, that theory does the job, that learning to see is already developed or that whatever perceptivity students have is adequate. Frankly, I believe the neglect of explicit attention to the development of connoisseurship is due, in part, to a tradition of neglect—it was not much a part of the preparation professors received when they were students. It is also due, in part, to the assumption that with experience observers will develop perceptivity on their own. I have been watching American football on television for thirty years and I still have a hard time seeing what goes on. Experience, to reiterate, *is achieved*. It is not an automatic consequence of maturation or merely a function of the number of times someone does something.

Representing What Is Seen

If the development of perceptivity is one side of the qualitative coin, the development of skills of representation is the other. The preparation of qualitative researchers must include exposure to the various ways in which the world is revealed. This means developing some sophistication in the epistemology of symbolic forms; here Nelson Goodman's (1976, 1978) work would be very helpful.

On the epistemological side, one wants students to understand that the need to represent is a fundamental part of the human condition. Humans have a basic need to externalize the internal, to communicate, to share their experience with others. The trick is to learn how to use a form of representation through which imagination, affect, and belief can be given a public, articulate presence. Art, music, dance, prose, and poetry are some of the forms that have been invented to perform this function. Each is nontranslatable; there is no verbal equivalent for Bach's *Mass in B Minor* and no literal equivalent for "Mending Wall." Thus part of the epistemological task is to try to understand the various uses of each form. What can be said in poetry that cannot be said in prose? What features of poetry account for this? By understanding the unique functions of forms of representation, by grasping the relationship between the form and the content that it can represent, we may achieve a fuller appreciation of what we now take for granted. We take prose for granted. Indeed, we seem to believe that literal prose can say it all. It can't. Since the aim of research is to reveal, understanding the limits and uses of the forms used to represent what connoisseurship has made available is important if for no other reason than to understand the way each form shapes content—that is, by leaving out what it cannot represent.

In another sense, it is important for students to develop an appreciation for the ways in which the world is represented, and for that to occur it is useful to encounter models that successfully represent the world in different ways. *Don Quixote* can tell us something about leadership; so can Machiavelli's *Prince. Hamlet* can reveal something about indecision; so can *Anna Karenina*. Wolcott's (1984) *The Man in the Principal's Office* provides one portrayal of what it is like to be a school administrator; John Fielders's (1981) *Profile: The Role of the Chief Superintendent of Schools* presents another view. Erving Goffman (1961) tells us about mental institutions in *Asylums*. Kesey's (1970) *One Flew over the Cuckoo's Nest* reveals a different picture. Howard Becker's (1963) *Boys in White* talks about professional socialization; Mel Konner's (1987) *Becoming a Doctor* tells a different story.

It is significant, I believe, that in recent years social scientists, particularly in sociology and anthropology, have developed a keen interest in the use of photography as a tool for conveying sociological and anthropological knowledge of the world. Howard Becker, a leader in this movement, regards photography as an important tool for understanding the social world. While recognizing the potential liabilities of the medium, he urges its full exploration and the epistemological possibilities it possesses (Becker, 1986).

Visual anthropologists have similar views and, in fact, Gregory Bateson and Margaret Mead (1952) used both film and photography in their very early efforts to reveal the life of Balinese families. And, of course,

Flaherty and Révillon Frères's (1922) *Nanook of the North* is a classic effort to help non-Eskimos appreciate the rigors of Eskimo life.

Models such as these, more directly than perhaps anything else, display to students the possibilities in qualitative inquiry. The standardized formats required of authors wishing to publish in some research journals have the virtue of facilitating comparison across research studies. They also have the liability of imposing upon researchers the constraints of a common framework, whether or not it is appropriate.

A particularly useful resource that displays the capacity of language to reveal nuance is the work of critics. The art critic, for example, copes with the task of rendering a painting vividly through the use of language. The critic must perceive the qualities the work possesses, understand their artistic antecedents, appraise the work's aesthetic merits, and then build a bridge through language that makes the work visible to less sophisticated viewers. When the critic's work is done well, the work becomes accessible. When it is done badly, the language itself becomes the object of admiration.

Critics of film come even closer to the work of the qualitative researcher. Consider a film by Lena Wertmüller, *The Seven Beauties*. Bruno Bettelheim, the late psychoanalyst whose initial training was in art history, reviewed it in the August 2, 1976, *New Yorker*. Bettelheim's review is an impressive demonstration of his ability to see, to penetrate, and to disclose the meanings embedded in the film and its larger social implications. The film is the story of two runaway Italian soldiers captured by the Germans during the last months of World War II. Bettelheim's critique focuses on the film's major theme, survival. The film vividly portrays these Italian soldiers trying to survive during their internment in a German concentration camp. Bettelheim analyzes not only the film, but also the background of its director, and he discusses the film's social implications. He compares the reactions of American and European audiences and puts the film's purported facts in a historical context. He brings to his work a vast understanding of historical detail and uses his background in both art and history to ground his criticism. After reading Bettelheim's (1979) "Surviving," we can no longer see Wertmüller's work in the same light as before. In some sense, not only has the work been "undressed," its social values have also been examined and the reasons for audience receptivity revealed. Bettelheim addresses the film not only as a work of art, but as a social document whose deeper message, he believes, was generally misunderstood.

It is clear that the work of the critic is qualitative, but is it research? Does it convey knowledge? Is it empirical? The work of the critic is clearly empirical since it addresses qualities in the empirical world. This is as empirical as anything can be. Its aim is to help readers come to know something about the world, the test of which resides in its referential adequacy. Does it convey knowledge? Only if it is effective. Is it research? If we are willing to call Erving Goffman's (1961) description of asylums research, or Tocqueville's (1898) portrait of America, or Lynd's (1929) *Middletown*, or Peshkin's (1986) *God's Choice*, then the critic's work must also be considered a genre of research. All share the common enterprise of describing and interpreting a small section of the world, with the aim of furthering our understanding of that world.

Questions of the kind I have raised, I believe, ought to be examined in programs preparing qualitative researchers. In some sense, it matters less that such questions be definitively answered than that they be asked during the course of training. The puzzlements that such questions raise have productive consequences. They deepen the intellectual conversation and broaden perspectives. Combined with models of the way the world can be portrayed, they contribute to a wider array of forms of inquiry that students can consider in doing research. With more drummers—and other instruments—the music becomes more interesting.

Skills in Using and Generating Theory

I have already alluded to the focusing role that theory performs in the perception and interpretation of social phenomena. Given its important functions, one of the critical tasks in the preparation of qualitative researchers is practice in using theory to account for what they describe. To use theory in this way is not easy, in part because of the generality of theory and the qualitative specificity of events. Nevertheless, it is a task worth attempting. Fortunately, we have good models of such work. Erving Goffman's work in sociology is a particularly powerful model of how theory can be related to the social world. What Goffman does is not only to apply theories already developed to the social situations he studies, he uses those situations to invent new theoretical concepts.

In the field of education Sara Lawrence Lightfoot's (1983) conceptions of the good high school are very helpful, as are Jackson's (1986) interpretations of teaching.

The analysis of the qualities of the social world is a rich source for theory construction. New concepts are more likely to be invented when new phenomena are experienced. When such invention occurs, another tool is added to the kit of the qualitative researcher. When one's practical interests are educational and when the setting is educational—say, a school or classroom—the conditions are right for generating concepts that are distinctively educational. It is through the process of framing new notions that more adequately address the phenomena of interest—in this case, education—that disciplines are created and refined. A discipline is an artifact, a product of the imagination designed to serve some useful function. There is no reason why there could not be a field called *educology*, the study of education, just as there is a field of *psychology*, the study of the psyche; or *sociology*, the study of the social world; or *biology*, the study of life; or *hematology*, the study of blood. Levels of abstraction and the subject matter of the discipline are arbitrary. We can slice the world in any way that makes sense.

I mention this because some people in the educational community believe that there cannot be, in principle, a discipline of education. Indeed, they regard the practice of education as an applied social science. Apparently they believe that disciplines are natural entities rather than cultural artifacts. I believe that the qualitative study of educational situations is one of the most promising ways to create a discipline of education.

My primary aim here is not to make the case for a discipline of education, but to discuss the importance of theory in the preparation of qualitative researchers and the role that theory can perform in doing qualitative work. It has been my experience that the application of theory in qualitative studies is often difficult and rather thin. There are several reasons for this. First, much of the theory that is available to educational researchers is either too general or ill-suited to the phenomena being described. The fit is not comfortable. Second, the particular features of the situation often require a more customized and context-specific interpretation than the theory available can provide. Third, most qualitative studies are undertaken not as hypothesis-testing enterprises, but as efforts that provide ex post facto explanations. That is, although researchers may have a general theme in which they are interested, the focus is usually emergent. Very often researchers do not really know what they are going to study until they have immersed themselves in the context. The task is more a matter of exploring what they have seen than of searching for qualities to test a theory.

In addition, in the analysis of practical affairs no single theory is likely to be adequate. As Schwab (1969) points out, there is a need for the arts of the eclectic, of putting things together, of multiple interpretations, of bridge building, of reasoning by analogy. Plausible interpretation and convincing insight rather than Truth are the major aspirations, even after one has spent, in some cases, years of field work in a particular setting.[3]

Yet, one of the primary reasons students have difficulty providing a convincing theoretical interpretation of the phenomena they study may be that they have little experience in doing so. Most graduate schools of education make little in-class use of simulation or realia. Making sense of print is still the major mode of communication. The print medium alone is to convey the message; analysis and theory are typically not applied to cases. What is needed, in my view, are videotapes, films, and visits to real settings in which theories can be applied for purposes of explanation. In fact, it would be useful for students to have the opportunity to apply more than one theory to a situation in order to illustrate the different ways in which the situation can be interpreted.

There is, of course, another reason why theory may be so difficult to apply to real life. The theories may simply be irrelevant or inadequate. In short, theory that can adequately provide a convincing explanation of the social or pedagogical scene in education may be scarcer than we believe.

What I have suggested so far regarding the preparation of qualitative researchers is, first, training in connoisseurship, through guided experience in the description, interpretation, and appraisal of educational situations, preferably ones in which comparisons and contrasts can be made. Second, I have identified the importance of encountering models of narrative or interpretation that can enable students to appreciate the various uses of different forms of representation. Third, I have described the importance of developing skill in the application of theories to socially complex situations as a means of accounting for the situations that have been described. The first need is for the cultivation of perception. The second is to understand the variety of ways in which the world can be described. The third is to acquire the ability to use theory so that it can explain what perception has provided. I have no doubt that university programs could develop courses in which such skills and understandings could be developed. At present they are rare.

Earlier I underscored the importance of developing some understanding of epistemology as a part of the training of qualitative researchers. I turn to this issue next.

Understanding Assumptions About Epistemology

One of the seductive features of professional socialization is that researchers seldom critically examine the assumptions and values into which they have been socialized. As a result, critical consciousness of the methods studied is seldom achieved.

Consider this question: Can everything, in principle, be measured? To answer it requires an analysis of the meaning of measurement. It also requires an understanding of what measurement describes and what it leaves out of its description. Yet most researchers do not undertake such analysis, and as a result think that what is measured represents its subject matter adequately. This is particularly egregious since the aim of measurement is to provide a precise, procedurally objective account of a set of qualities. Whether the qualities are measured with precision depends upon the nature of the instruments employed. Sometimes the instruments used are very precise, sometimes they are not. And if bias is to some extent a function of taking the part for the whole, measurement is *always* biased because it is always partial. Bias occurs because of omission as well as commission, and since there is no form of representation that includes everything, *in this particular sense,* all forms of representation are biased. Qualitative researchers as well as those trained in conventional research methods should not be strangers to such considerations. They are not merely philosophical musings, they bear directly on what we think we can believe.

How can knowledge be defined? What do we mean by cognition? What is affect? Can we know a cause on the basis of probable knowledge? Is there a difference between belief and knowledge? What constitutes adequate warrant for knowing something? And do all forms of knowledge result in true propositions whose warrant can be tested? If so, how shall we regard what people say they know but cannot articulate? What are the epistemological functions of different symbol systems or forms of representation, if any? On what grounds can epistemological status be given to what is represented in pictorial or poetic forms? Questions of the kind I have just raised are philosophical. Their importance is critical for developing a perspective on method, yet sadly many schools of education are losing enrollment in the philosophy of education and are not hiring new professors in this discipline to replace those who have retired or are about to retire. Unfortunately, philosophy is often considered marginal in the real business of educational research and practice. The long-range consequences of such short-term vision are troubling.

Preparing a Research Proposal

One of the most important aspects of doctoral training is the conceptualization and preparation of a proposal for a dissertation. The writing of the proposal and the researching and writing of the dissertation entail the toughest and most enduring contributions of doctoral training. Virtually all doctoral students worry about writing acceptable proposals and dissertations. And no wonder. Graduate students in general, but especially doctoral students, are in highly vulnerable positions. They often believe their entire career rests upon not only completing the degree, but on obtaining the high regard of their professors. They are not far wrong. What their professors regard as a significant topic and an appropriate method is critical in their doctoral work. What graduate students believe will be positively regarded, not only by members of their dissertation committee, but by those who sit on oral examination committees and write letters of recommendation looms very large in their choice of topics and method. Faculty attitudes toward qualitative work, the depth of the support provided to those doing it, and the ability of professors to avoid using inappropriate criteria for appraising proposals for qualitative studies are of the utmost significance in shaping the future of the field.

It has been my experience that more than a few doctoral students run into professors whose assumptions about research methods and criteria for the appraisal of their work reflect naivete about both qualitative research methods and the epistemology upon which they rest. When this happens, some doctoral students are frightened off into more conventional studies, even when their hearts are elsewhere. Other students get the message, sometimes exaggerated (as rumors often are), that qualitative studies are unacceptable. Often professors do not say that qualitative studies are unacceptable; they "simply" convey the message, often implicitly, that qualitative research must play by rules appropriate for other kinds of studies. For example, some professors expect qualitative studies to be replicable in the same way as quantitative studies. In fact, quantitative studies are seldom replicable the way people often think they are, and even if they were, such replicability would be inappropriate for most qualitative studies.

Matters pertaining to validity are often ill-conceived (Wolcott, 1990). The concept of referential adequacy is often misunderstood; epistemologies that pursue ontological objectivity as an achievable ideal still abound. There is too often little understanding of a transactional conception of knowledge or of the kinds of knowledge that are possible through educational research. As a result, proposals for qualitative research sometimes are reshaped to meet criteria that should not have been applied in the first place. In the process the research is often neutered. It doesn't make sense, for example, to expect graduate students, or a professor, to design a procedure for a qualitative study that is modeled after the kind that can be made in a psychological laboratory. One important part of qualitative research resides in researchers' ability to follow leads they did not know would emerge when the study began. Productive serendipity should not be prevented; on the contrary, it should be pursued.

Qualitative research proposals should have a full description of the topic to be investigated, a presentation and analysis of the research relevant to that topic, and a discussion of the issues within the topic or the shortfalls within the research literature that make the researcher's topic a significant one. They should describe the kinds of information that are able to be secured and the variety of methods or techniques that will be employed to secure such information. The proposals should identify the kinds of theoretical or explanatory resources that might be used in interpreting what has been described, and describe the kind of places, people, and materials that are likely to be addressed.

The function of proposals is not to provide a watertight blueprint or formula the researcher is to follow, but to develop a cogent case that makes it plain to a knowledgeable reader that the writer has the necessary background to do the study and has thought clearly about the resources that are likely to be used in doing the study, and that the topic, problem, or issue being addressed is educationally significant.

Lest these comments be interpreted by some to mean that no

planning is necessary in conducting qualitative research, or that "anything goes," as they say, I want to make it clear that this is not how my words should be interpreted. Planning *is* necessary. Nevertheless, it should not and cannot function as a recipe or as a script. Evidence matters. One has a responsibility to support what one says, but support does not require measured evidence. Coherence, plausibility, and utility are quite acceptable in trying to deal with social complexity. My point is not to advocate anarchy or to reduce the study of schools and classrooms to a Rorschach projection, it is to urge that the analysis of a research proposal or a research study should employ criteria appropriate to the genre. Professors who make such assessments should understand, as should graduate students, the nature of the genre, what constitutes appropriate criteria, and why they are appropriate.

The belief that one can prepare qualitative researchers in a school or department that demeans such work or misunderstands its features is simply without merit. It is reassuring to know that more and more institutions, often those with the strongest institutional ego, are receptive to qualitative research. What will undermine qualitative research, as Geertz (1973) has suggested, is for others to expect more from it than it can provide, or for its practitioners to do second-rate work. At the same time, it is unrealistic to expect that a form of research that is relatively new, at least in American education, will be conducted with the kind of technical finesse that some conventional research studies possess. The use of statistical analysis in the study of human behavior is more than eighty years old. Qualitative research in the field of education needs comparable time to mature.

Understanding Subject Matter and Value Orientation

I wish to make two other points regarding the preparation of qualitative researchers in education. One has to do with competence in a subject matter. The other pertains to the need to understand the various value orientations that can be legitimately used to guide the teaching of a subject matter. As Stodolsky (1988) has pointed out, the subject matter has a major influence on how teachers teach. Her work reveals that even the same teacher teaches different subject matters in different ways. This suggests that each subject has not only a structure or set of constraints or requirements, but also a tradition into which teachers have been socialized. We learn to teach arithmetic, in part, by the way in which we have been taught arithmetic. We also learn to teach arithmetic by the way we are taught to teach arithmetic. The way we are taught to teach arithmetic depends, in part, on the way in which arithmetic has been conceptualized as a subject and on the educational values that give direction to our teaching. For example, when the new math entered the American educational scene in the early 1960s what became important in the teaching of mathematics was not primarily helping students become accurate in computation but helping them learn the structure of mathematics. Understanding the meaning of *set* was considered more important than learning to recite the multiplication tables accurately by rote.

This conception of mathematics education was influenced, at that time, by the concept of the "structure of the disciplines" (Bruner, 1961) and by the idea that the best way to help a student learn a subject is by studying it in the way in which a scholar works in the field. Inductive thinking, learning by discovery, and problem-centered curricula were the educational fashion.

I mentioned this feature of the math curriculum because a qualitative researcher observing a math teacher or a classroom teacher teaching math needs to know about the assumptions and values animating the lesson to be able to provide a decent appraisal of what is going on. A teacher, for example, who puts little emphasis on accurate computation may believe that other educational values are more important. The rationale for the teacher's activities might be quite persuasive if the researcher understood the options and the basis for the teacher's selection.

Consider the teaching of art. A teacher might believe that the central goal of the teaching and learning of art is to enable students to perceive aesthetic qualities located in works of art and in the environment. The aim of art education, in this teacher's value system, is to refine vision, not primarily to develop creativity or to provide avenues for self-expression. As a result, the curriculum emphasizes looking, doing visual analysis, discussing, making comparisons between works of art, and seeing connections between the qualities found in paintings and sculpture and the qualities found in the environment at large. As a result students devote considerably less time to working with art materials and considerably more time to looking at and discussing the relationship of form to content in visual works of art.

A qualitative researcher observing this teacher might have a very different conception of what art classes should be like. Because what she sees does not fit her schema, she finds the teacher's work wanting. What is really wanting is the researcher's limited array of schemata. Her idea of pedagogical virtue in teaching art is simply too limited.

The fact that there are a variety of ways in which a subject can be taught is no reason for accepting just anything in the name of variety. Rather, the example of teaching art illustrates the variety of approaches that exist in any field. It is a mistake to appraise the teaching of any subject matter by a single "right" image.

The implications of this notion are substantial for qualitative researchers observing classroom practice. It means that to some significant degree those who observe classroom practice will need to know something about the subject being taught and about the ways in which it might be taught. I recognize that no one person can be an expert in every subject. At the same time, some aspects of teaching are common across virtually all teaching situations—the ability to keep students engaged, for example. Yet recognizing the variety of ways in which a subject can be taught will, I hope, increase the likelihood of greater tolerance for diversity in teaching.

In terms of preparing qualitative researchers, this notion means they should secure a background in the subject fields they will observe, one that familiarizes them with the different ways in which a subject can be taught and the rationale for each approach. Ideally it should include the videotape observation and analysis of such differences. Indeed, it is as important to provide this kind of background as to introduce qualitative researchers to theories in the social sciences that enable them to interpret the phenomena they observe. One limitation of social science theory with respect to the teaching of a subject matter is that it typically does not address the teaching of the subject matter or consider the various educational values that give the teaching of any subject a direction. Thus, if qualitative researchers are to be prepared to observe teachers teach a subject, they ought to know something about the ways in which that subject can be taught and, even more, something about the subject itself.

With respect to the preparation of qualitative researchers, it should not be assumed that all dissertations or research studies must have only one outcome, a written text. The text in the form of a dissertation or scholarly paper has, of course, long been what students and others are expected to produce as a result of conducting a study. It is also what libraries expect to shelve. But written text is only one way to inform someone about a school, a classroom, or some other aspect of the social world. Videotapes or films, for example, are other useful forms. As a matter of fact, videos and films are often richer resources for helping others understand a situation than a written narrative would be. With video, viewers can see the setting, hear the actors, observe the action "live." Researchers can also add commentary that is as analytical or theoretical as anything found between the covers of a book.

Doctoral research in which video and film have been used as central elements has been produced by McCutcheon (1976) and by Jones (1982) at Stanford. These visual resources, accompanied in each case by a written text, put the viewer in the classroom and at the school. They are far more vivid than any text alone could be. The "need" for a text to accompany each dissertation was not one that arose from the limitations of video, but from the traditions of the university. We expect doctoral students to *write* dissertations, a practice that has been going on for many years.

Although the availability of new technology makes new forms of representation possible, habit and tradition militate against their use as major vehicles for communicating research results. But I believe old habits and traditions will change. When they do, it will become important for doctoral students and others conducting qualitative research to develop the skills that will make film and video production not only possible, but truly useful. These skills are not now widely developed, but like computer skills, I believe they will be developed in the future.

The consequences of such development go well beyond the making of films and videos—they will also influence the kind of skills needed to assess what has been produced. They will affect the kinds of conferences that are held and the way in which work can be shared. They will influence the kind of work that is regarded as scholarly. They will affect the criteria that promotion committees use to assess the quality of what has been created. In short, the advent of new technologies—video and film—in the armamentarium of educational research will have a significant array of consequences for our conception of what the products of research look like and the criteria that are appropriate for their assessment.

Epilogue

I began this book by examining the relationship between qualitative thought and human understanding. I have devoted most of its pages to the ways in which the sensibilities and the imagination generate images and to the forms through which those images are given a public face. My emphasis on conceptual issues is intentional: I am primarily interested in opening up new ways of thinking about how we come to know and exploring the forms through which what we know is made public. Such forms as literature, film, poetry, and video have for years been used in our culture to help people see and understand important issues and events. They too rarely have been used in the conduct of educational research. We study teaching with high-powered statistical tools, but too seldom study it as a practical art. My aim is to create other visions of how inquiry into educational matters can be pursued.

The creation of new visions of educational inquiry can not only broaden the ways in which we study schooling, but even more important, can expand our conception of human cognition and help us develop new forms of pedagogical practice. When we come to understand that thinking is not mediated solely by language and that intelligence is not exhausted by tasks employing word and number, we are more likely, I believe, to provide more diversified and equitable programs in our schools. Such programs can help those whom our curricula now neglect to find a place in the educational sun. New models of mind, fresh conceptions of intelligence, and more generous views of knowledge ought to help us rethink the content of educational programs and the methods we use to mediate those programs with the young. Teaching practices, for example, that use resources from the visual world, from music and dance, and from poetry and literature can enable children to grasp what cannot be revealed in text. The creation and use of such resources, in all our programs, can do much to increase genuine educational equity in our schools. It is in this sense that method—whether it pertains to research or to teaching—is ultimately a political undertaking. The forms we employ exclude as well as invite. By broadening the forms through which the educational world is described, interpreted, and appraised, and by diversifying the methods through which content is made available and teaching methods are used, the politics of practice become more generous. Whether the field will pursue the ideas developed in these pages or remain on familiar waters remains to be seen. For me, at least, it is much more interesting to find new seas upon which to sail, than old ports at which to dock. My hope is that the leads offered in the foregoing chapters are sufficiently attractive to encourage at least some of us to chart the waters of these new seas and to see what the winds are like.

Notes

1. Egon Guba has, in particular, emphasized differences among research paradigms. For a wide-ranging discussion of these differences, see Guba (1990).
2. For a very useful discussion of the importance of understanding subject-matter content from a pedagogical perspective, see Lee Shulman (1987).
3. On this issue see Clifford Geertz's telling comments in *The New York Times*, May 11, 1988: "Anthropologist, Retracing Steps After Three Decades, Is Shocked," by Richard Bernstein.

References

Adler, M. (1982). *The Paideia proposal*. New York: Macmillan.

Adorno, T. W. (1950). *The authoritarian personality*. New York: Harper.

Apple, M. (1982). *Education and power*. Boston: Routledge and Kegan Paul.

Arnheim, R. (1969). *Visual thinking*. Berkeley: University of California Press.

Arnheim, R. (1986). *New essays on the psychology of art*. Berkeley: University of California Press.

Arnold, M. (1932). *The letters of Matthew Arnold to Arthur Hugh Clough*. Oxford: Oxford University Press.

Atkin, J. M. (1989). Can educational research keep pace with education reform? *Kappan, 71*(3) (November), 200–205.

Atkin, J. M., Kennedy, D., & Patrick, C. (1989). *Inside schools: A collaborative view*. London: Falmer Press.

Ausubel, D. (1978). *Educational psychology* (2nd ed.). New York: Holt, Rinehart & Winston.

Barker, R. (1968). *Ecological psychology*. Stanford: Stanford University Press.

Barone, T. (1978). Inquiry into classroom experiences: A qualitative holistic approach. Ph.D. dissertation, Stanford University, Stanford, CA.

Barone, T. (1983). Things of use and things of beauty: The story of the Swain County High School Arts Program. *Daedalus, 112*(3), 1–28.

Barthes, R. (1972). *Mythologies*. New York: Hill and Wang.

Barthes, R. (1985). *The responsibility of forms*. New York: Hill and Wang.

Bateson, G., & Mead, M. (1952). A Balinese family [Film]. New York: New York University Film Library.

Bateson, G., & Mead, M. (1954). Bathing babies in three cultures [Film]. New York: New York University Film Library.

Beauchamp, T. L., et al. (Eds.). (1982). *Ethical issues in social science research*. Baltimore: Johns Hopkins University Press.

Becker, H. (1963). *Boys in white: Student culture in medical school*. Chicago: University of Chicago Press.

Becker, H. (1986). *Doing things together*. Evanston, IL: Northwestern University Press.

Berliner, D. (1988). The development of expertise in pedagogy. Unpublished manuscript.

Bernstein, B. (1971). On the classification and framing of educational knowledge. In M. Young (Ed.), *Knowledge and control* (pp. 47–69). London: Collier-Macmillan.

Bestor, A. (1953). *Educational wastelands*. Champaign, IL: University of Illinois Press.

Bettelheim, B. (1979). *Surviving, and other essays*. New York: A. Knopf.

Boulding, K. E. (1956). *The image*. Ann Arbor: University of Michigan Press.

Boyer, E. (1983). *High school*. New York: Harper and Row.

Bridgman, P. (1936). *The nature of physical theory*. Dover: Louis Clark Van Uxem Foundation.

Broudy, H. (1976). Search for a science of education. *Kappan, 58*(1) (September), 104–111.

Broudy, H. (1987). *The role of imagery in learning*. (Occasional Paper No. 1). Los Angeles: Getty Center for Education in the Arts.

Bruner, J. (1961). *The process of education*. Cambridge: Harvard University Press.

Bruner, J. (1964). The course of cognitive growth. *American Psychologist, 19*(1) (January), 1–15.

Bruner, J. (1973). *Beyond the information given: Studies in the psychology of knowing*. New York: W. W. Norton.

Callahan, R. (1962). *Education and the cult of efficiency*. Chicago: University of Chicago Press.

Capote, T. (1965). *In cold blood*. New York: Random House.

Capouya, J. (1987). A gift for the game. *Sport, 79*(2), 59–60.

Cassirer, E. (1960). *The logic of the humanities*. London: Yale University Press.

Cassirer, E. (1961–64). *The philosophy of symbolic forms* (R. Manheim, Trans.; preface and introduction by C. W. Hendel). 3 vols. New Haven: Yale University Press.

Cattell, R. B. (1971). *Abilities: Their structure, growth, and action*. Boston: Houghton Mifflin.

Cohen, R. S. (1973). *Language and cognition*. New York: McGraw-Hill.

Connelly, F., & Clandinin, D. (1988). *Teachers as curriculum planners*. New York: Teachers College Press.

Cronbach, L. (1977). *Aptitudes and instructional methods*. New York: Irvington.

Cronbach, L. J. (1984). *Essentials of psychological measurement*. New York: Harper and Row.

Cross, R. C. (1964). *Plato's Republic*. New York: St. Martin's Press.

Cuban, L. (1988). *The managerial imperative and the practice of leadership in schools*. Albany: State University of New York Press.

Dewey, J. (1929). *The quest for certainty*. New York: Minton, Balch.

Dewey, J. (1934). *Art as experience*. New York: Minton, Balch.

Dewey, J. (1938). *Experience and education*. New York: Macmillan.

References

Dewey, J. (1931). *Philosophy and civilization* (rpt. 1963). New York: Capricorn Books.

Dickie, G., & Scalafani, R. (Eds.). (1977). *Aesthetics: A critical anthology*. New York: St. Martin's Press.

Digest of education statistics, 1989: Twenty-fifth edition. Washington, DC: U.S. Department of Education, Office of Educational Research and Improvement.

Donmoyer, R. (1980). Alternative conceptions of generalization and verification for educational research. Ph.D. dissertation, Stanford University, Stanford, CA.

Donmoyer, R. (1990). Curriculum evaluation and negotiation of learning. *Language Arts, 67*(3) (March), 274–285.

Dreeben, R. (1968). *On what is learned in school*. New York: Addison-Wesley.

Dretske, F. (1969). *Seeing and knowing*. London: Routledge and Kegan Paul.

Dunn, P. (1978). Teaching students through their individual learning styles. In *Curriculum materials*. Reston, VA: Reston.

Ecker, D. (1963). The artistic process as qualitative problem-solving. *Journal of Aesthetics and Art Criticism, 21*(3) (Spring), 283–290.

Eddington, A. S. (1929). *The nature of the physical world*. New York: Macmillan.

Edwards, B. (1979). *Drawing on the right side of the brain*. Los Angeles: Jeremy P. Tarcher.

Eisner, E. W. (1969). Instructional and expression objectives: Their formulation and use in curriculum. In W. J. Popham, (Ed.), *Instructional objectives* (pp. 1–31). (American Educational Research Association, Monograph on Curriculum Evaluation.) Chicago: Rand McNally.

Eisner, E. W. (1976). Educational connoisseurship and educational criticism: Their forms and functions in educational evaluation. *Journal of Aesthetic Education*, Bicentennial issue, *10*(3–4), 135–150.

Eisner, E. W. (1981). On the differences between scientific and artistic approaches to qualitative research. *Educational Researcher, 10*(4), 5–9.

Eisner, E. W. (1982). *Cognition and curriculum: A basis for deciding what to teach*. New York: Longman.

Eisner, E. W. (1985a). Aesthetic modes of knowing. In E. W. Eisner (Ed.), *Learning and teaching the ways of knowing: Eighty-fourth yearbook of the National Society for the Study of Education, Part II* (pp. 23–36). Chicago: University of Chicago Press.

Eisner, E. W. (1985b). *The educational imagination* (2nd ed.). New York: Macmillan.

Eisner, E. W. (1985c). *What high schools are like: Views from the inside*. Stanford CA: Stanford School of Education.

Eisner, E. W. (1986). A secretary in the classroom. *Teaching and Teacher Education, 2*(4), 325–328.

Eisner, E. W. (1988). The ecology of school improvement: Some lessons we have learned. *Educational Leadership, 45*(5) (February), 24–29.

Eisner, E. W., & Peshkin, A. (1990). *Qualitative inquiry in education: The continuing debate*. New York: Teachers College Press.

Eisner, E. W., & Walker, D. (1989). *Report to the Getty Center for Education in the Arts on the implementation of DBAE in four school districts*. Stanford, CA: Stanford University.

Elkind, D. (1988). *The hurried child* (rev. ed.). Reading: Addison-Wesley.

Epstein, T. (1989). An aesthetic approach to the teaching and learning of the social studies. Ph.D. dissertation, Harvard University, Cambridge, MA.

Erikson, E. (1963). *Childhood and society* (2nd. ed.). New York: W. W. Norton.

Feig, S., & McLelland, R. (Eds.). (1983). *Breast carcinoma: Current diagnosis and treatment*. New York: Masson.

Feilders, J. (1978). Action and reaction: The role of an urban school superintendent. Ph.D. dissertation, Stanford University, Stanford, CA.

Feilders, J. (1982). *Profile: The role of the chief superintendent of schools*. Belmont: Fearon Education.

First lessons: A report on elementary education in America. (September, 1986). Washington, DC: U.S. Department of Education.

Fish, S. (1980). *Is there a text in this class?* Cambridge, MA: Harvard University Press.

Fiske, D. W., & Shweder, R. A. (Eds.). (1986). *Metatheory in social science*. Chicago: The University of Chicago Press.

Flaherty, R., & Révillon Frères. (1922). *Nanook of the North* [Film]. Chicago: Dist. Facets Films.

Flinders, D. (1987). What teachers learn from teaching: Educational outcomes of instructional adaptation. Ph.D. dissertation, Stanford University, Stanford, CA.

Freud, S. (1933). *New introductory lectures on psycho-analysis*. New York: W. W. Norton.

Gage, N. (1978). *The scientific basis of the art of teaching*. New York: Teachers College Press.

Gardner, H. (1983). *Frames of mind: The theory of multiple intelligences*. New York: Basic Books.

Geertz, C. (1973). *The interpretation of cultures*. New York: Basic Books.

Geertz, C. (1988). *Works and lives: The anthropologist as author*. Stanford, CA: Stanford University Press.

Getzels, J. (1974). Images of the classroom and visions of the learner. *School Review*, 82(4) (August), 527–540.

Goffman, I. (1961). *Asylums*. Garden City, NY: Anchor.

Goodlad, J. (1984). *A place called school: Prospects for the future*. New York: McGraw-Hill.

Goodlad, J., & Anderson, R. (1959). *The non-graded elementary school*. New York: Harcourt, Brace.

Goodman, N. (1976). *The languages of art: An approach to a theory of symbols* (2nd ed.). Indianapolis: Hackett.

Goodman, N. (1978). *Ways of worldmaking*. Indianapolis: Hackett.

References

Goodman, P. (1960). *Growing up absurd.* New York: Vintage Books.

Goodman, P. (1964). *Compulsory miseducation.* New York: Horizon Press.

de Groot, A. (1946). *Thought and choice in chess.* The Hague: Mouton.

Guba, E. (1990). *The paradigm dialog: Options for social science inquiry.* Beverly Hills: Sage.

Gusfield, J. (1981). *The culture of public problems.* Chicago: University of Chicago Press.

Hagberg, H. (n.d.). Where to park. Unpublished manuscript, Stanford University.

Harper, W. A., & Meerbote, R. (Eds.). (1984). *Kant on causality, freedom and objectivity.* Minneapolis: University of Minnesota Press.

Harris, M. (1968). *the rise of anthropological theory.* New York: Thomas Y. Cravello.

Hawthorne, R. (1988). Classroom curriculum: Educational criticisms and teacher choice. Ph.D. dissertation, Stanford University, Stanford, CA.

Hellman, L. (1976). *Scoundrel time.* New York: Little Brown.

Heyns, B. (1988). Educational defectors: A first look at teacher attrition. *Educational researcher, 17*(3), 24–32.

Hintzman, D. (1978). *The psychology of learning and memory.* San Francisco: W. H. Freeman.

Hirst, P. (1974). *Knowledge and the curriculum.* London, Boston: Routledge and Kegan Paul.

Hockings, P. (Ed.). (1975). *Principles of visual anthropology.* Paris: Mouton.

Hoy, C. (Ed.). (1963). *Hamlet.* New York: W. W. Norton.

Hunt, J. (1961). *Intelligence and experience.* New York: Ronald.

Hunter, M. (1982). *Mastery teaching.* El Segundo, CA: T.I.P.

Jackson, P. (1968). *Life in classrooms.* New York: Holt, Rinehart & Winston.

Jackson, P. (1981a). Comprehending a well-run comprehensive: A report on a visit to a large suburban high school. *Daedalus, 110*(4) (Fall), 81–96.

Jackson, P. (1981b). Secondary schooling for children of the poor. *Daedalus, 110*(4) (Fall), 39–58.

Jackson, P. (1981c). Secondary schooling for the privileged few: A report on a visit to a New England boarding school. *Daedalus, 110*(4) (Fall), 117–130.

Jackson, P. (1986). *The practice of teaching.* New York: Teachers College Press.

Jensen, A. (1969). How much can we boost I.Q. and scholastic achievement? *Harvard Educational Review, 39*(1), 1–123.

Jones, J. H. (1981). *Bad blood: The Tuskegee syphilis experiment.* New York: Free Press.

Jones, K. (1982). The use of film in educational evaluation. Ph.D. dissertation, Stanford University, Stanford, CA.

Judd, C. H. (1915). *Psychology of high school subjects.* Boston: Ginn.

Kant, I. (1959). *Foundations of the metaphysics of morals* (L. W. Beck, Trans.). Indianapolis: Bobbs-Merrill.

Kesey, K. (1970). *One flew over the cuckoo's nest.* New York: French.

Kidder, T. (1989). *Among schoolchildren*. Boston: Houghton Mifflin.

Konner, M. (1987). *Becoming a doctor*. New York: Viking.

Kounin, J. (1970). *Discipline and group management in classrooms*. New York: Holt, Rinehart & Winston.

Kozol, J. (1968). *Death at an early age*. New York: Bantam.

Kuhn, T. S. (1962). *The structure of scientific revolutions*. Chicago: University of Chicago Press.

Kuhn, T. (1977). *The essential tension*. Chicago: University of Chicago Press.

Kuntz, J. F. (1986). The transmission of values in two Jesuit high school classrooms. Ph.D. dissertation, Stanford University, Stanford, CA.

Langer, S. (1942). *Philosophy in a new key*. Cambridge: Harvard University Press.

Langer, S. (1976). *Problems of art*. New York: Charles Scribner's Sons.

Lepper, M., & Greene, D. (Eds.). (1978). *The hidden cost of reward: New perspectives on the psychology of human motivation*. Hillsdale, NJ: L. Erlbaum Associates.

Levin, J., Shriberg, L., & Berg, J. (1983). A concrete strategy for remembering abstract prose. *American Educational Research Journal, 20*(2), 277–290.

Lifton, R. (1986). *The Nazi doctors*. New York: Basic Books.

Lightfoot, S. L. (1981a). Portraits of exemplary secondary schools: Highland Park. *Daedalus, 110*(4) (Fall), 59–80.

Lightfoot, S. L. (1981b). Portraits of exemplary secondary schools: St. Paul's School. *Daedalus, 110*(4) (Fall), 97–116.

Lightfoot, S. L. (1981c). Portraits of exemplary secondary schools: George Washington Carver Comprehensive High School. *Daedalus, 110*(4) (Fall), 17–39.

Lightfoot, S. L. (1983). *The good high school*. New York: Basic Books.

Lincoln, Y. S. (1990). Toward a categorical imperative for qualitative research. In E. Eisner & A. Peshkin (Eds.), *Qualitative inquiry in education: The continuing debate*. New York: Teachers College Press.

Lincoln, Y. S., & Guba, E. (1985). *Naturalistic inquiry*. Beverly Hills: Sage.

Luce, D. (1986). *Response times*. New York: Oxford University Press.

Lynd, R. S., & Merrell, H. (1929). *Middletown: A study in American culture*. New York: Harcourt, Brace.

MacDonald, B. (1977). A political classification of evaluation studies. In D. Hamilton et al. (Eds.), *Beyond the numbers game* (pp. 224–228). London: Macmillan Education Ltd.

Marx, G. T. (1988). *Undercover: Police surveillance in America*. Berkeley: University of California Press.

Mastropieri, M., Scruggs, T., & Levin, J. (1987). Learning disabled students' memory for expository prose: Mnemonic versus nonmnemonic pictures. *American Educational Research Journal, 24*(4), 505–519.

Mathieson, S. (1988). Why triangulate. *Educational Researcher, 17*(2) (March), 13–17.

Matson, J., & DiLorenzo, T. (1984). *Punishment and its alternatives*. New York: Springer.

McCarthy, B. (1987). *The format system: Teaching to learning styles with right/left mode techniques*. Barrington, IL: Excel.

McCutcheon, G. (1976). The disclosure of classroom life. Ph.D. dissertation, Stanford University, Stanford, CA.

McKeon, R. (Ed.). (1941). *The basic works of Aristotle*. New York: Random House.

Mead, M. (1928). *Coming of age in Samoa*. New York: William Morrow.

Meiland, J. W., & Krausz, M. (Eds.). (1982). *Relativism: Cognitive and moral*. Notre Dame, IN: University of Notre Dame Press.

Miles, M., & Huberman, M. (1984). *Qualitative data analysis: A source book of new methods*. Beverly Hills: Sage.

Milgram, S. (1974). *Obedience to authority*. New York: Harper and Row.

A nation prepared: Teachers for the 21st century. (1986). New York: Carnegie Forum on Education and the Economy.

Neisser, U. (1976). *Cognition and reality: Principles and implications of cognitive psychology*. San Francisco: W. H. Freeman.

Newell, R. W. (1986). *Objectivity, empiricism, and truth*. London: Routledge and Kegan Paul.

Nisbet, R. (1976). *Sociology as an art form*. London: Oxford University Press.

Noss, J. B. (1952). *Man's religions*. New York: Macmillan.

Peirce, C. S. (1931). *Collected papers* (Charles Harshorne and Paul Weiss, Eds.), vol. 1: *Principles of Philosophy*. Cambridge: Harvard University Press.

Peshkin, A. (1985). Virtuous subjectivity: In the participant observer's I's. In D. Berg & K. K. Smith (Eds.), *Exploring clinical methods for sound research*. Beverly Hills: Sage.

Peshkin, A. (1986). *God's choice: The total world of a fundamentalist Christian school*. Chicago: University of Chicago Press.

Phillips, D. (1983). After the wake: Postpositivistic educational thought. *Educational Researcher, 12*(5) (May), 5–12.

Phillips, D. C. (1987). Validity in qualitative research, or, why the worry about warrant will not wane. *Education and Urban Society, 20*(1) (November), 9–24.

Piaget, J. (1973). *The child and reality* (Arnold Rosin, Trans.). New York: Grossman.

Piaget, J., & Inhelder, B. (1964). *The early growth of logic in the child: Classification and sensation* (E. A. Lunzer and D. Papet, Trans.). New York: Harper & Row.

Pinar, W. (1988). *Contemporary curriculum discourse*. Scottsdale, AZ: Gorsuch Scavisbrick.

Polanyi, M. (1958). *Personal knowledge: Toward a post-critical philosophy*. Chicago: University of Chicago Press.

Polanyi, M. (1967). *The tacit dimension*. London: Routledge and Kegan Paul.

Popper, K. (1959). *The logic of scientific discovery*. New York: Basic Books.

Powell, A. G., Farrar, E., & Cohen, D. K. (1985). *The shopping mall high school*. Boston: Houghton Mifflin.

Raiffa, H. (1970). *Decision analysis: Introductory lectures on choice under uncertainty*. Menlo Park, CA: Addison-Wesley.

Ramist, L. (1985). Validity of the ATP tests: Criterion-related validity. In *Admissions testing program technical manual*. New York: College Entrance Examination Board.

Read, H. (1944). *Education through art*. London: Pantheon

Reese, W. L. (1980). *Dictionary of philosophy and religion*. Atlantic Highlands, NJ: Humanities Press.

Reichenbach, H. (1953). *The rise of scientific philosophy*. Berkeley: University of California Press.

Restructuring California education: A design for public education in the twenty-first century, recommendations to the California Business Round Table. (1988). Berkeley: B. W. Associates.

Rist, R. (1980). Blitzkrieg ethnography: On the transformation of a method into a movement. *Educational Researcher, 9*(2), 8–10.

Robeck, M. C. (1978). *Infants and children: Their development and learning*. New York: McGraw-Hill.

Rorty, R. (1979). *Philosophy and the mirror of nature*. Princeton, NJ: Princeton University Press.

Rosenberg, H. (1985). *Art and other serious matters*. Chicago: University of Chicago Press.

Rosenshine, B. (1976). Classroom instruction. In N. Gage (Ed.), *The psychology of teaching methods: Seventy-fifth yearbook of the National Society for the Study of Education* (pp. 335–371). Chicago: University of Chicago Press.

Rosenthal, R. (1986). *Pygmalion in the classroom*. New York: Irvington.

Rubin, L. (1985). *Artistry in teaching*. New York: Random House.

Rubinek, B. (1982). Writing about literature: Three instructional contexts. Ph.D. dissertation, Stanford University, Stanford, CA.

Schachtel, E. (1959). *Metamorphosis*. New York: Basic Books.

Scheffler, I. (1982). *Science and subjectivity* (2nd ed.). Indianapolis: Hackett.

Schepper-Hughes, N. (1979). *Saints, scholars, and schizophrenics: Mental illness in rural Ireland*. Berkeley: University of California Press.

Schoen, D. (1983). *The reflective practitioner: How professionals think in action*. New York: Basic Books.

Schutz, A., & Luckman, T. (1973). *The structure of the life world*. London: Heinemann Educational Books.

Schwab, J. (1969). The practical: A language for curriculum. *School Review, 78*(5) (November), 1–24.

Schwartz, B. (1975). *Cueing and waiting*. Chicago: University of Chicago Press.

Scriven, M. (1973). Goal free evaluation. In E. R. House (Ed.), *School evaluation: The politics and process*. Berkeley: McCutcheon.

Shabecoff, P. (1988, March 23). Head of E.P.A. bars Nazi data in study of gas. *The New York Times*, p. 1.

Shirer, W. L. (1959). *The rise and fall of the Third Reich*. New York: Simon and Schuster.

Shulman, L. (1987). Knowledge and teaching: Foundations of the new reform. *Harvard Educational Review, 57*(1), 1–22.

Shuy, R. (1986). Secretary Bennett's teaching: An argument for responsive teaching. *Teaching and Teacher Education, 2*(4), 315–323.

Siggers, W. (1980). Changing teacher correcting behavior: Using aversive and positive contingencies. *Educational Research Quarterly, 5*(3), 25–32.

Singer, M. (1990). Senses of history: An inquiry into form, meaning, and understanding. Ph.D. dissertation, Stanford University, Stanford, CA, in progress.

Sizer, T. R. (1984). *Horace's compromise: The dilemma of the American high school*. Boston: Houghton Mifflin.

Skinner, B. F. (1938). *The behavior of organisms*. New York: D. Appleton-Century.

Skinner, B. F. (1953). *Science and human behavior*. New York: Macmillan.

Slavin, R. (1983). *Cooperative learning*. New York: Longman.

Smith, J., & Heshusius, L. (1986). Closing down the conversation: The end of the quantitative-qualitative debate. *Educational Researcher, 15*(1), 44–53.

Smith, L. (1971). *Anatomy of educational innovation: An organizational analysis of an elementary school*. New York: John Wiley & Sons.

Smith, L., & Geoffrey, W. (1968). *The complexities of education in an urban classroom*. New York: Holt, Rinehart & Winston.

Stake, R. (Ed.). (1975). *Evaluating the arts in education: A responsive approach*. Columbus: Merrill.

Steinberg, L. (1972). *Other criteria: Confrontations with twentieth century art*. London: Oxford University Press.

Stephens, J. M. (1967). *The process of schooling: A psychological examination*. New York: Holt, Rinehart & Winston.

Sternberg, R. (1988). *The triarchic mind*. New York: Viking.

Stodolsky, S. S. (1988). *The subject matters*. Chicago: University of Chicago Press.

Stone, R. A. (1971). *John F. Kennedy: 1917–1963*. New York: Oceana.

Thorndike, E. L. (1910). The contribution of psychology to education. *Journal of Educational Psychology, 1*.

Thorndike, E. L. (1927). *The measurement of intelligence*. New York: Bureau of Publications, Teachers College, Columbia University.

Time for results: The governor's 1991 report on education. Washington, DC: National Governors' Association Center for Policy Research.

Tocqueville, Alexis de. (1898). *Democracy in America* (H. Reeve, Trans.). New York: Century. (Original work published 1835)

Tomorrow's teachers: A report of the Holmes Group. (1986). East Lansing: Michigan State University Press.

Toulmin, S. (1982). The construal of reality: Criticism in modern and post modern science. In W. J. T. Mitchell (Ed.), *The politics of interpretation* (pp. 99–118). Chicago: University of Chicago Press.

Tufte, E. (1983). *The visual display of quantitative information.* Cheshire, CT: Graphics Press.

Tyack, D. (1974). *The one best system: A history of American urban education.* Cambridge: Harvard University Press.

Uhrmacher, B. (1990). Waldorf schools marching quietly unheard. Ph.D. dissertation, Stanford University, Stanford, CA, in progress.

USA Research. (1984). *A nation at risk: The full account.* Cambridge, MA: Author.

Vallance, E. (1975). Aesthetic criticism and curricular description. Ph.D. dissertation, Stanford University, Stanford, CA.

Walker, D., & Schaffarzick, J. (1972). Comparing curricula. *Review of Educational Research, 44* (Winter), 83–112.

Waller, W. (1932). *The sociology of teaching.* New York: John Wiley & Sons.

Webb, E. J., Campbell, D. T., Schwartz, R. P., & Sechrest, L. (1966). *Unobtrusive measures: Nonreactive research in the social sciences.* Chicago: Rand McNally.

Weber, M. (1968). *On charisma and institution building* (S. N. Eisenstadt, Ed.). Chicago: University of Chicago Press.

What works [Educating disadvantaged children]. (1987). Washington, DC: U.S. Department of Education.

Who will teach our children? (1985, November). Sacramento: California Commission on the Teaching Profession.

Whyte, W. F. (1961). *Street corner society* (2nd ed.). Chicago: University of Chicago Press.

Wiesel, E. (1969). *Night.* New York: Discus Books, Avon.

Wiesel, E. (1970). *Dawn.* New York: Avon.

Wiesel, E. (1972). *Souls on fire.* New York: Random House.

Wiesel, E. (1978). *A Jew today.* New York: Random House.

Winch, P. (1958). *The idea of a social science and its relation to philosophy.* London: Routledge and Kegan Paul.

Wittrock, M. (Ed.). (1986). *Handbook of research on teaching* (3rd ed.). New York: Macmillan.

Wolcott, H. (1984). *The man in the principal's office.* Prospect Heights, IL: Waveland Press.

Wolcott, H. (1990). On seeking—and rejecting—validity in qualitative research. In E. Eisner & A. Peshkin (Eds.), *Qualitative inquiry in education: The continuing debate.* New York: Teachers College Press.

Wolfe, T. (1973). *The new journalism.* New York: Harper & Row.

Yolton, J. (1977). *The Locke reader.* Cambridge: Cambridge University Press.

Subject Index

Name Index

Adler, Mortimer, 73
Adorno, T. W., 185
Ahlbrand, W., 136, 148
Albers, Josef, 46
Alexander, L., 23n
American Educational
  Research Organization
  (AERA), 14, 129, 149,
  228
Anderson, R., 75
Apple, M., 73, 74
Arendt, Hannah, 121
Aristotle, 4, 57, 197, 203
Arnheim, Rudolf, 4, 24n,
  46, 179
Arnold, Matthew, 12
Atkin, J. M., 24n, 172,
  212n, 221

Barker, Roger, 74
Barone, Tom, 40, 168n,
  192
Barthes, Roland, 121,
  124–26
Bateson, Gregory, 188,
  235
Beauchamp, T. L., 214
Becker, Howard, 171, 235
Benedict, Ruth, 229
Bennett, William J., 10,
  23n, 129, 130–49, 177
Berg, J., 187
Berliner, David, 34, 90,
  189, 211n, 231
Bernstein, Basil, 76
Bernstein, Richard, 246n
Bestor, A., 9
Bettelheim, Bruno, 2–3,
  121, 236
Boulding, Kenneth E.,
  56–57
Boyer, E., 119
Branscomb, L. M., 23n
Broudy, H., 23n, 69
Bruner, Jerome, 46, 67,
  198, 199, 243

California Business
  Roundtable Report, 23n
Callahan, R., 12, 79
Campbell, D. T., See
  Webb, E. J.

Capote, Truman, 30, 37,
  39, 89
Capouya, J., 87
Cassirer, Ernst, 4, 50, 121
Cervantes Saavedra,
  Miguel de, 107
Clandinin, D., 14
Cohen, D. K., 104–5
Commons, D. I., 23n
Connelly, F. M., 14
Coulthard, R., 135, 149
Cronbach, L. J., 95
Cuban, L., 24n

Dewey, John, 4, 13, 16,
  17–18, 24n, 31, 38, 47,
  52, 60, 77, 83n, 85, 98–
  99, 101, 119n–120n,
  177, 206–7
Dilthey, Wilhelm, 4
Donmoyer, Robert, 103,
  168n, 194n, 211
Dreeben, R., 74
Dretske, Fred, 68, 83n
Dunn, P., 10

Ecker, D., 64
Eddington, A. S., 37–38
Edwards, B., 67
Eisner, E. W., 8, 14, 24n,
  33, 51, 55, 63, 72, 73,
  99, 110, 118, 130–35,
  173, 179, 184, 186,
  195n, 210, 221
Elkind, David, 55–56
Epstein, T., 179
Erikson, Eric, 210

Farrar, E., 104–5
Feig, S., 208–9
Fielders, John, 191–92,
  235
Fish, S., 90
Flaherty, R., 236
Flinders, D., 186
Foucault, Michel, 121
Freud, Sigmund, 108–9,
  185
Fromm, Erich, 121

Gage, N., 78, 208
Gallimore, R., 136, 147,
  148

Gardner, H., 105n, 209
Geertz, Clifford, 15, 35,
  43, 54, 97–98, 108–9,
  111–12, 186, 205, 229,
  242, 246n
Geoffrey, William, 13
Getzels, J., 71–72
Goethe, 197
Goffman, Erving, 2–3,
  121, 126–27, 185, 189–
  90, 235, 237
Gombrich, E. H., 46
Goodlad, J., 75, 119, 181
Goodman, Nelson, 4, 28,
  39, 46–47, 53–54, 60n,
  108, 111, 120n, 179,
  191, 203, 234–35
Goodman, Paul, 13, 15
Greene, David, 180, 195n
Greene, Maxine, 14, 168n
de Groot, A., 34
Grumet, Madelaine, 14,
  168n
Guba, Egon, 3, 14, 33, 82,
  246n
Gusfield, J., 113

Hagberg, Peggy, 90–95
Hawthorne, R., 77
Hellman, Lillian, 122
Heshusius, L., 14, 227
Heyns, B., 115, 118
Hintzman, D., 67
Hirst, P., 49
Hoetker, J., 136, 148
Holt, John, 15
Hockings, P., 188
Hoy, C., 112, 113
Huberman, M., 14
Hunt, J., 209
Hunter, M., 10
Hyland, J., 148

Inhelder, B., 199
Irvine, J., 135, 148

Jackson, Philip, 3, 13, 55,
  68, 112, 192, 237
James, William, 185
Jensen, P., 209
Jones, J. H., 214
Jones, K., 188, 244